GENDER AND POLITICAL IDENTITIES
IN SCOTLAND, 1919–1939

SCOTTISH HISTORICAL REVIEW

MONOGRAPHS SERIES

No. 17

GENDER AND POLITICAL IDENTITIES IN SCOTLAND, 1919–1939

ANNMARIE HUGHES

EDINBURGH UNIVERSITY PRESS

© Annmarie Hughes, 2010

Edinburgh University Press Ltd
22 George Square, Edinburgh
www.euppublishing.com

Typeset in 10 on 12pt ITC New Baskerville by
Servis Filmsetting Ltd, Stockport, Cheshire, and
printed and bound in Great Britain by
CPI Antony Rowe, Chippenham and Eastbourne

A CIP record for this book is available from the British Library

ISBN 978 0 7486 3981 6 (hardback)

Contents

Tables

Acknowledgements

Many people have assisted me in writing this book and in particular I owe a significant debt of gratitude to the men and women who agreed to share their memories of the inter-war years in Scotland with me, especially Mari Robertson who introduced me to a new way of looking at the past. I would also like to express my thanks to the staff at the Glasgow Regional Archive, the Glasgow University Archive, the Mitchell Library Glasgow, the Old Paisley Society, the Scottish National Archive, the Society for St Vincent de Paul, and Glasgow Caledonian University Archive, especially Audrey Canning who was a font of information. The book began its life as a Ph.D. thesis at the University of Strathclyde and I would like to thank my supervisors, Callum Brown and Arthur McIvor, for their enthusiasm and advice. I would also like to thank Bob Morris, Sarah Edwards and Eddie Clark at EUP.

Like many Scottish gender historians before me, I owe a tremendous debt of gratitude to Eleanor Gordon, not only for her work in opening the field of Scottish gender history, but also for her encouragement, guidance and most importantly her friendship. I am also fortunate to be a member of the Department of Economic and Social History at the University of Glasgow and I would like to thank my colleagues there for their collegiality. I am also indebted to Katie Barclay, Mark Freeman, Eleanor Gordon, Jim Phillips and Valerie Wright, who read and commented on parts of this book. I would also like to thank James McKay for his personal support and particularly for enduring a baptism in gender history! The book also benefited from the enthusiasm and lively discussions of undergraduate and postgraduate students in the department of Economic and Social History past and present, especially Valerie Wright, Fiona Skillen and Oliver Stockman. Finally, but by no means least, I would like to thank my friends, and most importantly my family, especially John and my sister Katrina for endless hours of transcribing oral histories. To my children Natasha, Amanda and Robert and to my greatest distraction, my granddaughter Kiera, I owe you most of all and I dedicate this book with love to you and in memory of my parents Ann and Richard McLaughlin.

Introduction

A man was brought into this world to be the breadwinner. No wife unless it's necessary should be out working. She should be at home attending to him and the children.[1]

According to many historians the separate spheres ideal reached its apogee between the wars in Britain. This book seeks to evaluate this hypothesis and the factors that may have influenced inter-war women to embrace the traditional worldview on womanhood quoted above that continued to position them in the private sphere as dependants of men. The investigation will consider the extent to which women did subjectify this vision of womanhood and how far this guaranteed their subordination. In other words, could women resist, defy or subvert dominant discourses to empower themselves? These questions, concerning power and identity, are central to this book and will be addressed by investigating how working-class women's political identities were influenced by the discursive context, but also by class, geography and the gender antagonism that existed in Scotland between the wars.

The inter-war years are identified with sexual antagonism in the workplace, politics, and everyday life that was intended to shore up the gendered public/private divide. Kingsley Kent argues that in the aftermath of World War I attempts to return to normality resulted in a backlash against women because 'the terrors' of war 'problematised masculinity, fragmenting it, causing men to question their relationship to a universal maleness'. The result of this was that 'towards the end of the war men perceived women to be emasculating them and began, at least rhetorically, to strike back'. Showalter insists that 'men's quarrels with the feminine element in their own psyches' were 'externalised as quarrels with women'. Represented as sexual disorder, this situation ensured that peace came to imply 'a return to traditional gender relationships' in which men dominated the public sphere and women were confined to the private sphere.[2]

---

[1] Interview with author: SOH/CA/019/06, born 1907, Glasgow. All interviewees have been given alternative names. References denote the archive deposit at the Scottish Oral History Centre, University of Strathclyde. There are profiles in the bibliography of the individual's transcripts used for this book.

[2] S. Kingsley Kent, *Making Peace, The Reconstruction of Gender in Inter-War Britain* (Princeton, 1993), 37–8, 70, 116–37 and 237, and E. Showalter, as quoted in S. Kingsley Kent, 'The politics of sexual difference: World War I and the demise of British feminism', *Journal of*

The aftermath of the First World War is also seen to have resulted in considerable male hostility towards women in the workplace as a result of fears generated by women's entry into hitherto male employment during the war. The changing nature of work between the wars that extended women's employment opportunities and the effects of the recession and depression also aggravated the perception that cheap female labour was the cause of depressed wages and men's unemployment. Trade unions contributed to this assessment by adopting defensive strategies against working women.[3] The state also colluded for a multiplicity of reasons ranging from anxiety over the declining birth rate through to concerns over the social and political effects of male unemployment in the 1920s and 1930s. State policies, particularly the Restoration of Pre-War Practices Act, were used as a counter-offensive against women workers. This legislation shored up domesticity by returning women to what was regarded as their 'rightful place', the home, or to 'women's work'.[4] The Anomalies Act followed and effectively barred married women from receiving benefits and underpinned the opinion that women should be dependants of their spouses. Marriage bars were extended between the wars and reinforced this view. They also upheld the perception that male occupations had to be protected from the infiltration of women, especially married women, and that married women should be dependants of men.

The labour movement, and feminist organisations, rather than allying with women, are identified as having contributed to the idealisation of domesticity by their complicity. Such organisations idealised housewifery, motherhood and the 'private sphere' for women. Thus, the state, politicians, state bodies, the clergy, the medical profession, the male-dominated labour movement and even feminists were all seen to have responded to the ruptures wrought by war by reinforcing traditional gender identities. The 'evolution' of the popular daily press with its discourse on modernity also contributed to the circulation of the idea that females were usurping men. Emerging as a result of the dislocations brought about by World War I, the 'flapper', as modern women were labelled, was seen as a physical manifestation of modernity and, although exaggerated, the idea of a 'new woman' who enjoyed greater access to public life, work and leisure opportunities was widely disseminated. The gaze of the media on young

---

British Studies, 27, 3: 252 (1988). See also J. Bourke, *Dismembering the Male: Men's Bodies, Britain, and the Great War* (Chicago, 1996) and M. Pugh, 'Domesticity and the decline of feminism, 1930–1950', in H. L. Smith (ed.), *British Feminism in the Twentieth Century* (Aldershot, 1990), 144–66.

[3] See J. Lewis, 'In search of a real equality: women between the wars', in F. Gloversmith (ed.), *Class, Culture and Social Change: A New View of the 1930s* (Brighton, 1980), 208–39 and S. Alexander, 'Men's fears and women's work: responses to unemployment in London between the wars', *Gender and History*, 12, 2: 401–25 (2000).

[4] See Lewis, 'In search of a real equality', 213 and Kingsley Kent, 'The politics of sexual difference', 232–53.

women contributed to the idea that traditional gender identities were being challenged by the onslaught of the 'new women' regardless of the fact that the representation was more myth than reality for the majority of women.[5]

In Scotland economic, social and political instability intensified the disruptions wrought by war, which ensured that additional factors held the potential to contribute to masculine insecurity. The decline of rearmament contracts after World War I, Britain's loss of foreign markets and the decision to return to the gold standard at pre-war parity guaranteed that Scotland's over-concentration on heavy industries, and their subsequent collapse, created economic stagnation in the 1920s. The introduction of 'new' industries did not compensate for this to any great extent. The situation was further exacerbated by the depression of the 1930s.[6] The ensuing high levels of unemployment created an environment that threatened the links between manliness, work and work-related expressions of male identity, while simultaneously undermining men's ability to provide for their families. The centrality of hard physical work, work culture and the wage packet to working-class male identity has been identified by historians of masculinity.[7] Alexander maintains that 'a workman felt less of a man without a job or a wage sufficient to support his family'.[8] In Scotland, although multiple masculinities coexisted, the hegemonic form which guaranteed men's domination over women linked the realms of the home, leisure and workplace through the power bestowed by the 'breadwinner's wage'. Men gained prestige from hard and hazardous physical labour which reproduced macho attitudes and masculine identity and formed the basis of male solidarity. In addition, the wage packet was a 'symbol of power' that facilitated 'entitlements' including 'preferential treatment in the home, and the right to recreation, leisure pursuits and mandatory sex'.[9] Thus, although men's responses varied, the precarious economic climate that threatened these privileges and exacerbated the idea that women were usurping men, led to considerable misogyny in the workplace, the political arena and particularly in the community, where men exploited aspects of

[5] A. Bingham, *Gender, Modernity, and the Popular Press in Inter-war Britain* (Oxford, 2004), 47–83. See S. Todd, *Young Women, Work and Family in England, 1918–1950* (Oxford, 2005), 195–225 and A. Bingham, '"An era of domesticity"? histories of women and gender in interwar Britain', *Cultural and Social History*, 1, 2: 225 (2004).

[6] See N. K. Buxton, 'Economic growth in Scotland between the wars: the role of production structure and rationalisation', *Economic History Review*, 33, 4: 549 (1980).

[7] See J. Tosh, 'Masculinities in an industrialising society Britain 1800–1914', *Journal of British Studies*, 44, 2: 332–3 (2005).

[8] Alexander, 'Men's fears and women's work', 404.

[9] R. Johnston and A. McIvor, 'Dangerous work, hard men and broken bodies: masculinity in the Clydeside heavy industries c.1930–1970', *Labour History Review*, 69, 135–51 (2004). See also R. W. Connel, *Masculinities* (Cambridge, 1995), 76–7 and P. Ayres, 'The making of men: masculinity in interwar Liverpool', in M. Walsh (ed.), *Working Out Gender Perspectives from Labour History* (Aldershot, 1999), 66–83.

popular culture to shore up their sense of masculinity. Vovelle stresses that popular culture

> is the most complex but strongest expression of resistance to change
> ... It contains a system of representations which constitute a series of
> defensive and subversive mechanisms fighting against the mutilating
> and mystifying forces of acculturation.[10]

Popular culture could reinforce and symbolise masculine identity at a time when other avenues were being blocked by the economic environment and when men were receiving discursive signals that women were being liberated at their expense. Such male insecurity may indicate the level of women's progress. However, it is more likely that there was a perception that women were making advancements at the expense of men and this was not a situation that men were prepared to tolerate.

In this discursive context feminists were apparently compelled to relinquish their demands for equal rights for women and this resulted in the fragmentation of first-wave feminism, signalling its demise.[11] Women's progress in the inter-war period was impeded because class divisions acted to the detriment of feminist unity. Pugh argues that the feminist movement faced adversity from the 'male dominance of the labour movement', who 'retained an abiding suspicion of all women's organisations as inherently middle class and divisive'. 'Socialist' women were seemingly discouraged from any involvement in feminist associations.[12] Class and political loyalties did lead to differences in ideas, aims and strategies between feminists in many localities in Scotland, as this book will highlight. However, although class caused fragmentation amongst feminists, the divisions were not merely the product of the male dominance of the labour movement. The political loyalties of feminists were also disruptive to gender unity. More importantly, it is clear that feminism was far from moribund, irrespective of the post-war backlash model which suggests otherwise.

In recent years feminism and the women's movement have been reappraised and this re-evaluation demonstrates that inter-war feminism was not waning.[13] The historiography also highlights the diversity of participants, as well as their different aims, objectives and strategies, which fused

---

[10] M. Vovelle, *Ideologies and Mentalities* (Oxford, 1990), 164–72.

[11] See Kingsley Kent, *Making Peace*, 37–8, 70, 116–37 and 237, and Pugh, 'Domesticity and the decline of feminism', 144–66.

[12] M. Pugh, *Women and the Women's Movement in Britain* (London, 2000), 134. See also P. Graves, 'An experiment in women-centred socialism', in H. Gruber and P. Graves (eds), *Women and Socialism, Socialism And Women: Europe Between The Two World Wars* (Oxford, 1998), 200 and J. Hannam, 'Women and politics', in J. Purvis (ed.), *Women's History: Britain, 1850–1945* (London, 1995), 238.

[13] See C. Law, *Suffrage and Power: The Women's Movement, 1918–1928* (London, 1997) and S. Stanley Holton, *Feminism and Democracy: Women's Suffrage and Reform Politics in Britain, 1900–1918* (Cambridge, 1986).

to cumulatively make up the first wave of feminism.[14] However, while this has expanded our understanding of feminism, inter-war feminism and feminists remain illusive categories. Delmar argues that such feminist categorisations are 'obstacles to an understanding of feminism in its diversity, in its differences, and in its specificity'. She shows how these terms are associated with anything from 'codes of dress, looks and behaviour' to a perception of feminism as 'an active desire to change women's position in society'. More frequently, 'feminism and the women's movement have been assumed to be coterminous'. This kind of institutionalisation of feminism is problematic. It disguises the diversity of 'ideas, aims and successes of feminist women'.[15] It also conceals other forms of feminism, including what has been identified as 'popular feminism'. This feminist behaviour 'does not name itself feminist' and is found in the 'narratives of popular fiction' and in the 'everyday' activities of women, including 'the battles over employment legislation and maternity rights'.[16]

Popular feminism is not a present-day manifestation: it was practised between the wars by a range of women, many of whom did not associate themselves with a feminist identity. Many first-wave feminists were bourgeois and this contributed to the disavowal of a feminist identity amongst working-class women, as did the 'negative threatening connotations' associated with feminism and feminists including the symbiotic vilification connecting the latter with lesbianism and the idea that feminism undermined family values.[17] Beaumont highlights how mainstream women's organisations disavowed a feminist identity to avoid the opprobrium from the negative images attached to the feminist movement. Feminism was seen to threaten the ideology of domesticity to which many of the members of such organisations adhered. Nevertheless, these organisations, many of which had working-class members, did act in feminist ways. They did so by using the concept of citizenship rather than feminist discourses to find ways to secure social and economic rights for women.[18] As this book will demonstrate, Scottish women were involved in such activities also. In addition, many working-class women in their everyday lives practised forms of popular feminism. In this sense, there may seem to be few historical precedents for working-class feminism or the ways in which working-class women

[14] See K. Offen, 'Defining feminism: a comparative historical approach', *Signs*, 1, 14: 119–57 (1988).

[15] R. Delmar, 'What is feminism?', in J. Mitchell and A. Oakley (eds), *What is Feminism?* (Oxford, 1986), 8–9, 13–24 and S. Kemp and J. Squires (eds), *Feminisms* (Oxford, 1997), 4–5.

[16] Kemp and Squires, *Feminisms*, 5.

[17] See K. Borland, '"That's not what I said": interpretive conflict in oral narrative research', in S. Berger Gluck and D. Patai (eds), *Women's Words: The Feminist Practice of Oral History* (London, 1991), 71.

[18] C. Beaumont, 'Citizens not feminists: the boundary negotiated between citizenship and feminism by mainstream women's organisations in England 1928–39', *Women's History Review*, 9, 2: 413–26 (2000).

might have responded to their gender oppression in a feminist manner. But where the actions of working-class women were compatible with a definition of feminism, even popular feminism, then the re-evaluation of feminism itself needs to be reappraised. This book contributes to this appraisal by adopting a wider interpretation of feminist aims, objectives and activities. It concentrates on gendered relationships of power, particularly those that were a product of sexual antagonism, to explore the ways in which inter-war transformations in gender relations, the economic climate and post-war masculine insecurity gave rise to greater gender conflict. This book also considers how women responded to such antagonism, often in feminist ways.

Riley, in her quest to seek the conditions behind a feminist consciousness, forwards the hypothesis that there might be enough ground to suggest that 'sexual antagonism can shape sexual solidarity', and that the 'assaults and counter-assaults' faced by women, 'with all their irritations', can lead to 'a rough kind of feminism'. Riley rejects this premise on the basis that women's 'estates divide them' much more than gender inequalities facilitate coalitions.[19] This may be the case, but although women have different interests, resources and identities, they could unite, even if only on a situational basis. This book will highlight the performative aspects of identities and how they can be enacted in different ways in a range of situations which offer individuals choice and agency. Identity is fluid, but the experiences of sexual antagonism could offer women a framework to overcome the constraints of generic convections of idealised womanhood. Drawing upon this hypothesis this book explores how the discourses experienced by working-class men and women who entered the First World War were contested by the exigencies of war, but were then returned to 'traditional' forms after the war. Yet the established discourses on masculinity and femininity became problematic for men and women as the economic and social climate undermined men's ability to meet the ideal male as depicted in the dominant gender discourse, to which women also broadly adhered. The result of this was that sexual antagonism was aggravated in Scotland in the workplace, politics, communities and homes. Women responded to sexual antagonism through expressions of a 'rough kind of feminism', a form of 'popular feminism'. But although they acted in a feminist manner this was merely one of a multitude of ways in which women's political identities were formed. Significantly, women's identities were both inspired, and also stalled, by the traditional gender discourses that permeated inter-war society.

Women's responses to discursive attempts to direct their behaviour, to masculine insecurity and to the sexual antagonism that they endured were complex and contradictory. However, although women were divided

---

[19] D. Riley, *'Am I That Name?' Feminism and the Category of 'Women' in History* (London, 1988), 10.

materially and ideologically, sexual antagonism did provide a basis for coalition on specific issues that affected them as a group. Women exploited and defied gendered norms and challenged male privilege and power over physical and psychological resources, whether that was men's domination of 'skill' in the workplace and political arenas or their 'right' to abuse families and 'family wages'. This book will show how women countered their potential powerlessness in a variety of ways and in particular by using an 'assertion of the feminine' as a 'political tactic'.[20]

Studies which argue that gender discourse drains women of individuality and agency tend to depict them in the abstract as metaphors of their own lives rather than as individuals who enjoyed varied and diverse lives. This has come under criticism in recent years. Klein highlights how, in the practice of constructing meaning through the use of dichotomies, there is scope for the mobility of meaning and thus the reinterpretation and confrontation of powerful discourses.[21] Kelber also notes that evidence that a 'women's sphere' existed as a construct rather than a lived reality 'lies in the hard and constant work required to build and repair its boundaries'.[22] In Scotland women extended and contested the boundaries of the discourse, particularly in the workplace, the political arena and the community, where they challenged the constraints of the 'separate spheres' ideal.

Innes and Randall maintain that 'women were neither challenging contemporary gender ideologies nor competing for power in a male sphere'. Rather, they were 'extending their familial responsibilities within civic society towards a broader terrain of social and national welfare' when they infiltrated the political world of nineteenth-century Scotland.[23] This strategy was extended after World War I, and by this period women did challenge gender discourse and male power and privilege in the political arena. Women exploited gendered discourses intended to marginalise them and constrain their agency. Just as they had done before World War I, between the wars a range of women's groups and organisations used a gendered concept of citizenship that emphasised the 'feminine' and embraced female-centred discourses on separate spheres and motherhood as a means of empowerment. Using these discourses women put forward

[20] See M. Barrett and A. Phillips, 'Introduction', in M. Barrett and A. Phillips (eds), *Destabilising Theory: Contemporary Feminist Debates* (Cambridge, 1992), 1–9 and N. Charles, 'Feminist Practices', in N. Charles and F. Hughes-Freeland (eds), *Practising Feminism: Identity, Difference, Power* (London, 1996), 1–22.

[21] See L. E. Klein, 'Gender and the Public/Private Distinction in the Eighteenth Century: Some Questions about Evidence and Analytic Procedure', *Eighteenth-Century Studies*, 29, 1 (1996). See also E. Gordon and G. Nair, *Public Lives: Women, Family and Society in Victorian Britain* (London, 2003).

[22] L. K. Kelber, 'Separate spheres, female worlds, woman's place: the rhetoric of women's history', *The Journal of American History*, 75, 1: 9–39 (1988).

[23] S. Innes and J. Randall, 'Women, gender and politics' in L. Abram, E. Gordon, D. Simonton and E. J. Yeo (eds), *Gender and Scottish History since 1700* (Edinburgh, 2006), 59–60.

demands for 'political representation, equal legal and employment rights, participation in civic society' and improved access to social and welfare rights on the basis of their special attributes as women and mothers.[24] They also demanded a reconstruction of the domestic sphere ideal by defining it as the 'workshop of wives and mothers' where women's roles should be, although separate from men's, equal in status. Kelber demonstrates how efforts at such a reconstruction 'severely challenge the traditional social order' and in this sense should be seen as feminist.[25]

The subversion of the traditional gender discourse was not restricted to the realm of formal politics. Working-class women used gender discourses in their daily lives to provide them with a sense of empowerment and also as a means of self-legitimisation that challenged male privilege and men's advantaged access to resources and power in the workplace, the neighbourhood and the home. They also used it to enhance their access to civic resources. Thus, these strategies were used against employers, working-class men and 'their organisations', politicians, landlords and a range of powerful civic institutions that held the capacity to subordinate women.

Women had other strategies of empowerment which included the potentially subversive use of emotions such as intuition and empathy. Indeed, the power of these particular strategies is evident in the ways in which they have been historically and culturally demonised in an attempt to marginalise and silence women and restrict their power.[26] Scottish women used emotive strategies; they were vital ingredients of women's politics. They were also an essential ingredient in the operation of the women's networks in Scotland between the wars. Berger Gluck argues that women's networks were based on a 'women's consciousness: women conscious of themselves as a group; aware of their own power and that of the collectivity, all of which is defined by their traditional roles'. She contrasts this with 'a consciousness about women's oppression which is a feminist consciousness'.[27] This is simplistic: a feminist consciousness does not have to be articulated and indeed can be situational. Nor does feminist behaviour have to be intentional. Between the wars, women used their collective power and exploited their traditional roles to challenge gender oppression in localities across Scotland so that the divide between a woman's consciousness and feminist behaviour was

[24] See C. Collette, *For Labour and for Women: The Women of the Labour League 1906–1918* (Manchester, 1990), E. Gordon, *Women and the Labour Movement in Scotland 1850–1914* (Oxford, 1991), J. Hannam and K. Hunt, *Socialist Women in Britain, 1880s to 1920s* (London, 2002) and S. Innes, 'Constructing women's citizenship in the interwar period: the Edinburgh Women Citizens' Association', *Women's History Review*, 13, 4: 621–7 (2004).

[25] Kelber, 'Separate spheres', 32.

[26] A. Jagger, 'Love and knowledge: emotion in feminist epistemology', in Kemp and Squires, *Feminisms*, 188–93.

[27] C. Smith-Rosenberg, in C. Smith-Rosenberg, E. Dubois, M. L. Buhle, T. Kaplan and G. Lerner, 'Politics and culture in women's history: a symposium', *Feminist Studies*, 6, 1: 55–64 (1980).

blurred. Women exploited their subordinate positions, gaining access to resources that determined levels of power in the workplace, the political arena, the family and community. By Charles' definition these women were acting in feminist ways because they challenged areas of social and economic life that had been 'systematically structured to give men advantages over women', enabling men to 'exclude women from avenues of power'.[28] Thus, where women, individually and as a collective group, adopted survival strategies or used women's consciousness to challenge male domination of resources, physical or psychological, or as a means of self-legitimisation, then they were behaving in a feminist manner, even if they did not do so consciously.

Gender was a significant force in shaping women's identities in Scotland, but so too was class. The west of Scotland was a highly populated region with a distinctly working-class constituency that has been identified as having a powerful class awareness which gave rise to extreme militancy immediately before, during and in the years after the First World War. This has generated a debate over Scotland's radical and 'revolutionary' potential. In Scottish labour historiography it prevails that no legend is as strong in the history of the Scottish labour movement as that of Red Clydeside, and Scotland's radical left, and that story has been a masculine narrative.[29] The inclusion of women's experiences in this narrative is another purpose of this book. This insertion will fundamentally alter and challenge the narrative of working-class history in the inter-war period.

Scottish women's participation in formal and informal political struggle between the wars has been largely ignored. This is partly due to the fact that labour historiography is guilty of measuring 'class consciousness' by studies based on levels of industrial militancy and party political identity.[30] Exclusionary policies, marriage bars and the idea that women should refrain from employment after marriage are amongst the factors which can make these criteria irrelevant as a measure of women's 'militancy'. The same critique can be applied to research on women's class awareness which has been evaluated on perceptions of voting behaviour.[31] This approach neglects how class is gendered: not only were women denied equal voting rights until 1928, but many females were reluctant to participate in formal

---

[28] N. Charles, 'Feminist Practices', 23.

[29] See I. McLean, *The Legend of Red Clydeside* (Edinburgh, 1983), R. Duncan and A. McIvor (eds), *Militant Workers: Labour and Class Conflict on the Clyde 1900–1950. Essays in Honour of Harry McShane* (Edinburgh, 1992) and W. Kenefick, *Red Scotland! The Rise and Fall of the Radical Left, c. 1872 to 1932* (Edinburgh, 2007).

[30] See S. Bruley, 'Women', in J. McIlroy, A. Campbell and K. Gildart (eds), *Industrial Politics and the 1926 Mining Lockout, The Struggle for Dignity* (Cardiff, 2004), 229 and M. Nolan, '"The women were bloody marvellous": 1951, gender and New Zealand industrial relations', *Historical Studies in Industrial Relations*, 16: 132 (2003).

[31] Notable exceptions include Gordon, *Women and the Labour Movement* and J. Melling, *Rent Strikes: People's Struggle for Housing in West Scotland 1890–1916* (Edinburgh, 1983).

politics or political activity because it was seen as intimidating and unfamil-iar, a masculine world in which women's own forms of political behaviour and political priorities were not considered.[32] Nonetheless, the discursive and structural realities of class helped shape Scottish women's identities and how they viewed their place within society Gender, culture, religion, environment and everyday experiences also fashioned women's images of class and thus their political identities, which in turn determined their political behaviour.

Historians investigating the realities and experiences of everyday life during the inter-war period have access to the recollections of working-class people. Hannam argues that 'it is through an understanding of the complex inter-relationship between different forms of politics that the process by which women became politicised' and the choices that they made become evident.[33] To explore the intersection of different forms of politics in the everyday lives of women and how this politicised them this book draws on a selection of oral histories conducted between the years 1995 and 2000 as well as archive material. The narratives have been used to analyse the politics of everyday life which shaped political identi-ties. The respondents, twenty-five women and nineteen men, reflect the religious profiles of Scotland. Born between the years 1895 and 1920, with the mean year of birth being 1906, the men and women interviewed came from towns and cities with economies characterised by maritime, mining, textile and heavy industrial occupations to reflect the diversity of the Scottish economy. These individuals were also engaged in a range of jobs in the heavy industries and the new occupational employments of the inter-war years. The narratives are also supplemented by oral history projects conducted by other organisations with individuals who lived through the inter-war years in Scotland.

There are many problems associated with the use of oral history. Criticisms highlight how a lack of objectivity in the use of material can stem from an individual's potential to embellish, misremember and 'axe-grind'.[34] The omission from memory which is as important as what is remembered is also a consideration when using such sources. Memory is shaped by the discourses of time and place, and by what was, and is, deemed acceptable or unacceptable in a given society. Thus, what is remembered or forgotten can tell us about power relations and oppression and how the latter was resisted over the course of an individual's life. Furthermore, an evaluation of nostalgia in the narratives, which is a 'strategy of resistance to a world

---

[32] A. Coote and P. Patullo, *Power and Prejudice: Women and Politics* (London, 1990), 28.

[33] Hannam, 'Women and politics', 218.

[34] See S. Berger Gluck, 'Reflections on oral history in the new millennium: roundtable com-ments', *Oral History Review*, 26, 2: 1 (1996) and P. Summerfield, *Reconstructing Women's Wartime Lives: Discourse and Subjectivity in Oral Histories of the Second World War* (Manchester, 1998), especially introduction.

that deemed an individual's agency as lacking in significance', can also contribute to our understanding of the workings of power in given societies.[35]

Oral histories also form part of people's 'hidden transcripts'. Scott argues that in relations of domination and subordination there is a zone of constant struggle evident in a whole range of practices including speech. Memories of defiance, of hidden criticism, the use of ritual and of flattery to extract gains form part of those relations.[36] In this sense, whilst conventional sources may provide a medium to elicit the ways in which attempts were made to direct people's behaviour and determine their identities, the narratives reveal the level of subjectification, resistance, and the forces which shaped the latter. Hence, although not unproblematic, the narratives of Scottish men and women contributed immensely to the analysis of 'the politics of everyday life' at the centre of this book, including the manifestations of the culture and ideologies, and the signifiers for the symbolic arrangements of everyday life.

Summerfield also identifies the importance of recognising the power relations laden in the interview process. I share the same national and class profile as my respondents and for many the same gender. More significantly, I concur with Iacovetta that we 'cannot possess objective knowledge, but we can choose to try and write about others even if the final product is incomplete, uneven and filtered through us'. We may also have

> considerable power as producers of knowledge and no device or desire will ever make entirely egalitarian the relationship between the researcher and the subject but the cost of the silence of scholars from minority or working-class backgrounds is complicity in the re-silencing of neglected and marginal groups.[37]

Scottish women have been neglected and, although improving, the lack of Scottish gender studies, particularly those looking at the twentieth century, continues to be manifestly evident. British gender historiography has done little to alleviate this situation because it generally fails to include an analysis of Scottish women within a British context.[38] This book not only considers Scottish gender relations, but it also offers a comparative analysis of British experiences of gender in the workplace, politics, the community and the home. It highlights how the construction of gendered identities and the way in which their legitimisation shaped experience provided a

---

[35] L. Passerini, 'Memory', *History Workshop Journal*, 15: 195–6 (1983) and N. Norquay, 'Identity and forgetting', *Oral History Review*, 26: 1 (1999).

[36] J. C. Scott, *Domination and the Arts of Resistance: Hidden Transcripts* (New Haven, 1990), 1–18 and passim.

[37] F. Iacovetta, 'Post-modern ethnography, historical materialism, and decentring the (male) authorial voice: a feminist conversation', *Histoire Sociale/Social History*, 53, 64: 289–93 (Nov. 1999).

[38] See E. Breitenbach, A. Brown and F. Myres, 'Understanding women in Scotland', *Feminist Review*, 58: 44–65 (Spring 1998); J. Purvis, 'From "women worthies" to poststructuralism? Debates and controversy in women's history', in Purvis, *Women's History*, 14–20.

means by which women could contest extremely unequal power relations. Individuals and groups of women may have been fragmented, but they nevertheless challenged gender and class oppression in a variety of ways and, regardless of the means, much of their behaviour was identifiable as a 'rough kind of feminism'.

CHAPTER ONE

Usurpers of Men? Gender, Work and Political Identities

The gendered nature of employment and women's experiences of work between the wars remains a relatively neglected field of study, especially in Scotland. There is research on the changing patterns of women's work and the institutional impediments women endured in the workplace at this time, but generally the imagery of the 'hungry thirties', the impact of the depression and the fortunes of men in the labour market and the labour movement take precedence. Contemporary depictions of working women in the inter-war period often present them as cheap labour and 'usurpers of men's jobs', while historical representations of women tend to portray them as embracing a reconstructed domesticity. British labour historiography continues to ignore women's workplace experiences, instead giving priority to women's exclusion from work. Indeed, women have been sidelined by the 'inherent and often unacknowledged bias of labour history towards men'.[1] Thus, the perspectives that women were a politically apathetic and docile workforce which employers exploited to the detriment of male workers' wage levels and employment opportunities remains unchallenged. However, Scottish women's employment patterns, work experiences, trade union membership, industrial activism and political consciousness in the workplace, although failing to fit within labour historiography's male-centric framework, do nevertheless subvert the stereotypes that inter-war working-class women were politically apathetic or that they had the potential to undermine male employees. What the nature of women's work and trade union organisation does highlight are the considerable obstacles that working women had to overcome to achieve progress and avoid exploitation in the world of work.

Many of the impediments women faced in the inter-war years were due to their penetration of the labour market in greater numbers during the First World War which was seen as a threat to male occupations. World War I provided multiple employment opportunities for women beyond the narrow range of jobs classified as 'women's work', and this was not confined to munitions work. Women of all ages substituted for men in the perceived 'safer' occupations of retail, transport, commerce and general employment. Women also joined their male colleagues in a range of

---

[1] See Bruley, 'Women', 229 and Nolan, 'The women were bloody marvellous', 132.

occupations in factories, bakeries, shops, post offices, street cleaning, lamp lighting and policing. Indeed, 'to the amazement and shock of the old carters and officials', women had to be accepted as drivers of horse-drawn vehicles and motors.[2] Women did enter male sex-typed jobs, especially in munitions work, and this caused insecurity amongst male workers, but most female workers did not substitute for men. Many women workers were situated in factories purpose-built to accommodate war work and a great deal of the work they did was sex-typed 'women's work'.[3] Mrs Harrison recalled her employment in munitions. 'It was sewing! There was a treadle on a table and there was a weighing machine. We measured it out, cordite, just as if you were weighing out sweets.'[4] It was not the substitution of men that caused concern, but rather the evidence of women's capacity to engage in such work and the knowledge that employers might exploit this situation in the post-war years. Thus, when women replaced men at a Lanarkshire print works in 1914, rather than addressing the fact that wage rates fell from between 20/- and 28/- per week to 8/3, the labour movement, to dissuade women from considering such work on a more permanent basis, warned them that the work would 'brutalise' and 'demoralise' them and make them 'unfit for motherhood and social life'.[5] The Union of Shop Assistants was worried about replacing men with women because 'temporary expedients have a nasty knack of becoming permanent features'.[6] The perception of women as a threat to male employment caused sexual antagonism in the workplace, but expediency was often adopted during the war rather than outright hostility because of the necessity to employ female labour. The Amalgamated Society of Engineers demanded that the National Federation of Women Workers 'ensure that there would be no cheap labour' and enforce 'the just claim of women for equality of treatment with men be made good' – at least for the duration of the war![7]

After World War I, women were subjected to verbal and ideological assaults from the industrial wing of the labour movement, employers, the state and male workers which was intended to undermine their contribution to industry and condone their expulsion from wartime occupations. In 1920 the Operative Bakers and Confectioners Union supported male members who placed strike notices that demanded the removal of female employees. The women were not ousted without protest. They argued that the growth of firms in this sector had provided greater employment opportunities for both men and women and also pointed out that because of

[2] A. Tuckett, *The Scottish Carter* (London, 1967), 130.

[3] J. Liddington, *The Long Road To Greenham, Feminism and Anti-Militarism in Britain since 1820* (London, 1989), 109 and J. Hinton, *The First Shop Stewards Movement* (London, 1973), 63.

[4] SOHCA/019/09/Glasgow, b. 1900. See also G. De Groot, *Blighty: British Society in the Era of the Great War* (London, 1996).

[5] *Forward*, 16 May 1914.

[6] *Forward*, 20 Feb. 1915.

[7] *Forward*, 18 Dec. 1915.

men's exclusionary policies they would be unable to leave a job to further their prospects. Females would be forced to remain tied to their present employer, regardless of working conditions, because length of service indicated that they were not encroaching upon male territory. These women were also aware of the source of their exploitation. They stressed that 'men would not tolerate this! Trade unions are imposing restrictions that did not exist prior to the war.'[8] Public and private sector employers expressed negative opinions about Scottish women's wartime work performance at the end of the conflict. It was identified as 'inferior' to men's. Women workers were accused of having no 'initiative', and 'no sense of duty and moral responsibility'.[9] The manager of Glasgow's Tramway Department stated of his 430 female employees that they were 'more likely to have accidents', after which 'owing to nervous breakdown they had to be relieved for the rest of the day'.[10] Male attitudes towards women's wartime work highlights the pressures placed on women to restrict themselves to what was identified as 'women's work' and for married women to refrain from employment.[11]

Yet it has been suggested that women entered male occupations during the war largely by invitation and that this explains their relative acquiescence to their expulsion thereafter.[12] The situation was more complex and contradictory than this hypothesis suggests. Many munitions jobs were discontinued; protest in this context was fruitless. At the same time, in some occupations women did contest their expulsion, whilst others were content to be expelled. Some women remained in the occupations they had secured during the war.[13] Therefore, experiences varied immensely. Like the female workers 'invited' into the world of work in the Second World War, women had to adjust to the ruptures created by World War I. In the post-war years women were torn between multiple and contradictory ideals of femininity, ranging from the wartime vision of the woman worker to the post-war re-establishment of the traditional ideal on womanhood.[14] Mrs Harrison was distraught when she lost her job in munitions, but felt sympathy for men who lost their jobs to women. 'The jobs were all taken up before the boys came home. They never got their job back. My younger brother, it was a shame, he was working in an office when he joined the army, and he could hardly get a job. Needless to say women were scared.

---

[8] *Forward*, 13 and 27 Nov. 1920.

[9] J. Arnot, 'Women workers and trade union participation in Scotland, 1919–1939', Ph.D. thesis (University of Glasgow, 1999), 27–9.

[10] D. Cairns, 'Women and the Clydeside labour movement', M.Phil. thesis (University of Strathclyde, 1996), 38–41.

[11] Lewis, 'In search of a real equality', 212–13.

[12] Cairns, 'Women and the Clydeside labour movement', 197.

[13] J. D. Young, *Women and Popular Struggles: A History of Scottish and English Working-class Women 1500–1984* (Edinburgh, 1985).

[14] Summerfield, *Reconstructing Women's Wartime Lives*, Chapter six.

They didn't want to give up their jobs.'[15] These ruptures affected men too, as did the labour movement's discourse on the female usurper. Mr Davidson was a baker between the wars. He claimed that

> After the war a lot of jobs were taken over by women and that suited some of the bosses, cheaper labour. The men could never get their jobs back again. The women were kept on. As a matter of fact practically every shop you went into, it was always men that were serving, bakers, you name it, grocers, but all these shop-keeping jobs died out with regards a man working.[16]

The omission from Mr Davidson's memory of the concerted attempts to exclude women from the bakery trade may be this man's attempt to find interview composure, but clearly the labour movement's inter-war discourse as it related to working women as a threat to men's jobs is also present.

The idea that women might usurp men in the world of work by offering their services at a cheaper rate had penetrated the discourses of the industrial wing of the labour movement long before the inter-war years. Between the wars this intensified when the 'breadwinner ideal' was being reaffirmed and was simultaneously vulnerable to high levels of unemployment, the threat from women's lower pay and the changing nature of work. Thus, exclusionary policies designed to ensure the sex-segregation of employment and the exclusion of women from work increased. Eleanor Rathbone, an inter-war feminist, felt compelled to warn women that 'only when there is work for all is it relatively easy for men to be magnanimous'.[17] Nevertheless the pressure of the dominant gender discourse and relative improvements in working-class standards of living may have influenced some married women to refrain from paid work. Seemingly some women also refrained from undertaking paid employment willingly to maintain a family wage as a form of resistance to capitalist exploitation. This is seen as having been a conscious strategy to sustain working-class households under conditions of dangerous exploitation rather than evidence of false gender consciousness.[18] Families also depended on children's earnings rather than the wages of wives so as not to undermine the breadwinner ideal.[19] While it is clear that married women faced considerable pressure to refrain from undertaking paid work this should not detract from the experiences of single women or those married and widowed women who were either

[15] SOHCA/019/09/Glasgow, b. 1900.

[16] SOHCA/019/030/Glasgow, b. 1900.

[17] Quoted in B. Harrison, *Prudent Revolutionaries: Portraits of British Feminists between the Wars* (Oxford, 1987), 314.

[18] Pugh, *Women and the Women's Movement*, 81, 140, E. Roberts, *A Woman's Place: An Oral History of Working-class Women 1890–1940* (Oxford, 1984), 10 and A. Campbell, *The Scottish Miners, Vol. One* (Aldershot, 2000), 235.

[19] S. Pederson, *Family Dependence and the Origins of the Welfare State: Britain and France* (Cambridge, 1993), 311–12.

compelled to or chose to work. In Scotland although 50 per cent of all married women who worked in 1931 were between the ages of thirty-five and fifty-four, suggesting that they had raised their families before return- ing to work, the other 50 per cent of married working women were largely among those of child-rearing age who were evidently undermining the breadwinner ideal.[20]

Moreover, in some regions of Scotland, especially textile areas, an alter- native family ideal, the dual-income family, was evident. This model actively encouraged married women to work and understood women and men's incomes to be of equal importance. The ideal was spreading between the wars and was accompanied by important demographic changes. Scottish women married later than their English counterparts and although fer- tility rates were falling less slowly in Scotland, the declining birth rate contributed to an increase in the number of married women undertaking work in the formal economy.[21] The dual-income ideal, smaller family size and more frequently material impediments ensured that many married women worked in the formal and informal economies. Not all married women had equal access to the economic means to ensure that they could embrace the ideal that a woman's place was in the home as a dependant of her spouse. Mr Armstrong was born out of wedlock in December 1905, because his father, a hewer, could not afford to marry his mother until he secured work. His parents had nine children. Mr Armstrong recalled how his mother, a seamstress, supplemented his father's earnings. 'She had a contract with the rag trade. She got practically coppers for it, but she was actually manufacturing dresses, working in the house. She got about 3d for a dozen dresses.'[22] Mrs Kilpatrick returned to work because 'I would have been hungry many a time and my children, but I went out to work. I did house-cleaning.'[23] Mr Parsonage recalled:

> I was the oldest of seven and I had to look after them all. I had to be able to feed them because my mother was doing a cleaning job. She had to. She went to the private houses and scrubbed steps for a loaf of bread.[24]

Elizabeth Wheeler was born in the mining village of Cowie in 1924 and she recalled a widowed mother of two young children who had to take in a lodger, clean two offices and do the shopping for two bachelors to 'make ends meet'.[25] While it has been acknowledged that poor women worked out of necessity, it is also maintained that this ensured that women were

[20] *Census for Scotland* [hereafter *Census*], 1931.
[21] A. McIvor, 'Gender apartheid? Women in Scottish society', in T. M. Devine and R. J. Finlay (eds), *Scotland in the Twentieth Century* (Edinburgh, 1996), 190.
[22] SOHCA/019/027/Glasgow, b. 1905.
[23] SOHCA/019/012/Glasgow, b. 1907.
[24] SOHCA/019/026/Cardiff, b. 1915.
[25] E. Wheeler, *Growing Up in Cowie and Bannockburn* (Stirling, 2006), 37.

not interested in their jobs and this vindicated men's negative impressions of women workers. It justified lower wages, even though 'women were compelled to work and could not afford the luxury of dissenting from employers' opinions'.[26] Necessity ensured that many married women worked, but as it will become clear, single and married women were interested in their jobs, but they faced considerable institutional discrimination.

State policies limited women's employment opportunities after World War I. The Restoration of Pre-War Practices Act was followed by a drive to re-situate females into 'women's work', primarily domestic service. Women who refused this employment were denied benefits.[27] Discrimination of this nature doubly disadvantaged women because those who had secured work during World War I in the manufacturing sector, which was generally insured employment, often found themselves relocated after the war into uninsured sectors of employment, especially domestic service.[28] Because of this, and the extent to which 'women's work' remained uninsured, structured gender inequality in access to unemployment insurance and to unemployment benefits ensued. This situation was aggravated by the Anomalies Act which effectively barred married women from receiving unemployment benefit. Labour exchanges, which supplied prospective employers with workers, only kept records of the unemployed in receipt of benefits thus reducing women's ability to secure employment. Protective legislation also limited the hours women could work, further disadvantaging access to paid employment.[29] Consequently unemployment was not the masculine problem that it is often presented as in the literature documenting the period. The 1931 census recorded 11.3 per cent of Scottish women as unemployed, but in Glasgow the rate of female unemployment was 20 per cent, and this excludes uninsured workers such as domestic servants. Female unemployment was much higher in textile regions. In Dundee, by 1931, female unemployment rates stood at 41.2 per cent in contrast to male unemployment rates which were 37.6 per cent.[30]

Marriage bars also affected the employment of women and these became increasingly important in the depressed 1920s and 1930s when unemployment rates averaged 10 per cent, a rate which was greater in Scotland.[31] Women were conditioned or forced to leave their place of employment on marriage. Mrs Edwards worked in the hosiery trade before marriage. After her marriage she and her sister applied to work in a factory making

---

[26] C. Chinn, *They Worked All Their Lives: Women of the Urban Poor in England, 1880–1939* (Manchester, 1988), 87–88.

[27] Lewis, 'In search of a real equality', 213.

[28] See N. Whiteside, *Bad Times: Unemployment in British Social and Political History* (London, 1991).

[29] M. Savage, 'Trade unionism, sex segregation, and the State: women's employment in new industries in inter-war Britain', *Social History*, 13, 2: 223–5 (1988).

[30] Arnot, 'Women workers', 239.

[31] J. Humphries, 'Women and paid work', in Purvis, *Women's History*, 100.

cardboard boxes. They were refused on the grounds that they were married women. Mrs Edwards remembered, 'it was supposed to be you got married and brought up a family and looked after your man, and it was silly, it was foolish, because you were young and you were able to work'. Indeed, in March 1931 Wishaw Co-operative Society in Lanarkshire proposed to disqualify married women and argued that they should not be eligible to receive insurance money. Other employers used pronatalist discourses to justify married women's exclusion from work. Margaret Allen worked for a company which dyed furs in Barrhead; they refused to employ married women because the work was too heavy for women who might fall pregnant. In this environment there were women who postponed marriage to avoid the marriage bar. Mrs Galbraith, an office worker, recalled, 'I'd a very good job and as far as I was concerned my wages were so good and I was having such a wonderful life that there was no point in rushing into getting married.'[32] Trade union demands for a family wage also discriminated against women by shoring up the perception that women should be dependants of men. Indeed, inter-war feminists argued that the family wage was designed to promote 'full employment for men'.[33] In the persistently slack labour markets of the inter-war Scottish economy this resulted in protective labour relations that underpinned an understanding between employers and unions that women should regard themselves as housewives and dependants of men.[34]

At the root of Scotland's economic problems lay its over-concentration on heavy industries. Staple industries had faced rising foreign competition before 1914. During World War I, armament contracts helped to disguise the extent and force of foreign competition, but at the same time they allowed employers to take advantage of the Excess Profit Duty. Established in 1915, the duty was designed to impede war profiteering by imposing a tax of 100 per cent on excess profits. However, this could be evaded through the loophole that allowed profits to be redirected into capital expenditure, thus contributing to the geographical concentration and over-commitment to heavy industry. After the short post-war boom, the loss of markets became visibly apparent. Britain's return to the gold standard at pre-war parity, which caused the pound to be overvalued at a time when world prices were falling, also adversely affected industry, especially those which were heavily export-orientated. This, and the high interest rates and taxation used to maintain parity, impeded investment. The spread of 'new

---

[32] SOHCA/019/06/Glasgow, b. 1907, L. Sinclair, '"Silenced, suppressed and passive": a refocused history of Lanarkshire women, 1920–1939', Ph.D. thesis (University of Strathclyde, 2005), 131, The Barrhead People's Story Group, *It's Funny Whit Ye Remember: Shared Memories of Life Experiences from 1920 to the 1950s* (Essex, 2002), 142 and SOHCA/019/08/Glasgow, b. 1916 respectively.

[33] Harrison, *Prudent Revolutionaries*, 125.

[34] See P. Hudson and W. R. Lee, *Women's Work and the Family Economy in Historical Perspective* (Manchester, 1990), 34.

industries' in inter-war Britain did not compensate for unemployment in heavy industries: new industries contributed only 11 per cent of total net output in Scotland between the wars.[35] In 1947, the Labour activist John Taylor, commenting on the Government White Papers on the Scottish economy, claimed that inter-war Scotland was 'the most depressed of depressed areas, with the highest unemployment percentages' and that 'the whole country, with the exception of some agricultural districts, was in a state of decay'.[36]

In regions characterised by staple industries economic decline played a significant role in creating a sense of vulnerability amongst male workers. Although some 'new industries' were introduced that corresponded with technological progress and alternative managerial strategies, such as quasi-Taylorist methods, work processes remained relatively static. For most of the inter-war years the 'gospel of hard work' remained the predominant managerial strategy because 'indivisibility of plant' and the dearth of 'new industries' ensured that traditional practices were maintained. Wages were cut and work intensified. Reducing labour overheads also inhibited reconstruction by curtailing domestic demand.[37] Rationalisation entailed a concerted attack on labour with unemployment assisting an employers' offensive as economic circumstances reduced the bargaining power of workers and trade unions. This commenced with the rooting out of militants. By 1922 John Brown's shipyard on the Clyde had no shop stewards. Foremen had their powers increased and the status, privileges and restrictive practices of skilled workers were undermined.[38] In engineering, which employed a vast number of men, routinisation, mechanisation and work-related payment systems were introduced as a result of experimentation during World War I, resulting in a 28 per cent decline in jobs classified as skilled. However, trade unions continued to influence local and national government policy. They demanded the expulsion of women from engineering and the skilled workers' power base in the STUC 'guaranteed that even during the depression non-union shops were refused government contracts if they did not recognise nationally negotiated wage levels and conditions'.[39] In printing, by contrast, according to the STUC, work that had formerly been done under trade union conditions was being threatened by the introduction of 'multigraph' machines that cheapened printing processes because it could be used by 'non-unionist girls' on extremely 'poor wages'.[40] A trade

---

[35] Buxton, 'Economic growth in Scotland', 549.

[36] *Labour Women*, 15 Sep. 1947.

[37] W. W. Knox, 'Class, work and trade unionism in Scotland', in A. Dickson and J. H. Treble (eds), *People and Society in Scotland, Vol. III* (Edinburgh, 1992), 114.

[38] A. McKinlay and A. Hampton, 'Making ships, making men: working for John Brown's between the wars', *Oral History*, 19, 1: 24–5 (1991).

[39] Knox, 'Class, work and trade unionism', 115–29.

[40] A. Tuckett, *The Scottish Trades Union Congress, the First 80 Years, 1897–1977* (Edinburgh, 1986), 237.

union's strength determined the extent to which workers could resist management's encroachment at the point of production, including the infiltration of female labour and Taylorist managerial strategies, which were the principal features of 'rehabilitation'. The number of women working in engineering in Scotland declined from 11,290 in 1924 to 10,230 by 1933. In London, by contrast, the introduction of 'new industries' and a process of work degradation resulted in an increased female labour force. In 1924, 41,170 females worked in engineering in London. By 1933 this figure had risen to 73,670.[41]

The relative absence of new industries, state policies and the political mobilisation of men partially offset the appeal of cheap female labour in Scotland. Nevertheless, the vulnerability that ensued from the possible effects of capitalism in transition, facilitated by structural unemployment, was spreading as men were compelled to seek work in the growth sectors of white-collar, retail and the 'new' industrial occupations. The idea that women were a menace to male jobs therefore occurred in an environment of intensification, rationalisation and substitution in the principal heavy industries, which raised the significance of work for men that was less rigidly sex-typed masculine. In 1929, the Lord Privy Seal, Mr Thomas, a linchpin 'moderate' of the TUC and leader of the Railwaymen's Union, gave an address that encapsulated the discourse of the labour movement towards women in the workplace, especially married women. He stated:

> Despite the tremendous volume of unemployment and the absolute necessity for some women to work in industry, it is not only uneconomic, it is not only unfair, but it is against the nation's interests for women to work for what they call 'pin money' and to deprive other working people of legitimate work. It is morally wrong.[42]

The state also subscribed to this politically expedient worldview. If successful it would reduce male unemployment and therefore contribute to the maintenance of social stability. Thus, state schemes were introduced to train young women in domestic service, many with the intention of encouraging them to emigrate to the Dominions.[43] Yet these conditions corresponded with changes in the nature of work which expanded the range of jobs open to women. As Table 1.1 highlights, more women were entering formal employment in mining, maritime and industrial and commercial towns and cities.

In 1931, 38 per cent of women worked in the formal economy in Aberdeen and in Edinburgh 41 per cent of women were gainfully employed. In Dundee 55 per cent of women worked in the formal economy.[44] Textile

---

[41] M. A. Hamilton, *Women at Work, A Brief Introduction to Trade Unionism For Women* (London, 1941), 136–7.

[42] *Glasgow Herald*, 25 Nov. 1929.

[43] *Glasgow Herald*, 16 and 17 Oct. 1928.

[44] *Census*, 1931.

Table 1.1 Women enumerated as gainfully employed in selected areas of Scotland, 1921–31.

Region	1921			1931		
	Total enumerated	Gainfully employed	Percentage gainfully employed	Total enumerated	Gainfully employed	Percentage gainfully employed
Clydebank	16,426	4,429	26.9	16,739	5,416	32.3
Glasgow	404,888	146,022	35.7	424,857	165,868	39.0
Greenock	29,032	8,701	29.9	28,389	9,548	33.6
Motherwell and Wishaw	23,627	5,364	22.7	22,272	5,904	26.5
Paisley	35,292	15,012	42.6	34,884	14,947	42.8
Port Glasgow	7,347	2,129	28.9	6,679	2,269	33.9

Source: *Census of Scotland*, 1921 and 1931. The school-leaving age was raised from twelve to fourteen years between both censuses.

areas, like Paisley and Dundee, continued to have the greatest proportion of women workers and these employees were largely confined to traditional female sectors of employment in the mills. Nevertheless, Table 1.2 below indicates that from 1911 the number of women employed in commerce, the service and retail sectors, food production, drink and tobacco, and to a lesser extent standardised production in 'new industries' was increasing.

White-collar and commercial occupations together with the jobs in the 'new industries' were less susceptible to unemployment. Women were able to penetrate these sectors not only because of the expansion of these jobs, but because they were either non-unionised or weakly unionised occupations.[45] Therefore, while many male jobs were opened to the force of unemployment, the new occupations were 'sheltered' and often labelled or re-labelled 'women's work'. Thus, the changing nature of work held the potential to embed the idea of the female usurper. Yet, women's expanding occupational opportunities were often accompanied by a 'degrading' rather than a 'deskilling' of the job's classification to justify women's lower pay.[46] The contemporary Mary Agnes Hamilton stated, 'women who earned 50 per cent of what men earned counted themselves lucky'.[47] In 1928, 70 per cent of the 3,000,000 British workers who had their wages set by the Trades Board were women.[48]

For employers the appeal of standardisation and the subsequent substitution of more expensive male labour with women and youths would have been immense, but many were not in a position to implement these changes. Employers were also divided over the benefits of such strategies. The arrival of monopoly capitalism was a very gradual process in Britain. This was particularly so in Scotland because the economy served a specialised demand incompatible with standardisation. 'Skill' remained vital to production because 'transaction costs outweighed efficiency concerns when combined with market demand'.[49] A rejection of the high-wage strategy and the administration costs implicit in scientific management and standardisation characterised Scotland's workplaces. Yet where cheap labour, especially young workers, could be used to cut costs, it was as Table 1.3 below highlights.

The number of juveniles employed fell, along with the number of workers in every age group, because of unemployment. Despite this, there were changing patterns within the trend. The nature of work and the appeal of women workers as cheap labour increased the range of jobs open

---

45 S. Walby, *Patriarchy at Work, Patriarchal and Capitalist Relations in Employment* (London, 1986), 2–3 and passim.

46 D. Simonton, *A History of European Women's Work 1700 to Present* (London, 1998), 254.

47 Hamilton, *Women at Work*, 151.

48 *Forward*, 4 Feb. 1928.

49 A. McIvor, 'Were Clydeside employers more autocratic? Labour management and the "labour unrest"', in A. McIvor and W. Kenefick (eds), *The Roots of Red Clydeside* (Edinburgh, 1996), 47.

Table 1.2 Strathclyde employment statistics, 1911–31.

Occupation	Male			Female		
	1911	*1921*	*1931*	*1911*	*1921*	*1931*
Agriculture, forestry and fishing	31,672	31,604	32,174	7,625	6,813	4,402
Mining and quarrying	82,406	90,217	71,622	1,048	2,201	983
Food, drink and tobacco	13,678	21,951	24,120	8,775	18,614	20,948
Coal and petroleum products				844		147
Chemicals and allied industries	5,495	8,040	7,866	1,471	2,424	2,309
Metal manufacturing	48,748	68,127	50,214	150	1,831	1,396
Electrical engineering	4,560	5,027	5,130	50	702	751
Shipbuilding and marine engineering	45,314	95,976	65,884	268	2,242	1,230
Vehicles	6,685	10,000	19,461	82	711	882
Metal goods not elsewhere specified	25,784	10,279	9,337	1,462	2,460	2,134
Textiles	20,052	19,779	19,206	45,082	42,008	42,366
Leather, leather goods and fur	2,825	2,476	2,627	427	1,058	1,068
Clothing	15,597	13,279	10,657	36,894	26,129	20,040
Bricks, pottery, glass, cement etc.	6,539	6,311	9,608	1,497	1,924	1,902
Timber, furniture etc.	14,702	17,825	19,287	3,292	3,214	3,504
Paper, printing and publishing etc.	8,699	9,728	12,486	8,711	8,229	9,136
Other manufacturing industries	2,300	3,322	5,328	1,690	2,147	2,646
Construction	52,682	31,783	48,174	67	1,374	1,831
Gas, electricity and water	4,885	10,037	9,703	7	598	374
Transport and communications	88,441	81,294	85,012	7,033	4,755	8,332
Distribution trades	52,611	71,386	10,012	7,033	4,755	8,332
Insurance, banking, finance and business	10,936	10,298	12,577	269	4,350	3,851

Table 1.2 (continued)

Occupation	Male			Female		
	1911	*1921*	*1931*	*1911*	*1921*	*1931*
Professional and scientific services	17,388	14,407	20,993	16,497	13,074	28,505
Miscellaneous services	5,427	23,540	31,066	68,228	62,254	73,559
Public administration and defence	12,713	43,495	35,551	543	21,700	9,278
Total employed	716,239	781,802	772,614	226,250	300,530	324,094

Source: C. Lee, *British Regional Employment Statistics* (Cambridge, 1979).

Table 1.3 Occupation of juveniles in selected regions of the west of Scotland, 1931.

Region	Male	Female
Scotland	81.9	69.3
Clydebank	81.8	71.4
Glasgow	82.0	76.9
Greenock	81.0	66.9
Motherwell and Wishaw	77.1	58.7
Paisley	84.9	82.7
Port Glasgow	79.8	68.4

Source: *Census for Scotland*, 1931.

to women, but this varied regionally. Young women fared more favourably in Paisley where textile employment remained dominant. However, while employers continued to hire comparatively large numbers of young men, in Clydebank and Glasgow they were increasingly showing a greater propensity than was the average in Scotland to employ young women. Jessie Dreghorn, a shop assistant between the wars, recalled, 'in those days bosses were all powerful and if they could get someone cheaper you were out'.[50]

The trend towards employing young women was facilitated by rise of the tertiary sector and changes in merchandise. Women did not substitute for men; instead, a combination of new forms of employment and the extension of work already sex-typed 'women's work' widened their employment opportunities. The physical appearance of young women also became an increasing consideration for employers of office and retail workers. Yet the construction, by employers, of a discourse characterising the female worker and women's 'work culture' as 'docile, politically apathetic and

[50] Glasgow Regional Archive [hereafter GRA], Workers' Educational Association [hereafter WEA], *Growing Up in Shettleston between the Wars* (1985), interview with Jessie Dreghorn, born Shettleston, Glasgow 1910.

easily managed' was also an important feature of women's work opportunities.[51] Scottish women's employment in clerical occupations increased significantly between the wars, but the majority of women who worked in commerce were employed as typists and message girls. Moreover when it was recognised that female white-collar workers could work as effectively as their male colleagues and by association compete with them, a 'pink-collar ghetto' was created in which women faced vertical and horizontal segregation.[52] This was obviously with the tacit support of employers. In Glasgow, of the 15,802 women employed in commerce in 1921, 8,479 were typists. By the 1930s white-collar female employees were largely confined to routine work, denied promotion and expelled from work on marriage. Local and national governments were major employers of civil servants. In 1925, Greenock councillors presented a motion to the Parish Council that was 'unanimously' supported by the Greenock Trades and Labour Council. The motion requested that the female Assistant Inspector be given a month's notice that her services would be dispensed with, and that the Council 'appoint in her stead a suitable man with large family obligations'.[53]

Although women continued to be confined to jobs characterised by low pay, less standing and few, if any, promotional prospects, they did not accept this placidly. When attempts were made by male workers to drive women from the telegraph service the women made it clear at trade union conferences that they would fight against this and their inability to achieve promotion. These female employees stated that they desired 'positions even as high as Postmasterships. We place no limit to our ability and ambitions.'[54] It is clear that women did show an interest in their work and that there was no vindication for men's negative impressions of these workers. However, it is also clear that men were supported in their opinions by employers. In 1931, the Civil Service maintained that it was unable to find a woman 'with the essential qualities for management'.[55]

In the retail sector the situation was more complex. Increased employment opportunities for women became available because of the growth of chain stores and department stores, but this corresponded with the 'deskilling' of work processes in retail implicit in the shift to self-service and pre-packed food. Thus, a growing numbers of women workers were entering 'new' jobs in retail but these jobs were afforded low status and were poorly paid.[56] Work also remained sex-typed: by 1931 there were 5,701 men and

---

[51] Simonton, *Women's Work*, 254.

[52] G. Wilson, 'Women's work in offices and the preservation of men's "breadwinning" jobs in early twentieth-century Glasgow', *Women's History Review*, 10, 3: 461–82 (2001), especially 478.

[53] *Census*, 1921 and *Greenock Parish Records*, General Report 1925.

[54] *Scotsman*, 7 Jan. 1933.

[55] *Scotsman*, 24 Feb. 1931.

[56] J. Cushman, 'Negotiating the shop floor: employee and union loyalties in British and American retail, 1939–1970', Ph.D. thesis (University of Glasgow, 2003), 195–9.

5,412 women employed in department stores in Glasgow. However, men dominated areas such as the meat and grocery trade, and women areas such as confectionery and clothing. In 1911, there were 2,652 male butchers and 183 females employed in the retail of meat. By 1931, the numbers were 4,605 and 502 respectively.[57] Mr Davidson, a baker, maintained that 'there were no women in the bread factory. You'd get them in pastry, not bread. The work was too heavy', or more appropriately, the work was sex-typed male.[58]

In professional occupations there was an increase in the number of female teachers and nurses because of the sex-typing of some areas of the teaching and medical professions. Improvements in health care and education were a phenomenon influenced by the labour movement's growing electoral support and by concerns for a healthier and more productive workforce due to fears of foreign competition. This opened opportunities in these fields of employment for both sexes, but within gendered demarcations. In 1931 there were 970 physicians and surgeons in Glasgow, but of these only 154 were women. In 1901 there were 2,573 women teaching in Glasgow and by 1931, there were 4,642.[59] While women did make some progress, it was curtailed. For example when the Lanarkshire Education Board appointed a woman as 'first assistant' to the New Stevenson Roman Catholic School in 1932, the Board faced a deputation from male teachers objecting to her appointment.[60]

Many of the 'new' jobs that emerged in the inter-war years also grew out of older industries, sex-typed as male. In these occupations male trade unionism already had a tradition of using exclusionary policies against women, especially in engineering. In 1936 the engineering trade unionist Mr O'Haloran stated that he was 'opposed lock, stock and barrel to the employment of women in the industry'. He believed that the feeling of his fellow countrymen was that 'the proper place for women is in the home'. Women were identified as 'a danger to members and wage standards'. O'Haloran asked engineers, 'should we not be ashamed of ourselves to talk about the conditions of women in the industry, when there are over a million men who are unable to find employment'.[61] Working men agreed with his assessment. Mr Gordon, a shipbuilder from Clydebank, felt that there were more jobs for women in factories such as Singers sewing machine factory, a 'new industry', because 'women got poorly paid'.[62]

The labour movement and male workers did not identify equal pay as a means of uniting workers against exploitative work environments. In 1938 the National Union of General and Municipal Workers maligned women

---

[57] *Census*, 1911, 1921 and 1931.
[58] SOHCA/019/030/Glasgow, b. 1900.
[59] *Census*, 1921 and 1931.
[60] *Daily Record*, 2 Jun. 1932.
[61] *Scotsman*, 5 Jun. 1936.
[62] SOHCA/019/07/Clydebank, b. 1920.

as a 'menace to industry' because in some jobs women received wages as low as 4/6 for a fifty- to sixty-hour week and consequently this was seen to be forcing down the wages of young men to £1 per week.[63] However, by the later 1930s some unions, especially those representing occupations where men and women worked alongside each other, began to support equal pay 'in theory if not in practice'. But this was also a strategy to displace female workers: women would no longer be cheap labour. In 1938, the Railway Clerks Association stated, 'the low standard of pay granted to women is a menace to the welfare of the community. The time has come when women should demand equal pay with men for similar duties.'[64] While there were progressive unions, it is also evident that the impending Second World War would guarantee women's greater participation in the labour market, as well as their entry into traditional male employment. These forces resulted in demands for equal pay, just as they had done in World War I, not to promote equality but to safeguard future male employment interests. Women workers were therefore naturally suspicious of men's support and because of this they were more inclined to moderate their demands for higher wages as opposed to equal wages.[65] Women were not deluded about men's perception of equal pay. Mrs Anderson, a textile worker, argued that 'men got more money. Men always do right enough. There'd have been a hue and cry if the women had been making the same money as the men. They'd have been going out on strike.'[66] Eleanor Rathbone complained in 1936 that there was no progress on equal pay and opportunity for women because the 'exceptional unemployment has intensified masculine jealousy'. Rathbone identified the barriers to women's progress as trade unions and 'professional exclusiveness'.[67] The expansion of 'women's work' may have appeared to provide 'opportunity, liberation and independence' for women. In reality it was usually the product of 'different definitions of labouring activity', based on 'ascribed gender differences' which were generally accompanied by the 'degrading of work' and wages for women.[68] Moreover, improved opportunities largely benefited single women as table 1.4 indicates.

The number of married women working in the formal economy in Scotland rose by 4.8 per cent between 1911 and 1921. In the next decade the number of married women working in the formal economy rose again by 6.4 per cent. This was lower than the British average of 10 per cent for the 1930s.[69] Thus, the number of married women in work remained marginal.

[63] *Scotsman*, 2 Jun. 1936.
[64] *Scotsman*, 21 Sep. 1938.
[65] Arnot, 'Women workers', 61, 210–12.
[66] SOHCA/019/02/Glasgow, b. 1908.
[67] Quoted in Harrison, *Prudent Revolutionaries*, 314.
[68] Simonton, *Women's Work*, 2, 231–54, 269.
[69] Lewis, 'In search of a real equality', 210.

Table 1.4 Occupied married women in selected regions of Scotland as enumerated in the Census, 1921–31.

Region	1921			1931		
	Total number of married women	Gainfully employed	Percentage gainfully employed	Total number of married women	Gainfully employed	Percentage gainfully employed
Clydebank	8,484	150	1.7	9,016	278	3
Glasgow	181,531	11,103	6.1	201,430	14,843	7.3
Greenock	13,693	278	2	14,079	474	3.3
Motherwell and Wishaw	11,919	160	1.3	12,087	818	6.7
Paisley	14,542	998	6.9	15,720	1,331	8.4

Source: *Census for Scotland*, 1921 and 1931.

Furthermore, in Britain between 1921 and 1931 the number of widows employed in the formal economy declined by 4 per cent, while the decrease in Scotland was 3 per cent.[70] The declining number of widows in work was due to the introduction of widows' pensions in 1925, which allocated 10/- per week to widows, 5/- for the first child and 3/- for subsequent dependent children.[71] Yet evidence from the families of widows in this study suggests that these sums of money were insufficient to maintain a family so that many women were obliged to seek employment, albeit in the informal economy. Indeed, it may well be the case that this benefit reduced any sympathy employers had for hiring widows, pushing them into the informal economy. Thus, although the nature of work was in transition, the effects of this did not result in women becoming a real threat to male employees between the wars. Work in the formal economy remained for the majority of women a temporary experience until marriage. Employment opportunities were proscribed and harnessed by the operation of formal and informal marriage bars. This reinforced horizontal segregation that denied women opportunities for training and promotion. Advancement was slight: the majority of women remained narrowly confined to a small group of occupations associated with their gender.

Except where textile employment continued to dominate, by 1931 domestic service was the main occupation of Scottish women. In Edinburgh, like Glasgow, where a declining number of women were taking up employment in domestic service between 1911 and 1921, and regardless of increasing employment opportunities, the number of domestic servants rose from 20 per cent of the total female workforce to 22 per cent between 1921 and 1931. In 1931, 16 per cent of women workers were employed in commerce in Glasgow, 14 per cent worked in offices and a further 19 per cent in personal services. This trend continued throughout the 1930s with the number of women in these sectors increasing. In rural and mining areas, including Shetland, Lanarkshire and Fife, this pattern was replicated. In some mining communities over a third of women enumerated were employed as domestic servants.[72] By 1931, women workers in Motherwell were situated thus: 28 per cent worked in commerce, 21 per cent in personal service, 12 per cent in an office and 11 per cent in textiles or making textile goods. Even in Dundee the number of domestic servants increased, rising from 7 per cent of the female workforce in 1921 to 8 per cent by 1931. Like the heavy industries that employed men, Scotland's textile workforce was at the forefront of rationalisation and unemployment between the wars. In 1921, 7,905 Paisley women were classified as textile workers, more than 50 per cent. By 1931 this figure had fallen to 4,717, just over one-third. At this time, 8 per cent of women enumerated in Paisley worked in an

---

[70] *Census*, 1921 and 1931.
[71] Lewis, 'In search of a real equality', 209.
[72] *Census*, 1921 and 1931 and Campbell, *Scottish Miners*, 232.

Table 1.5 Trade union membership in selected regions of Scotland, 1923–4.

Region	Female members	Percentage of all women employed	Male members	Percentage of all men employed
Scotland	78,470	18.8	457,962	37
Glasgow	15,487	14.2	117,212	41.4
Renfrewshire, Lanarkshire and Ayrshire	11,710	13.7	117,264	37.9

Source: *Report on the extent and structure of the Trade Union Movement in Scotland*, STUC Annual Report, 1925, 33–4.

office, 12 per cent in personal service and a further 10 per cent in commerce.[73] Women were not a threat to men in the world of work, although their improved opportunities, if relative, may have contributed to such a misperception.

Trade unions did little to undermine this perception or to safeguard women's jobs. Indeed, there was greater misogyny from the industrial wing of the labour movement between the wars, this being evident in a male backlash against women.[74] The Scottish labour movement excluded women, and where it did not, it denied women representation and ignored women's issues with the effect that it contributed to the continuation of women's comparatively poor working conditions and wage rates.[75] This was not because women refused to join trade unions. In 1925 there were 78,470 female trade union members in Scotland and 15,487 in Glasgow.[76] Yet, as Table 1.5 highlights, there were regional variations in women's access to trade unionism linked partly to the nature of work and the composition of the labour force in a given locality.

In Scotland, almost twice as many employed men than employed women were represented by a trade union. In Glasgow, Renfrewshire and Lanarkshire, areas dominated by heavy industries, men were nearly three times more likely than women to be members of a trade union, but in Dundee 75 per cent of the Jute and Flax Union – 15,000 members – were women.[77]

Many female trade unionists were in mixed-sex unions and according to Miss Brand of the National Union of Clerks, 'some mixed unions neglected women'. Miss Mewhort of the Edinburgh Trades Council insisted that this

[73] *Census*, 1921 and 1931.

[74] M. Savage and A. Miles, *The Remaking of the British Working Class 1840–1940* (London, 1994), 74–87. See also Alexander, 'Men's fears and women's work', 401–25.

[75] McIvor, 'Gender apartheid', 154–6.

[76] William Gallacher Memorial Library, Scottish Trades Union Congress, 28th Annual Report [hereafter STUC A/R], 1925, 33–4.

[77] Arnot, 'Women workers', 118.

resulted in women having 'a natural distrust of male protection'.[78] The way in which prominent trade union activists articulated their perception of the benefits of trade unions for women was unlikely to mediate this or inspire confidence amongst female trade unionists or prospective female members. In 1932, Ernest Bevin, then General Secretary of the Transport and General Workers' Union, addressed the readership of *Labour Women*. He stated, 'To nobody do the women owe more for their advancement and for the maintenance of standards of living, than to the Trade Union and Labour Movement' because

> In every fight and dispute which the Movement has been engaged, our thoughts have always been of the home. It is not merely to advance the position of men that the Trade Union Movement defends wage standards; it is in order that homes may be brighter; that the task of the women may be made easier.[79]

Two years later Eleanor Stewart of the Transport and General Workers Union and chairman of the STUC's Women Organisation Committee [WOC] used the same publication to argue that

> Women are anxious to be accepted as fellow workers and to share in the responsibilities and difficulties of building up an organisation necessary to solve our economic troubles. We must not allow the presence of women in industry to develop into a sex war as that would be playing into the hands of employers.[80]

The WOC was established by the STUC in 1926 to enlist female members, promote discussion on topics of interest to women, accommodate coordination between female trade unionists, women of the Labour Party and members of the Co-operative Women's Guild, facilitate propaganda and advance local activities. But, as formidable as Stewart's sentiments were, the WOC did little to alter the male-dominated structures of trade unionism. By Stewart's own admission there were significantly fewer female officials in Scotland than in England.[81] In fact, it would arguably have needed a 'sex war' to alleviate women's peripheralisation in the trade union movement and thereby their marginal positions in the workplace rather than mere accommodation as espoused by Stewart.

Women's involvement on the STUC General Council and at the highest levels of trade unionism in Scotland was weak. Few women were nominated as delegates to the STUC annual conference and those who did attend were sidelined. Moreover, although the STUC's WOC was established in 1926 and successfully promoted women's trade union groups,

---

78 STUC, 23rd A/R, 1920, 114 and 31st A/R, 1928, 83.
79 *Labour Women*, 15 Jan. 1932, 8–9.
80 *Labour Women*, 15 Apr. 1934, 58.
81 STUC, 32nd A/R, 1929, 70.

its conferences were ineffective in bringing women's issues into the mainstream of trade union policymaking. The efforts of the WOC were frustrated because of a lack of support from trade unions, officials and the rank-and-file members alike. Opposition to this organisation was rife.[82] At the first conference of the WOC, the Labour party activist Ellen Wilkinson protested against the lack of organisation and the agenda, stating that she 'deplored the fact that more reality had not been imported into it'. Miss Horen, a delegate of the Transport and General Workers' Union, claimed that 'it savoured of a happy evening for the poor', while Miss House, the delegate of the Post Office Workers Union, insisted that it was a 'farce to call them together under such circumstances'.[83] The WOC's neighbourhood meetings and special visitations to workplaces by rank-and-file female members proved more effective in membership drives.[84] The same is true for visits to local organisations, including the Co-operative Women's Guild, Women's Guilds and religious organisations, which enabled members to enlist the support of working-class mothers 'to teach their daughters what their fathers had disregarded', the benefits of trade unionism. This was in contrast to the STUC's proposal to provide 'a marriage dowry' to entice women to join a trade union, particularly as marriage generally resulted in women leaving or being made to refrain from work in the formal economy.[85]

Trade unions' attitudes towards women workers ensured that there was widespread ignorance of trade unionism amongst women, even those who had male family members in positions of power in trade unions. This was an issue raised by the National Union of Tailors and Garment Workers. It was apparently 'difficult to organise girls and women' because of 'the apparent indifference of trade union fathers to impart the knowledge, of why trade unionism is so important'.[86] However, such an approach merely reinforced the perception of women workers as dependants rather than as autonomous workers who had agency. Women were also made to feel that trade unions were male preserves. Ms Anderson stated, 'I joined this union and at first they said they didn't have women; they didn't welcome women.'[87] Mrs Jones believed unions 'helped the workers because my grandfather was a great union man', but she also recalled how before World War II

> The men didn't want women coming into the union. When the war started and they were on fire watching duty they demanded that we take a turn of fire watching duties. But they wouldn't let us in at the

---

[82] Cairns, 'Women and the Clydeside labour movement', 56.
[83] *Glasgow Herald*, 8 Sep. 1926.
[84] Tuckett, *Scottish Trades Union Congress*, 271.
[85] *Scotsman*, 20 Feb. 1928.
[86] STUC, Organisation of Women Committee, 27 Dec. 1934.
[87] SOHCA/019/02/Glasgow, b. 1908.

beginning and then when they thought they were getting done out of something they said the women had to join the union.[88]

These attitudes caused mixed feelings towards trade unions. Some women regarded unions as 'probably your only saviour'. Mrs Edwards believed unions were 'the only thing that helped you when anything happened'.[89] Other women had ambivalent feelings towards unions, even the most 'socially progressive' of them. Margaret Quaile worked for the Barrhead Co-operative Laundry. She remembered how 'on a Friday night when you got your wages and the woman came round for the money for the union she nearly got annihilated'. Many of the female workers objected to paying for a union they believed did nothing for them. Regardless of the fact that women felt that the union did not serve their interests and was not worth 4d from wages of as little as 9/6 each week, the manager of the laundry decided to educate the women on the benefits of the union. Margaret remembered that the women were all 'marched up to the office'. Mr Botherstone 'told us about all the good things the union was doing for us'. Then,

> Annie Connelly started to laugh, it was the excitement. I started to laugh, we all started. He said, 'You all find this amusing. You are all guilty of dumb insolence. I've a good mind to suspend you all.' We nearly all went down on our knees because everyone needed their job more than the next one.[90]

There were also women who displayed complete apathy towards trade unions and were not compelled to join. Married women, in particular, had most to fear from the ultimate weapon of industrial action, the strike. Young women, trained for their future roles as wives and mothers no doubt had an affinity with these concerns. One of the reasons Margaret Quaile 'nearly went down on her knees' was because her mother was a widow with three children to maintain. Margaret was frequently reminded by her mother of the significance of her contribution to the household economy.[91] Ms Anderson was also the daughter of a widow. She recalled ignoring grievances at work because 'I'd probably have been too scared to go and tell in case I'd get the sack. I'd have dreaded that. An awful lot depends on your circumstances.'[92]

Women, particularly married women, experienced extreme hardship during periods of industrial action and this was both acknowledged and used by the labour movement as a sympathy tactic during periods of industrial militancy. The Independent Labour Party (ILP) activist Kate Beaton

---

[88] SOHCA/019/011/Glasgow, b. 1917.
[89] SOHCA/019/02/Glasgow, b. 1908 and SOHCA/019/06/Glasgow, b. 1907.
[90] The Barrhead People's Story Group, *It's Funny Whit Ye Remember*, 124–5.
[91] The Barrhead People's Story Group, *It's Funny Whit Ye Remember*, 125.
[92] SOHCA/019/02/Glasgow, b. 1908.

stated, 'women and children in every case bore the real brunt of the battle'.[93] The people interviewed for this book concurred. Mrs Parsonage stated,

> Wives and families suffered the most. The mothers had the worst job. With any little money that came in they were the ones that had to make do and mend and help get food for the children. They went without themselves.[94]

Mrs Johnson, a miner's wife, stated,

> The wives suffered most because they'd to do without to give to their bairns, they'd to do without to give to their men. Men took it for granted that women would go short to give to them. I mean a mother had to make a cold pot of porridge and give them it without milk because she hadn't any milk. I remember I sat in the house many a time and hadn't a penny to put in the gas. I couldn't put the light on. I'd to keep the penny for the gas in the morning to make porridge. I used to say, 'What's the point in it? What are we getting out of it?' 'Oh, it's going to make a New World.' But I sat many a night – I dare say dozens of women did. I suppose that was just a way of life. We just took it for granted. When I look back, women were very silly in they days.[95]

Mr Ewart, a docker, recalled how male workers often conducted themselves during a strike. 'Oh they'd go to the pub.' Mr Gordon confirmed this. 'A lot of men on strike had a few pound handy, but the wives didn't get it.'[96] Although many women recognised the benefits of trade unions, the internalisation of this discourse, often based on experience, along with trade union attitudes towards women, may have resulted in the dissemination of the idea amongst women that trade unions were complicit in the burdens endured by women and this could contribute to women's perceptions of the movement as adverse to their interests.

Nevertheless, there were women who were committed to the ideals of trade unions and direct action, even amongst those who did not vote for the labour movement. Indeed, women's opinions of what direct action should achieve were not significantly different from men's; nor were their perceptions of the value of trade unions determined by the type of work they were employed in. Mrs Kilpatrick was unable to join a trade union between the wars. She worked in an office in close proximity to her employer, which is a situation often regarded as having a negative impact on class awareness. Yet this woman expressed an instrumental appreciation of the role of trade unions. She felt that office workers 'needed someone at that time

---

[93] *Forward*, 29 Mar. 1924.
[94] SOHCA/019/026/Glasgow, b. 1917.
[95] SOHCA/019/025/Paisley, b. 1914.
[96] SOHCA/019/031/Glasgow, b. 1908 and SOHCA/019/07/Clydebank, b. 1920.

to fight for them. They really needed them, because the wages were very low.'[97] Mrs Campbell was also in a non-unionised job; she was employed in food production in the Camp Coffee Company. She demonstrated that wage levels, working conditions and solidarity with fellow workers were influential considerations in whether women would join a trade union. She indicated that she would have joined a trade union 'if they were fighting for bigger wages. The conditions we had: we got 12/6 and some of them were away in Auchinairn and they'd their fares to pay and sandwiches to make up. It used to be very hard on 12/6.'[98] When women contemplated joining a trade union or participating in industrial action, economic considerations and a desire for protection were the main factors that directed them. They were no different from most men. These considerations were related to their everyday concerns. Working-class people's material conditions determined the circumstances of their everyday lives, hence they could connect economic well-being and perceptions of powerlessness, all linked through the wage they earned to the life they lived. This suggests that there was a large and promising constituency of women who were persistently neglected throughout the inter-war years by the trade union movement.

Political work cultures and trade unions, generally male preserves, did influence class consciousness. In contrast to women's silence on this issue, Mr Davidson recalled what the period identified as 'Red Clydeside' meant to him. 'That's when everything changed on the Clyde. Men were being forced to join unions to make a better fight of it. That was Labour getting started. It was just a minor revolution.' Mr Bruce recalled being threatened during the 1926 General Strike, stating that, 'There were heavy men that would come up to you and say that union's not worth it. Drop it!' He refused because he 'saw labour as the hounded mob in any strike, because they would rather take a shilling off your pay than give you one'. When asked what the strikers had hoped to gain, Mr Bruce insisted, 'A bit of power. Labour got more publicity and at the next election we went into a good majority.' Mr Armstrong, a transport worker, joined the Communist Party because 'we had the finest work conditions outside of Great Britain. They can talk till they're blue in the face, but the Communists were the greatest shop-stewards.'[99]

Women could be similarly affected by work experiences. Jane Rea was involved in the 1911 strike at Singers sewing machine factory in Clydebank and was sacked for her participation. She went on to join the ILP, became a town councillor and was involved with the Clydebank Housing Association and the rent strikes it orchestrated against 'landlord profiteering'. She participated in anti-war demonstrations during World War I and was a

---

[97] SOHCA/019/08/Glasgow, b. 1916.
[98] SOHCA/019/04/Glasgow, b. 1910.
[99] SOHCA/019/030/Glasgow, b. 1900, SOHCA/019/028/Glasgow, b. 1905 and A/019/027/Glasgow, b. 1905 respectively

member of the Co-operative Women's Guild.[100] Political cultures, trade unions and industrial action were catalysts of working-class political identity which women were largely denied. This represented a loss to the labour movement that ultimately disempowered the working-class politics of the workplace, but it was a loss of the labour movement's own making.

The changing nature of work created opportunities for women to enter the formal workplace in greater numbers and facilitated an increased range of employment opportunities. Although this transpired, opportunities for women's progress in the world of work remained extremely proscribed. Employment in many of the traditional jobs that women undertook was also affected by the adverse effects of the economic climate and by the defensive responses of men and trade unions that resulted in women workers being displaced from employment rather than men. In addition the new employment opportunities open to women did not offer equal pay, status or promotional prospects and the labour movement failed to challenge this, and indeed where it could it defined work as masculine. Thus, trade unions contributed to women's subordination in the workplace by upholding a discourse that identified women as temporary workers rather than regarding them as working women. An archaic worldview based upon the idea of women as competition was advanced by trade unions in Scotland, a view that had little basis in reality. In this way, defensiveness negated sustained broader militancy. Focusing upon women and identifying them as a major source of men's potential subordination to capitalism mediated the possibilities of unity with women. The aftermath of war, the influence of women's penetration of hitherto male occupational preserves and the adverse economic climate also affected women's relationship with the political wing of the labour movement and it is to this we now turn.

---

[100] Women at http://www.theclydebankstory.com/, accessed 1 Apr. 2008.

CHAPTER TWO

Socialist Women, the ILP and the 'Politics of the Kitchen'

In contrast to the years before World War I, the inter-war years are often portrayed as a barren period for women of the labour movement. The challenges women had mounted against the sexual division of labour and the male dominance of their movement, like their interests in general, were apparently sidelined. This has been attributed to the reassertion of traditional gender ideals, the economic climate and the need for class unity in the face of the reactionary Conservative or Conservative-dominated governments.[1] In addition, women's political agency was largely confined to domestic issues and restricted within the sphere of local government with the implication that it was less significant than that of their male counterparts operating in national politics. While this may be an accurate description of the politics of women of the labour movement, they did contribute immensely to improvements in social welfare between the wars. Indeed, it was women who were responsible for placing welfare on the Labour Party's agenda. This benefited both political women and the labour movement, but restricted women to what was labelled 'the politics of the kitchen'. However, these women also challenged the sexual division of labour by adopting strategies intended to guarantee that marriage and the breadwinner ideal did not 'subordinate and silence women'. They did so by placing value on the home and 'home workers' without simultaneously devaluing women's paid work. They may not have enjoyed immense success, but nonetheless many women did not lose their 'radical and feminist edge'.[2]

Socialist women faced many constraints when advancing their policies,

---

[1] See C. Rowan, '"Mothers, vote Labour!" The state, the Labour movement and working class mothers, 1900–1918', in R. Brunt and C. Rowan (eds), *Feminism, Culture and Politics* (London, 1982), 80–2, P. Graves, *Labour Women, Women in British Working Class Politics 1918–1939* (Cambridge, 1994), 10 and Graves, 'An experiment in women-centred socialism', 181–214, G. Scott, *Feminism And The Politics of Working Women: The Women's Co-operative Guild 1880s to the Second World War* (Sussex, 1998) and Harrison, *Prudent Revolutionaries.*

[2] P. Thane, 'Visions of gender in the making of the British welfare state: the case of women in the British Labour Party and social policy 1906–1945', in G. Bock and P. Thane (eds), *Maternity and Gender Policies: Women and the Rise of the European Welfare States 1880s–1950s* (London, 1991), 95–99. See also P. Thane, 'The women of the British Labour Party and feminism 1906–1945', in Smith, *British Feminism*, 124–43.

but women's experiences differed over time and across parties and place.[3] In Scotland the ILP's domination of labour politics until the party's disaffiliation from the Labour Party in 1932 influenced women's experiences. After the extension of the franchise in 1918 to include women over the age of thirty, the ILP identified itself as the 'Real Women's Party' and suggested it would advance policies to effect greater equality between men and women. In the immediate post-war years the ILP asserted that it would promote equal pay for equal work, the unionisation of female workers and full adult suffrage. It also stated that it would 'reject imposed marriage bars', arguing that 'to dismiss married women if their husbands work if carried to its logical conclusion will cloister all women after marriage. This is based on a stupid argument originating from male fears of feminine influence and enterprise.'[4]

The Scottish ILP may have presented itself as a women-friendly party but Helen Gault, a feminist and ILP councillor, who wrote a women's column for the ILP's newspaper *Forward*, was not alone in the view that 'among socialists the belief in equality is only skin deep'.[5] The political manifesto of the ILP was underpinned by the party's belief in social justice and a desire to improve the material conditions of the working classes which resulted in what has been identified as a 'wives and weans' socialism rather than one that promoted real equality for women.[6] The party failed to contest women's unequal positions in the workplace and the home and prioritised the trade union movement's concerns over women's issues. Yet many contemporary socialist women, including the feminists Selina Cooper and Hannah Mitchell, did identify the ILP as more woman-friendly than other branches of the labour movement, although they recognised the gap between 'equality in theory and equality in practice' within the party's rhetoric.[7] Nevertheless, the ILP compared more favourably to continental and other British socialist organisations in its relations with women and women's issues.[8]

[3] See J. Hannam and K. Hunt, 'Gendering the stories of socialism: an essay in historical criticism', in Walsh, *Gender Perspectives*, 102–18.

[4] *Forward*, 7 Dec. 1919 and 1 Jul. 1922.

[5] *Forward*, 28 Feb. 1925. See also Hannam, 'Women and politics', 217–43, J. Hannam, '"In the comradeship of the sexes lies hope of progress and social regeneration": women in the West Riding ILP, 1890–1914', in J. Rendall (ed.), *Equal or Different* (Oxford, 1987), 214 and Cairns, 'Women and the Clydeside labour movement', 197.

[6] R. Findlay, 'The Labour party in Scotland, 1888–1945: pragmatism and principle', in G. Hassan (ed.), *The Scottish Labour Party* (Edinburgh, 2004), 26.

[7] G. Mitchell, *The Hard Way Up: The Autobiography of Hannah Mitchell Suffragette and Rebel* (London, 1977), 178, 189; J. Liddington, *The Life and Times of a Respectable Rebel: Selina Cooper 1864–1946* (London, 1984), 123, 159, 300. See also J. Liddington and J. Norris, *One Hand Tied Behind Us* (London, 1977), 44–6.

[8] See C. Sowerwine, 'Socialism, feminism and the socialist women's movement from the French Revolution to World War II', in R. Bridenthal, S. M. Stuard and M. E. Wiesner (eds), *Becoming Visible: Women in European History* (New York, 1998), 375–7.

As well as facilitating a domesticated form of politics which women could use as a political platform the ILP was 'less authoritarian and bureaucratic than the Labour Party' and its branches were 'small and intimate'.[9] Such an environment was an asset to women entering the political arena because they were generally fewer in number and had less well developed political resources to promote themselves and their aims than their male counterparts. These factors explain why 'most of the grass roots activities' of Scottish women were undertaken 'under the auspices' of the ILP. The ILP also had its own women's sections and established a Scottish Women's Advisory Council, which also acted as a forum for the provision of classes in politics for women. In the 1920s, the ILP made deliberate attempts to attract and involve more women within the party. By 1921, women represented up to 25 per cent of the total membership of some branches and this figure was growing. At the 1925 conference, the ILP reported that 'women delegates were numerous and capable' and that women were gaining 'more confidence'. In 1925, the ILP's membership reached its highest level in Scotland, attributed to the increased number of women being enlisted into the party.[10] For example, between 1923 and 1926 the number of ILP branches in Edinburgh rose from ten to twenty-six.[11] The ILP also developed links with a wide range of left-wing organisations, many of which represented women. This, along with its emphasis on social justice and domestic aspects of politics, provided a platform for women from the ILP, the Labour Party and the Co-operative Women's Guild to advance their programme. These 'socialist women', as they were defined and defined themselves, including the ILP councillor, Kate Beaton, saw their programme as 'expressions of our social commonsense'.[12]

However, although women commanded the platform of domesticated politics and their membership of labour movement organisations was rising, the selection of women for national elections was unimpressive. Scotland produced two female MPs, Agnes Hardie and Jennie Lee. Hardie was an advocate of 'sex equality' and one of the ILP's earliest pioneers as well as a founding member of the Shop Assistants' Union. She was the first woman member of the Glasgow Trades and Labour Council and of the Glasgow School Board. Other women were selected to stand in national elections but were unsuccessful, including the 'housewives'' representative, Jean Mann, who was defeated in the West Renfrewshire constituency. Barbara Woodburn, a teacher, who married the prominent socialist Arthur Woodburn, was unsuccessful in the South Edinburgh seat

---

[9] See W. W. Knox and A. McKinlay, 'The Re-making of Scottish Labour in the 1930s', *Twentieth Century British History*, 6, 2: 174–93 (1995).
[10] Cairns, 'Women and the Clydeside labour movement', 113 and *Forward*, 30 Apr. 1921.
[11] *Scotsman*, 11 Jan. 1926.
[12] *Forward*, 29 Mar. 1924.

and Agnes Dollan was unsuccessful in Ayr.[13] However, Scottish women fared slightly better than their British counterparts and in comparison with members of the Scottish Co-operative Women's Guilds, women from the ILP were doing well. The Guild claimed to be making successful inroads in Parish and Town Council elections, but lamented in 1931 their inability to gain a seat in the national elections.[14]

The selection of socialist women to stand in local elections, especially by the ILP, was more progressive in Scotland. In 1920 eight female labour movement candidates were elected to Glasgow City Council. By 1925, 24 per cent of the Council's labour representatives were women. These figures, whilst not remarkable, compare favourably with many regions in England.[15] The ILP sponsored more women as candidates in municipal elections in Scotland between the wars than any other branch of the movement. Indeed, for a party with limited resources, exacerbated by rising unemployment, the prior experience, reputation and recognition of a candidate was important. These candidates included the prominent socialist-feminist women who had led the 1915 Rent Strikes in Scotland, Mary Barbour and Agnes Dollan. As well as being feminists and 'pioneers' of the ILP, these women worked in unison with other labour movement organisations including the Women's Labour League and the communist Labour Housing Association. They also helped establish the Women's Peace Crusade in 1917. Mrs Thompson was also a local councillor who assisted in the establishment of the Labour Housing Association. She was also the secretary of the Govan branch of the Co-operative Women's Guild. Other distinguished socialist-feminist activists elected to Glasgow City Council included the suffragette Elizabeth MacLean and Kate Beaton, a feminist and member of the National Executive of the Labour Party. Helen Gault, a local councillor, ILP propagandist and feminist, was also amongst these women. So too was Laura Maclean, a local councillor for Kingston and the wife of John Maclean, the ILP MP for Govan, Glasgow. Jean Roberts, also a feminist, was elected as a Kingston Councillor. Jean Mann, who did not adopt a feminist identity but promoted women-focused policies earning herself the title 'the housewives' MP', became a baillie of Glasgow Council in 1934 and Convenor of the Housing Committee between 1935 and 1938. Mrs Hay, wife of the ILP MP for Cathcart, and Christine Moodie, President of the Glasgow Labour Housing Association, were also elected as local councillors, as were Agnes Lauder, Alice Cullen, Christine Muir and Florence Morrison. There were also eighteen unsuccessful female candidates who stood between the wars for Glasgow City Council as well

[13] *Scotsman*, 30 Oct. 1935 and W. W. Knox (ed.), *Scottish Labour Leaders 1918–1939* (Edinburgh, 1984), 90.

[14] C. Burness, 'The long slow march: Scottish women MPs, 1918–1945', in E. Breitenbach and E. Gordon (eds), *Out of Bounds: Women in Scottish Society* (Edinburgh, 1992), 169 and *Scotsman*, 30 Oct. 1935.

[15] Cairns, 'Women and the Clydeside labour movement', 106 and *Labour Women*, Jan. 1952.

as a significant number of women who represented the labour movement on the Parish and Education Boards such as Margaret McKell, Annie Clark and Jeanie Ross.[16]

The same patterns were evident in the east of Scotland as highlighted by the career of the prominent ILPer and Co-operative Guild member Mrs Swan Bunton. She was elected as one of the first ILP members of Edinburgh Parish Council and the Edinburgh Education Board before she was elected to the City Council as a Co-operative Guild representative. These women were joined by a younger generation of activists who were not noted for their feminist sympathies, such as Jennie Lee, the left-wing MP for North Lanarkshire and the trade union activist and local councillor Eleanor Stewart. This list is not exhaustive, but other women who gained 'national recognition' included Clarice McNab, who married William Shaw, secretary of the Glasgow Trades Council. By 1918 she was president of the Scottish Labour Party Executive Committee. There was also Stephanie McGill, the ILP Women's Sections organiser and Mary Shannon of the National Executive of the ILP.[17]

Significant numbers of women infiltrated the political arena with the support of the ILP, but there were differences across Scotland. Women seem to have been more successful in Fife, Glasgow and Lanarkshire, considered the 'reddest' areas of the country. These were also areas dominated by the ILP. By contrast, in 1929 the National Council of Women in Dundee and the Dundee Women Citizens' Association held discussions on how to overcome the fact that Dundee had had no women councillors. These organisations attributed this to the double burden carried by many Dundee married women who looked after families and worked in the mills and therefore had little time for the duties demanded by serving on Town and Parish Councils.[18] The strength of the Communist Party in Dundee's Trades and Labour Council may have contributed to socialist women's exclusion from political power in Dundee. It was certainly an impediment to political women in Greenock and Paisley.[19]

The ILP took account of women and women's interests not only because these complemented the party's political agenda, but because from around 1910 there was an increasing awareness within the labour movement of the potential benefits of women's enfranchisement. At the 1910 Scottish

---

[16] Cairns, 'Women and the Clydeside labour movement', 96–116 and Knox, *Scottish Labour Leaders*, 51, 136–7, 197–9, 254.

[17] F. W. S. Craig, *British Parliamentary Election Results 1918–1949* (Chichester, 1983), 571–634, *Govan Press*, 7 Jan. 1926, *Scotsman*, 27 Oct. 1927, 11 Apr. 1930, 17 Oct. 1931, 16 Mar 1932.

[18] *Scotsman*, 9 Mar. 1929.

[19] For Greenock see P. G. Clark, 'The Greenock labour movement and the General Strike', B.A. dissertation (University of Strathclyde, 1986), 3–11. For Paisley see C. M. M. Macdonald, *The Radical Thread, Political Change in Scotland, Paisley Politics, 1885–1924* (Edinburgh, 2000). For Dundee see Knox and McKinlay, 'The Re-making of Scottish Labour', 17 and *Scotsman*, 22 Oct. 1931.

Trades Council meeting the Women's Conciliation Bill was discussed and fifty-three of the seventy trade union delegates voted to support the enfranchisement of women.[20] Also indicative of the importance attributed to the potential female electorate was the appearance and maintenance of a weekly 'Suffrage Column' in *Forward* from 1912 to 1914. This signified the value afforded the potential constituency that the extended franchise would represent to the labour movement. However, it also corresponded with the National Union of Women's Suffrage Societies [NUWSS], and the Women's Freedom League [WFL], joining forces with the Labour Party to fight for a woman's right to the vote on the same property basis as men. The ILP were more conscious of the suffrage question because of the influence of their radical suffrage members.[21] Radical suffragettes who influenced the Scottish ILP included Helen Crawfurd, Agnes Dollan and Jessie Stephens.[22]

Of equal significance to the question of women's suffrage was the second factor; the ILP was actively attempting to secure municipal representation. It was noted by the Glasgow Women's Labour League that women held sufficient voting power in two-thirds of Glasgow's municipal constituencies to alter the fortunes of the ILP. Women not only had voting power at municipal level, but having contested the bourgeois ideology of the 'angel in the home' by embracing the moral causes of philanthropy, they had penetrated the 'social' area of politics. Ethical politics complemented the ILP's heritage of radical liberalism, providing scope for women to enter the formal world of Labour politics. Hence tradition ensured that both sexes contributed to a definition of 'women's politics' as the 'politics of the kitchen' that was compatible with the ILP's manifesto on social reform. Within this framework socialist women could also assert their value and that of working-class women as home workers. Thus, women came to be the subjects of, and participants in, a revolution of ideas in which there was an increasing recognition that it was

> selfish to fight for more leisure, more pay and better working conditions for working men if the wives and mothers of the working class are to linger on forever under a system of bondage to which most of them are at present subjected.[23]

By advancing the politics of everyday life socialist women also assisted in nurturing the success of the Scottish ILP, helping the party gain the support of the working classes, while contributing to the formation of the enfranchised women's political consciousness. Indeed, having gained the extended franchise, the working classes sought to forward their interests, and increasingly those related to their everyday concerns. Where the labour

[20] *Forward*, 24 Sep. 1910.
[21] C. Rowan, 'Women in the Labour party, 1906–1920', *Feminist Review*, 12: 77–8 (1982).
[22] *Times*, 10 Apr. 1928.
[23] *Forward*, 1 Jun. 1911.

movement supported these issues, there was a favourable correlation in voting behaviour, as there was across many areas of Scotland.[24] The *Times* attributed the election successes of 'Socialism in the Clyde' in 1922 to the propaganda of the 250 members of the Glasgow and Lanarkshire Socialist Teachers' Societies, the majority of whom were women.[25] Political women's use of their domestic skills in campaigning and fundraising also brought the labour movement 'together as a community, reinforcing a sense of purpose and keeping morale high', while their involvement in May Day Parades, their bands and banners and 'proud proclamation of labour's cause' encouraged other women to join them.[26] However, socialist women's support for the ILP was not unconditional. The ILP reported that 'anyone who has been through an election knows the supreme value of the Co-operative Women's Guild', but only 'if their conscience [could] be convinced' of the utility of the campaign could their 'activity be enlisted'.[27] Women may have been on the periphery of the power structures of the political wing of the labour movement, but they were never completely marginalised or silenced. They continued to find ways to advance their causes, working within the bounds of limited social, economic and cultural constraints.

The ILP was acutely aware of the contribution socialist women could make to their electoral success, although this was contained through the party's endeavours to generate a female political constituency narrowly fenced within the social sphere of politics. In 1922, the ILP appealed directly to women to stand for election for the Education Boards, stating, 'women are especially required, as the work of education administration will never be adequately or efficiently under-taken until there is a considerable proportion of women'.[28] The ILP acknowledged that municipal elections were regarded as 'Cinderella' elections, but it was a political arena that the party was determined to penetrate between the wars. Thus, prominent male members including James Maxton, who became MP for Bridgeton, stood as a candidate for the Education Boards.[29]

The remit of the Education Boards included overseeing the clothing, feeding and medical care of children in need and the provision of free school textbooks and spray baths. These were major concerns in a city like Glasgow which, by 1921, had 70,000 registered unemployed, estimated to be responsible for 100,000 dependants. By February 1922, unemployment had risen to 86,000. According to Patrick Dollan, leader of the Labour group on Glasgow City Council, those out of work and on short time accounted for

[24] M. Savage, 'Urban politics and the rise of the Labour party', in H. Corr and L. Jamieson, *State, Private Life and Political Change* (London, 1990), 204–15.

[25] *Times*, 28 Dec. 1922.

[26] V. Hall, 'Contrasting female identities: women in coal mining communities in Northumberland, England, 1900–1939', *Journal of Women's History*, 13, 2: 118–19 (2001).

[27] *Forward*, 24 Sep. 1922.

[28] *Forward*, 25 Feb. 1922.

[29] *Forward*, 18 Feb. 1920 and *Glasgow Evening Times*, 2 Nov. 1922.

a quarter of the populace of Glasgow and they lived in destitution.[30] Many people lived on the margins of poverty in overcrowded housing conditions lacking sanitary facilities in urban Scotland. Overcrowding and poor sanitation contributed to the high incidence of infant mortality and disease. Paisley had a poor record in public health and a reputation as the dirtiest and most unhealthy town in Scotland. It was not until 1923 that a drainage system was installed there.[31] In Lanarkshire, a medical inspection of 74,818 children was undertaken in 1931. It found that 36.6 per cent had some disability and 70 per cent required dental treatment. *Forward* issued an article in 1932 highlighting how 'Greenock's poor lived'. It reported that 'thirty-six people share one lavatory. The houses are rat infested. There is one washhouse for forty-eight households and up to eleven of a family residing in single apartments. Sewage runs from the upstairs flats into the homes below.'[32] Mr Coyle was a teacher in Greenock in 1929. He recollected, 'Children were coming into the school in their bare feet. One of the earliest jobs I had to do was to arrange for them to be measured and supplied with boots by the local school boards. Some of the children used to be sewn into their clothes for the winter!'[33] As late as 1935 Dundee Education Committee were dealing with children who had indeed been sewn into their clothing for the winter.[34]

By the ILP's own admission it was women who placed these concerns on the political agenda. *Forward* reported:

> The growing political power of women and their intense desire for better home conditions will be a great aid in effecting the peaceful revolution in civic administration. Women are practical and more concerned about securing a fuller life for their children. We are on the threshold of tremendous developments. Politics are being rapidly domesticated.[35]

Women were encouraged by the ILP to realise and develop their governing and administrative powers for the well-being of the community. Local government was the centre of the ILP's political activity until the early 1930s and for a third party local politics was also the best arena to promote socialism and show how it would work on a national scale. It was also an effective arena for the 'pragmatic and principled politics of protest' that the ILP favoured.[36] In 1929, Patrick Dollan insisted that it was in local government that legislation was made effective.[37]

---

[30] *Forward*, 21 Apr. 1921, 4; 25 Feb, 15 Jul. and 2 Sep. 1922; 11 Feb. 1922.
[31] See Macdonald, *The Radical Thread*, 109.
[32] *Forward*, 18 Apr. 1931 and 2 Apr. 1932.
[33] SOHCA/019/022/Greenock, b. 1906.
[34] *Scotsman*, 13 Feb. 1935.
[35] *Forward*, 7 Nov. 1922.
[36] See J. Smith, 'Labour traditions in Glasgow and Liverpool', *History Workshop Journal*, 17: 44 (Spring 1984), J. Gyford, *The Politics of Local Socialism* (London, 1983), 3 and Findlay, 'The Labour party', 26–7.
[37] *Glasgow Herald*, 23 Sep. 1929.

However, labour historians often neglect the importance of local politics between the wars and by doing so they ignore the political agency of
socialist women in the areas of health, housing, education, public assistance relief and other welfare services. From the 1920s, public services were
transferred to local authority control and were supported by Exchequer
grants. At this time, much of the legislation pertaining to welfare services
was permissive rather than compulsory in nature and thus the provision
and quality of welfare and housing was susceptible to the pressure of local
protests. Socialist women therefore operated in a political space with the
capacity to allow them to considerably improve the lives of their constituents and by doing so advance the progress of the ILP. Women were aware
of their influence. At the 1920 Scottish Labour Women's Conference in
Hamilton female activists agreed to 'urge local authorities to promote
their permissive powers to improve the welfare of women and children'.[38]
In 1926, at the Labour Women's Advisory Council, Mary Sutherland
addressed several hundred activists and stressed the importance of women
taking a 'keener interest and a larger share' in politics, especially in the
work of public bodies because 'this was how they would get the things they
longed for'. It was also the means by which the 'opinions of women on
those matters upon which they were better able to speak than men could
be thoroughly ventilated'.[39] In 1930, the Labour Party activist Marion
Phillips also pointed out that 'male members of the party' were only
'sympathetic to feminine questions' when women brought them to their
notice. She added that it was women who most influenced public opinion
on welfare matters.[40]

However, socialist women were impeded in influencing public opinion
and ILP policy by the effects of the economic depression. Economic hardship contributed to the declining membership of various labour movement organisations. In 1921, the Co-operative Women's Guild had 230
members in their Greenock Central branch. The Guild had 302 members
in Hutchesontown and Lauriston, Glasgow. The Govan branch in Glasgow
had 310 members and in Paisley there were 460 members. By 1927 there
were 105, 82, 135 and 286 respectively.[41] The financial problems were so
intense in Scotland for women's organisations that the Scottish Women's
Sections of the Labour Party were unable to send delegates to the national
Labour Women's Conference in 1932. Yet, throughout the period 1920
to 1930 the Co-operative Women's Guild never had fewer than 25,000
members in Scotland.[42] In 1929, fourteen new branches were established

[38] *Forward*, 5 Mar. 1920.
[39] *Scotsman*, 4 Jun. 1926.
[40] *Forward*, 2 Apr. 1932.
[41] Scottish Co-operative Women's Guild [hereafter SCWG], 29th Annual Report and
      Statement, 1921, 23 and 1927, 23.
[42] *Labour Women*, Jun. 1932, 87, SCWG, 29th Annual Report and Statement, 1921, 23 and
      35th Annual Report, 1927, 23.

and Scottish membership reached 27,380. Membership increased as the Guild exploited hitherto neglected localities such as Edinburgh which had forty branches by 1932.[43]

Women's membership of the ILP and Labour Party also expanded in the 1920s. For example, in Lanarkshire women's sections of the ILP were instrumental in raising funds to build the first ILP hall in Rutherglen in 1920; by 1924 there were women's sections of the party in Bothwell, Coatbridge, Hamilton, Bothwellhaugh and Kilsyth and in 1926 another five sections were added in the region. In the later 1930s the Labour Party began a recruitment drive that resulted in increased female membership of the party. Like the Guild, the Labour Party concentrated on relatively neglected regions, such as Greenock. By 1932, Greenock acquired its first two female Labour councillors, Mrs McDonald and Mrs McLeod.[44] In 1935, four Women's Sections of the Labour Party were set up in Greenock and a Central Committee was formed under the secretaryship of Mrs O'Neil. Membership drives also took place in Labour strongholds including the Glasgow constituencies of Bridgeton, Camlachie, Gorbals and Shettleston with relative success.[45] By 1932, Scottish Labour Women's membership had increased by 10,000 and at the same time delegates to the Scottish Labour Women's Annual Conference rose from around 200 in 1930 to 350 by 1934. In the latter year there were 180 women representing the Labour Party, 150 from the Co-operative Women's Guild and a mere 20 from the trade unions.[46]

Membership of women's labour movement organisations was increasing in the 1930s but the new members were often drawn from professional and white-collar jobs. It seems that these women had not experienced poverty first hand and that they tended to be anti-feminist and against single-sex women's groups; this undermined the promotion of 'women's issues'.[47] Anti-feminist sentiment and hostility to women-only groups was not confined to the 'new women'. When discussing the benefits of women-only forums, Mrs Mann, a prominent ILPer who was amongst the 'pioneers' of the movement, carried the vote when she maintained that 'women should be socialist first, women second'.[48] Moreover, younger women may have been less interested in single-sex labour movement organisations and feminism, but they had as yet to make their presence felt within the structures and the hierarchy of the labour movement. In 1935, Mary Sutherland, in an article in *Labour Women*, asked her colleagues,

[43] *Glasgow Herald*, 17 May 1930 and *Scotsman*, 16 Mar. 1932.

[44] *Forward*, 10 Dec. and 8 Oct. 1932 respectively and Sinclair, '"Silenced, suppressed and passive"'.

[45] *Labour Women*, Jan. 1935, 16 and Jul. 1935, 80.

[46] *Forward*, 10 Dec. 1932 and *Labour Women*, Jan. 1934, 16.

[47] Graves, *Labour Women*, 43–53.

[48] *Forward*, 16 Jan. 1926.

How can we appeal more effectively to the women wage-earner; attract a larger number of young married women? It is generally true that the great majority of our members, at least those who attend meetings and carry on the work of the Party, are not so young.[49]

Continuity as well as change is also apparent within the politics of the Scottish Co-operative Women's Guild. It has been suggested that women of the Guild lost their radical and feminist approach and their independence and autonomy by the 1930s because of socio-political changes and changes in the Guild's leadership. Under the new secretary Eleanor Barton, women who did not sympathise with the Labour Party, including Communist Party members, were ousted.[50] At the 1926 Annual Meeting of the Scottish Co-operative Women's Guild a discussion was held over whether the organisation should 'keep their platforms for the principles of the Guild, and not open them for people who were not going on the same lines'. The President stated that 'where speakers were to address branches they should find out if they were in sympathy with the aims of the Guild'. Any doubt was to be 'communicated' to the 'session secretary'. However, Mrs Pittendreigh, of the Greenock branch, asked 'what about members of Guild who are communists, can they speak?' It was made clear that the Guild

did not suggest that members of the branches should not be allowed to speak, but we did indicate that outside organisations which are seeking to use our branches for purposes which are not in line with our own, should be excluded.[51]

Moreover, many Scottish women were members of the Communist Party, the Guild and, through this, affiliated to the Labour Party or more aptly the ILP, which had a strong tradition of working with other left-wing groups including communists.[52] In this environment members who were communists were not ousted and their views continued to influence local branches. Janet Kerr Reid was a Clydebank communist councillor. She was also involved in the management of the Clydebank Co-operative Society and was a member of the Co-operative Women's Guild.[53] In Glasgow, a fellow Communist Party member introduced Mrs Glover, also a Communist Party activist, to the Guild. She stated that communists and Guild members worked together because 'we all had the same aims'. Mrs MacIntosh was also a member of the Women's Co-operative Guild, a Communist Party activist and a member of the National Unemployed Workers' Movement and she saw no contradiction in this.[54] Family networks also cemented

[49] *Labour Women*, Oct. 1935, 153.
[50] Scott, *The Women's Co-operative Guild*, 147.
[51] SCWG, 27th Annual Report and Statement, 29 May 1926.
[52] See Knox and McKinlay, 'The Re-Making of Scottish Labour', 175–6.
[53] 'Women' at http://theclydebankstory.com/, accessed 1 Apr. 2008.
[54] Interview with author, Mrs Glover, born Govan, Glasgow 1919 and SOHCA/019/014/ Glasgow, b. 1911.

alliances. Mrs McLeod, one of Greenock's first female Labour councillors, and Mrs Stone, a Labour councillor for Govan, were both related to
notable Communist Party activists.[55] Such links between different branches
of the movement and the capacity to unite was not limited to Scotland. The
Labour Party activist Selina Cooper found herself working with members of
the ILP and the Communist Party between the wars, increasingly sympathis-
ing with some of their criticisms of her own party.[56] In local politics women
could share aims, ideals and strategies, particularly the ideal that they could
improve the everyday lives of working-class women and enhance the status
of womanhood.

The contemporary socialist Kate Beaton argued that socialist women's
political propaganda was effective because it came 'from the experience of
the common lot of working-class mothers and housewives'.[57] Many prominent inter-war Scottish socialist women came from working-class backgrounds. Alice Cullen, who would become Britain's first female Catholic
MP in 1948, was a French polisher to trade before her marriage. She was
widowed and left to bring up young children on her own. Agnes Hardie
was a shop assistant before embarking on a political career and the ILPer
and prominent Co-operative Women's Guild activist Mary Barbour, who
became Glasgow's first woman councillor and baillie, had been a textile
worker. The Lanarkshire MP Jennie Lee was also from a working-class background in mining. Agnes Dollan was one of eleven children. Her father was
a blacksmith and poverty ensured that she had to find employment first in a
factory and then as a telephone operator. In fact, her personal experiences
of poverty, the low wages, long hours and lack of promotional opportunities that women endured were what prompted Dollan to become involved
with trade unionism, feminism and ILP politics.[58] These women had experienced poverty and this formed the basis of their political agitation and
demands.

Although these women could empathise with working-class women,
many of their constituents were politically ignorant and this proved to be
an impediment to socialist women. In this sense the argument that socialist
women underestimated the voting potential of working-class women may
have been overstated. Contemporary women, even those from families
deeply involved in the labour movement, did not always gain the education and socialisation to absorb political concepts. Mrs Bruce's father was
a signatory of a trade union in John Brown's shipyard. She left school at
the age of ten to take over the running of the household from her ailing
mother. She attended an ILP Sunday school but, Mrs Bruce was 'ashamed

---

[55] *Labour Women*, Jun. 1936, 192–3.
[56] Liddington, *Selina Cooper*, 372.
[57] *Forward*, 14 Feb. 1925.
[58] See *Oxford Dictionary of National Biography* at http://www.oxforddnb.com, *Scotsman*, 8 Sep.
1937 and Knox, *Scottish Labour Leaders*, 89.

to say' she did not understand 'socialism' or what issues the ILP had been interested in because 'I might read something but a hundred times to one I don't know what it means'.[59]

Working-class women were also subject to 'habituation and socialisation into sex stereotyped roles', in which formal politics was identified as a male domain. Mrs Duncan stated of politics, 'women really had nothing to do with it. It was more the men. They were the masters and we took a back seat.' Mrs Jones believed that 'the women weren't interested. I don't think women were interested in politics because it didn't help them. They had too much to worry about trying to scrape by to the end of the week for their wages.' Mrs Jones recollected how politicians 'came round the doors with leaflets or if you had kids they used to make a fuss. They didn't mean it either. They were a lot of two-faced baskets.' Mrs Campbell recalled, 'they were always round the door. You never saw them in your life and then they were coming and chapping your door wanting your vote.'[60] Thus, many working-class women's political identity derived partly from the way they identified with the characteristics of the traditional vision of womanhood which the male-dominated labour movement actively promoted, and partly from their awareness that they would have to challenge more than the 'system'. Mrs Harrison maintained of politicians that 'they didn't bother, because when we were young, and more so for females, unless you happened to be in a job that would benefit them, I don't think they were ever round a lot trying to get members, things like that.'[61] This woman voted for the Conservative Party indicating this was not confined to the politics of the labour movement. Women's expectations from politics and politicians differed from those of their male counterparts and this was something that socialist women understood and had to contend with. Laura McLean and Jean Roberts won the Kingston municipal seats for the ILP in 1929. Roberts attributed her success to her accessibility and visibility, made possible by the fifty back-court meetings she held in the last week of her campaign.[62]

Socialist women also understood that the requirements of working-class women differed from those of working-class men. According to Kate Beaton, at their conferences 'all the things they discussed related to their homes and everyday work'. However, she also pointed out that 'home questions are political questions today' due to 'our' efforts.[63] The ILP considered consumption a domestic concern and therefore a women's issue, but apparently the social, economic and political environment that emerged during World War I ensured that consumption, and in particular the cost of rent and food, were submerged within the party's wider political

[59] SOHCA/019/03/Glasgow, b. 1907.
[60] SOHCA/019/05/Glasgow, b. 1912, SOHCA/019/011/Glasgow, b. 1917 and SOHCA/019/04/Glasgow, b. 1910.
[61] SOHCA/019/08/Glasgow, b. 1916.
[62] *Govan Press*, 29 Nov. 1929.
[63] *Forward*, 14 Feb. 1925.

concerns over standards of living. This, it has been argued, guaranteed that although some women 'imagined a socialism' which included a politics of consumption it remained a possibility rather than a reality. With the exception of the Co-operative Women's Guild socialist women failed to develop a 'politics of consumption', although the potential had existed before the inter-war years.[64] However, many ILP women were also members of the Scottish Co-operative Women's Guild and social policy cannot be simply categorised under broad headings. The demands for welfare improvements and a social wage sought by socialist women from both organisations were related to working-class women's standards of living and to their consumption. The social wage was a redistribution of income from taxpayers to non-taxpayers and married women were invariably non-taxpaying citizens. Family endowments, maternity benefits, widows' pensions and healthcare provisions were all aspects of the social wage that socialist women demanded. Socialist women may have been impeded from developing a politics of consumption, but they continued to promote 'a domesticated version of socialism' that challenged the ways in which the ILP 'privileged production over consumption'.

For example, from 1915 Scottish socialist women challenged rent prices and the cost of food and fuel, involving themselves in demonstrations and protests and, as Chapter five will highlight, housing costs and conditions remained central to socialist women's politics throughout the inter-war years. The price of food was another issue that commanded the attention of socialist women throughout the period under review. For example, in 1920, at the Labour Women's Conference held in London, 400 delegates discussed 'The Question of Bread Prices'. Socialist women also challenged their own movement over these issues. In 1924 the Labour government set up a Royal Commission on Food Prices because it was estimated that the price of food had increased by 79 per cent between July 1914 and December 1924. In May 1925 the Committee's report recommended that a 'Food Council' be established in a move towards 'harmonising the interests of producers, distributers and the consumers of food'. It was also recommended that the Council should act as an advisory body and watchdog which would intervene in the interests of the consumer and would report directly to the Board of Trade. The Council was to consist of twelve members, two of whom would be 'practical housewives'. Two others were to come from the trade union movement and one other was to be the director of the Co-operative Wholesale Society who was seen to have wide business experience. The proposed Food Council was attacked by the Scottish media on the grounds that 'it [was] a definite advance in the direction of state socialism'.[65] Socialist women disagreed. At the first conference held under the auspices of the Women's Advisory Council of the Glasgow ILP,

---

[64] Hannam and Hunt, *Socialist Women in Britain*, 136–60.
[65] *Scotsman*, 11 Dec. 1924 and 9 May 1925 and *Forward*, 14 Feb. 1925.

Mrs McLean, the presiding officer, made it clear that they were there to discuss the 'high price of food' and the 'breadbasket of the housewife'. Mary Shennan accused the government of 'not dealing with the rising price of food' and 'profiteering' and condemned the Food Commission's inquiry. Mary Laird and Helen Gault both argued that the Labour Party should go further along the road of 'state socialism' and Mrs Gault put forward a motion that

> This conference deems it advisable that all working-class women should rouse an intense agitation in all districts and adopt all means in their power to combat the high price of food, and, if necessary, organise boycotts against the buying commodities that can be easily dispensed with, and by this means start a movement which, if sufficiently supported, can be the direct means of reducing the high cost of living.[66]

Mrs Gault was not just an ILP councillor; she was also a prominent member of the Knightswood West branch of the Co-operative Women's Guild. Mrs Laird was a member of the Co-operative Women's Guild as well as President of the Glasgow Women's Housing Association.[67]

Both the Co-operative Women's Guild and the Women's Housing Association supported a politics of consumption, which continued to permeate socialist women's political concerns, as did working-class standards of living. After the extension of the franchise in 1928, which enfranchised women over twenty-one years of age, socialist women took the opportunity to argue that 'henceforth politics will be bread and butter politics. The test of a government will be whether or not it has put more food on the plates of the people.'[68] Furthermore, although the labour movement focused on social policy rather than consumption, the Labour Press Committee attributed the party's success in 1929 to women voters, claiming that 'the women of Glasgow have led the men'. Socialist women asked readers of the *Glasgow Evening Times* to 'remember what politics was before women entered' and brought 'housing, unemployment, child welfare and rents' into the world of politics.[69] Social policy and a politics of consumption overlapped and although socialist women were impeded from placing it on the political agenda from the late 1920s, this was not necessarily due to the ILP's emphasis on standards of living. Rather, it can be attributed to the impact of recession and depression, to the debacle of the second Labour government of 1929, and to deflationary policies that reduced the cost of food and fuel, but which corresponded with the introduction of the means test. Safeguarding working-class incomes and standards of living from the effects of reduced benefits can also be seen as part of the promotion of a social wage.

[66] *Scotsman*, 4 May 1925.
[67] *Forward*, 9 and 16 Jan. 1915.
[68] *Forward*, 8 Jun. 1929.
[69] *Glasgow Evening Times*, 16 Nov. 1929.

Throughout the period under review socialist women consistently sought to promote a social wage and one of the strategies they used was to exploit inter-war concerns about the quality and quantity of the British race. Protesting in pragmatic and 'prudent' ways, socialist women avoided direct conflict with their movement and the appearance of subverting the 'bread-winner ideal'. They adopted this approach when they demanded improvements to the Widows' Pension Act 1925, framing their requests in terms of the capacity of such a benefit to ensure that men's wages were not undercut by women seeking work because they were desperate to feed and maintain their families.[70] Socialist women were aware that in trade union circles and in the Labour Party opinions on widows' pensions found more favour than endowments for mothers because any assistance received by widows did not undermine the breadwinner ideal. In 1929 the Labour Party extended the scope of the 1925 Old Age and Widows' Pensions Contributory Act. Widows of those men insured prior to the enactment of the Widows' Pension Act of 1925 were granted this benefit by the Labour government of 1929.[71]

When socialist women articulated these demands their aim was to see the roles of working-class women in the family elevated to the status of the male breadwinner. Thus, they did not directly challenge the sexual division of labour. They did, however, contest its effects when demanding acknowledgement of women's roles as guardians of the home, which they identified as a 'sacred place', and when they promoted motherhood and housewifery as occupations deserving recognition and improved conditions.[72] To gain assistance for their constituents and provide working-class women with economic independence, in kind or in the form of an endowment, these women emphasised the link between the welfare of the child and the future of the race. Intervention by the state on the part of the child had a longer tradition and raised fewer fears of subverting the male breadwinner's responsibility than intervention on behalf of wives.[73] Yet, although Scottish socialist women framed many of their demands within the signifiers of this discourse they did not do so when they demanded an endowment for women.

For many socialist and feminist women a family endowment was to provide the housewife with economic freedom and security.[74] Thus, social-ist women in Scotland merged their feminist rhetoric with class signifiers – demanding that women should have economic freedom and the same

---

[70] SCWG, 27th Annual Report and Statement, 1919, 15–16 and 33rd Annual Report and Statement, 1925, 18.

[71] P. Thane, *The Foundations of the Welfare State: Social Policy in Modern Britain* (New York, 1982), 197–9.

[72] SCWG, 34th Annual Report and Statement, 1926, 10.

[73] J. Lewis, *The Politics of Motherhood: Child and Maternal Welfare in England 1900–1939* (London, 1980), 165–90.

[74] SCWG, Central Council Minutes, 7 Jan. and 4 Feb. 1931 and ILP, Women's Section Minutes, 2 Mar. 1925 and 6 Sep. 1926.

rights as the rich to maintain their families. Annie Maxton stressed that family endowments should be established to provide women with independence but she maintained that this 'economic freedom' should be facilitated within a 'reconstructed social order' as proposed by the ILP.[75] In April 1929 the Scottish Advisory Council of the ILP adopted a resolution in favour of family allowance for schoolchildren to be given to mothers or guardians. This was to be paid for through the taxation of the wealthy.[76] Family endowment was sidelined by both Labour governments elected between the wars and the possibility of being seen to subvert the breadwinner's economic responsibility for the family was far from being the dominant perspective of the labour movement. Although demands had been forwarded from 1920 at the STUC Annual Conferences for family endowment, maternity and child welfare schemes and widows' pensions, it was unions with female members, or those representing unskilled labour that issued these demands. It was not until 1930 that the STUC's Organisation of Women Committee showed any support whatsoever for family allowance, and hostility from trade unions and the Labour Party prevailed throughout the period. Thus, ILP women contested the discourses promoted by men and women of their own movement.[77]

However, the ILP support for family endowments was part of the party's advancement of a so-called family wage, a 'living wage', and this allowed women to use class signifiers when demanding economic independence for married women in the form of a 'mother's wage'. Although the idea of a family wage was supported by significant numbers of ILP women it has been pointed out that such an aim had 'utterly no relevance for working women'.[78] Most women expected to marry and give up their employment; thereafter they would be beneficiaries of the 'living wage'. The majority of the women who attended ILP meetings and the ILP's female constituency were married women. Of equal significance, the concept of a 'family wage' had different meanings in different settings.

> The lack of work for women, high levels of unemployment, wages which were seldom high enough to maintain a family with dependent children above the poverty line, low levels of unionisation in most industries, and state polices which did little to ameliorate the inadequacies of the wage system for the support of families all channelled the choices of workers.[79]

Most of these conditions affected Scottish women at some time or other between the wars and as such there were realistic benefits to be gained from

[75] ILP, Women's Section Minutes, 19 Oct. 1925.
[76] *Forward*, 12 Apr. 1929.
[77] STUC, 23rd A/R, 1920, 93.
[78] Cairns, 'Women and the Clydeside labour movement', 115.
[79] C. Creighton, 'The rise of the male breadwinner family: a reappraisal', *Comparative Studies in Society and History*, 38, 2: 330–4 (1996).

supporting a 'living wage'. Gender socialisation and the obstacles married women faced in gaining employment were unlikely to result in housewives, in the midst of rising unemployment, calling for emancipation of women to compete on equal terms with their spouses, especially if this liberation could affect a husband's already vulnerable employment. In addition, working-class mothers were generally responsible for controlling the family income. Therefore, although feminists, including those within the ILP, supported equal pay for equal work, they also fought for a living wage that reinforced the breadwinner ideal but also acknowledged women's right to economic independence through the endowment of motherhood.

The concept of family endowment is a useful medium that highlights how the demands of women of the labour movement were subverted. Whilst the Scottish ILP and the Labour Party had accepted the idea of family allowance by 1930, it generally had very different meanings for the men and women of the labour movement. What the feminist women of the labour movement sought when they advocated an endowment for married women was based on traditional arguments put forward by pre-war feminists and by the Family Endowment Society. This was a payment to women to provide them with economic freedom and to enhance their status as 'home workers'. The vast majority of the men in the movement, by contrast, tended to oppose the introduction of a monetary family endowment based on the perception that such a benefit was a wage subsidy. Indeed, employers, Liberals and some Conservatives, by the 1930s, had come to support the idea of family allowance because of the economic climate. They believed that such a state payment would help maintain a low wage strategy, while helping to invigorate the economy by reducing labour overheads, and thereby the cost of production, and at the same time increase consumer spending. In addition, it was felt that the benefit could enhance social stability and contribute to 'national efficiency' by improving the stock of 'human capital'.[80] Support from employers increased male hostility and encouraged the labour movement to support a family endowment that took the form of feeding and maintaining schoolchildren so that the school-leaving age might be raised to alleviate unemployment by reducing the pool of cheap labour. Thus, although not confined to the Labour Party, civic concerns and the meanings attached to the demands of women guaranteed that a policy intended to emancipate women was frustrated. When family allowance was finally established under the coalition government of 1945 it had little to do with feminist objectives and the benefit was far from liberating for women. The introduction of family allowance had more to do with the arguments promoted by advocates of pronatalism, imperialism and 'national defence' and as an alternative to a statutory minimum wage rather than as a response to the demands of feminists of any persuasion. Yet feminist debates and the demands of socialist women surrounding family

[80] Thane, *The Foundations of the Welfare State*, 150, 216–17, 241–2.

endowments should not be discounted because through their campaigns these women 'educated public opinion on the issue'.[81]

Socialist women were more successful when they exploited concerns over the quantity and quality of the race. This contributed to the extension of maternal and child welfare schemes, which were vital in Scotland, where incapacity and debility caused by multiple pregnancies were rife. The admission records of Redlands Hospital for Women for 1925 show that pregnancy-related illness and debility account for almost 50 per cent of all cases of hospitalisation in that year.[82] In mining districts women's death rates were 20 per cent higher than their husbands', regardless of the dangers of men's work, because of frequent pregnancies and the polluted environment in which the women lived.[83] Unquestionably this motivated activists like Mary Barbour, Glasgow's first female baillie, and an ILP councillor for Govan not only to try and improve the 'workshop' of the housewife but to increase women's access to health care. In 1926 Glasgow Corporation built new premises for the West Govan Child Welfare Association and agreed to contribute 50 per cent of the maintenance cost. At its opening it was acknowledged that Barbour's influence on the Corporation had been instrumental in the decision to support the extension of child welfare services. Barbour took the opportunity at its opening to challenge Govan men. She stated that the new clinic 'was not merely a child welfare clinic, but an institution for mother-craft and father-craft too'. She also let it be known that the clinic 'would see its first meeting for fathers', asking 'health visitors to turn out' to make sure that the meeting was a success.[84] Using pronatalist discourses did not undermine feminist aims and objectives within the labour movement.

Although socialist women were more successful when they adhered to the labour movement's emphasis on child welfare when advancing women's issues this ensured that considerations of child welfare were increasingly separated from women's interests within the movement, creating a further impediment to socialist women when they tried to promote women's issues.[85] However, the most significant obstacle women had to overcome to achieve their aims was the labour movement's representation of womanhood that reflected the traditional gender discourses of inter-war Britain. The ILP saw women's roles in creating the 'brave new world' as that of 'guardians of the race; shrines of human life'.[86] When the ILP addressed women it was more often as wives and mothers who

[81] J. MacNicol, *The Movement for Family Allowances* (London, 1980), 138–60 and Harrison, *Prudent Revolutionaries*, 110–11.
[82] GRA, HB10/4/3, Redlands Hospital for Women, Admissions Records, 1925. See M. Spring Rice, *Working-class Wives: Their Health and Condition* (London, 1987), 21–7.
[83] Hall, 'Contrasting female identities', 114.
[84] *Govan Press*, 26 Nov. 1926.
[85] See A. Digby and J. Stewart (eds), *Gender, Health and Welfare* (London, 1996).
[86] *Forward*, 11 May and 22 Jul. 1922.

were expected to support a largely male-dominated politics. Yet the ILP did not do so in an overt sense as the coalitionists did by asking women to vote for them to 'please their husbands' and by appealing to the budgeting role of the housewife who needed to understand the need for 'strict economy'.[87] The ILP was aware that the majority of working-class women were already only too familiar with strict economy. Instead it directed its attention to familial concerns and the promotion of 'ethical socialism' which, although gendered, did relate directly to many of the everyday concerns of working-class women. The ILP noted that 'women suffer most in unemployment in the unequal combat between poverty and necessity', but as wives and mothers, not workers.[88] Unemployment was seen as a male problem, and one which the ILP hoped to alleviate by introducing direct labour schemes, mainly housebuilding, a male occupation. In 1929, Patrick Dollan proposed that Glasgow Corporation spend £3,000,000 to help the unemployed. The proposal aimed to employ four thousand men for four years to build roads and houses.[89] Housebuilding, in a region with dire housing conditions, however, was also promoted as a woman's concern and as a medium to offer women political power. Women's committees were to oversee housing because women councillors had proved 'capable' of this. According to the ILP, women's 'speciality was domestic reform' and any improvements in the housing situation was 'indebted to them'.[90] Thus, housing was a political issue accommodating many signifiers while entrenching the sexual division of labour.

Unemployed women had little to thank the ILP for. Highlighting the ways in which women's language was muted and how they were unable to articulate a worldview that did not mirror that of the male dominance of the party was the male derision that ILP women endured when they advanced direct labour schemes for women. The schemes that female ILP activists proposed were intended to benefit both single and married women. Female ILPers argued that household drudgery should be eliminated through the establishment, in all new houses, of labour-saving applications. In addition, communal restaurants, laundries, bakeries and nurseries could be formed to relieve married women of the drudgery of housework, while at the same time creating work opportunities for unemployed females. Socialist women argued that by releasing housewives from the burdens of housewifery and mothering they would be in a position to take their 'proper share of the duties of citizenship'.[91] Although the proposed employment would entrench the sexual division of labour, this was a challenge to the signification that unemployment was a male problem.

---

[87] *Glasgow Evening Times*, 9 Nov. 1922.
[88] *Govan Press*, 9 Aug. 1929.
[89] *Govan Press*, 9 Aug. 1929.
[90] *Forward*, 19 Mar. 1922.
[91] See *Forward*, 1 Jul. 1922 and ILP, Women's Section Minutes, 6 Sep. 1926.

It was also feminist in its demand that women should have equal access to, and share in, the duties of citizenship. These schemes were a pragmatic attempt to accommodate a diverse constituency of working women, wives and mothers, but they were also an expression of the emphasis socialist women placed on the coexistence of gender equality with separate but equal status for the roles of each sex.

Some male ILPers did acknowledge the problems of women's unemployment but within gendered discourses. David Kirkwood, the Clydebank ILP MP put forth an impassioned plea to Margaret Bondfield, Minister for Labour, and architect of the Anomalies Act that effectively barred married women from receiving state benefits. He asked her to

> Remember the women, thousands of them, who are sitting at home breaking their hearts because they are cut away from the Employment Exchange without a friend in the world. Thousands are looking to you to relieve them of this terrible nightmare.[92]

Kirkwood's plea had no impact. In 1932, Mrs Brand of the Transport and General Workers' Union catalogued how the government was 'penalising the woman worker'. Married women were denied benefits and single women's benefits were substantially reduced.

From 1919 there had been concerns expressed by female activists regarding the level of women's unemployment, particularly in relation to demobilisation. In 1921 the Scottish Council for Women's Trades complained that the government and local authorities assumed unemployment was an 'evil' which afflicted men and on that assumption 'made large grants, forwarded schemes and appointed committees which left women out of the account'. The ILP MP for Lanarkshire, Jennie Lee, also contested the ways in which women were compelled to accept work as domestic servants or lose unemployment entitlements. She was particularly vocal when she argued that if such work was well paid it would be more popular and she went on to insist that domestic service should be an insured trade.[93] Inequalities in access to, and the level of remuneration of unemployment benefits were consistently challenged. In 1926 at the STUC Annual Congress, Miss Evans of the Association of Women Clerks and Secretaries moved a resolution demanding that there be no differentiation between the rates of unemployment insurance benefit paid to single men and single women. She complained that the Congress was supposed to be pledged to equality and she also pointed out that single women felt the burden of unemployment just as much as men.[94] The resolution was defeated on the grounds of the 'complications that would ensue' if women were to receive the same ben-

---

[92] *Forward*, 20 Jul. 1929.

[93] *Forward*, 14 May 1932 and Sinclair, '"Silenced, suppressed and passive"', 127.

[94] Sinclair, '"Silenced, suppressed and passive"', 116, Tuckett, *Scottish Trades Union Congress*, 144 and *Scotsman*, 7 Sep. 1926.

efits as men. At the Scottish Labour Women's Conference in Hamilton in 1932 female activists condemned the government and local authorities, claiming that they were less concerned to find ways to alleviate women's unemployment in comparison to men. Although these women did put forward a critique of unemployment policy their criticism did little to alleviate the problem, which was essentially conceptualised as masculine.[95] Unemployment was not only signified as a 'public' concern, but through direct labour schemes, the proposed policies to tackle the issue, it was also identified as a masculine problem.

These impediments ensured that socialist women from the ILP, the Co-operative Women's Guild and the Labour Party faced difficulties when expressing an alternative vision of society that undermined that of the male-dominated labour movement, but they nonetheless continued to question the dominant ideology of gender norms. They used a variety of strategies to promote a politics of consumption and to challenge gender inequalities and women's unemployment. In doing so, socialist women had to develop a political agenda with many signifiers to appeal to the diversity of their constituents and at the same time challenge class and broadening gender discrimination. The increasing force with which the male agenda was forwarded hampered women as did the economic situation and the gendered culture that shaped their constituents' worldviews in Scotland. Moreover, as the next chapter will highlight, socialist women were also impeded in advancing their political aims by the fragmented nature of the Scottish working-class electorate.

[95] *Forward*, 5 Mar. 1932.

CHAPTER THREE

Class Fragmentation: Respectability, Religion and Residence

In 1924 the Labour activist Mary Sutherland warned the female electorate that

> It is you as a *woman* who will be blamed. It is your affairs because as a rule it is your job to run a house, see your family is fed and clothed. When unemployment comes, the kind of men *you* send to the Parish Council will decide if the children are fed.[1]

The Scottish labour movement was benevolent in its praise of working-class women when they were successful in electoral campaigns but they were also quick to suggest that women did not vote 'properly' and to blame them for any 'election fiasco'.[2] This worldview has resonance in labour history literature and popular discourse which continues to identify women as being more inclined to vote Conservative.[3] It also correlates with accusations that socialist women failed to recognise the potential of the newly enfranchised women's vote as a lever to forward women's issues. Many working-class women did vote for parties of the left in Scotland, but like men, there were Scottish women in the inter-war period who voted against it for a variety of reasons, which included perceptions of self based on the concept of 'respectability' and the influence of religious identity. The adoption of the hierarchal model of class in Scottish communities that linked economic well-being to 'respectability', a classification system that measured working-class status, merged with religious divisions to shape political identities.[4] Women have also been identified as more vulnerable to the hierarchal model of class because, unlike men, they faced impediments in absorbing a consciousness of class from workplace experiences which facilitated the more adversarial 'them and us' vision of class. Thus, women are seen to have developed their class identities from contact with their communities

---

[1] *Forward*, 24 Oct. 1924 (her italics).

[2] *Forward*, 21 Feb. 1930.

[3] See Pugh, *Women and the Women's Movement*, 150–3 and I. G. Hutchison, 'Scottish issues in British politics 1900–1939', in C. Wrigley (ed.), *A Companion to Early Twentieth Century Britain* (Oxford, 2002), 82–3. From the inception of the ILP many leading men like Keir Hardie rejected this view of women voters. See J. J. Smyth, *Labour in Glasgow 1896–1936: Socialism, Suffrage and Sectarianism* (Edinburgh, 2000), 159.

[4] Cannadine, *Class in Britain* (London, 2000), 1–23 and passim.

and communities were replete with tensions that could fracture class awareness. These tensions increased between the wars because of greater access to home ownership and to council housing, which held the potential to undermine the traditional community-based working class, displacing it with a more materialistic and individualistic working class.[5] In Scotland housing developments were mediated by structural, economic and cultural forces. Nevertheless, aspirations as well as access to improved housing fused with the forces which fractured class awareness to aggravate the fragmentation of the working classes.

There are a number of reasons forwarded to explain why women may have identified with political parties other than those of the labour movement. The newly enfranchised women of the inter-war years seemed to be less inclined to support the Labour Party because of the party's concentration on male-centric policies of production and unemployment which women were less concerned with because of their marginalisation from work and trade unions after they married.[6] Whilst the majority of women did marry, most worked before marriage and many experienced unemployment directly and indirectly as workers and wives. For example, the maritime towns of Greenock and Port Glasgow depended on heavy industry, especially shipbuilding, dock work, textiles and ancillary employment in sugar refineries and rope works.[7] In these towns ancillary employment was affected by the problems facing the main industries, including textiles. Thus, women's work in textiles, sugar refineries and rope works was severely hit, especially during the depression of the 1930s. In 1927 the *Glasgow Herald* reported that Greenock had a larger number of able-bodied unemployed in receipt of benefits than any other parish in Scotland and more importantly, the authorities did not think this was influenced by fraudulent claims.[8] Many of the unemployed were women, as highlighted by the 'terrific amount of women in the National Unemployed Workers' Movement from the local mills and sugar refineries'.[9]

However, in Greenock it was the Communist Party that dominated the National Unemployed Workers' Movement, as well as the Trades and Labour Council and the Labour Housing Association at least until 1925. The Communist Party has also been identified as extremely male-dominated in this area.[10] Unlike other left-wing parties, the Communist Party failed to link unemployment to wider concerns over standards of living, including housing, and this may have contributed to the loss of a

---

[5] Savage and Miles, *The Remaking of the British Working Class*, especially Chapter 3.

[6] Pugh, *Women and the Women's Movement*, 150–3.

[7] See A. Hughes, 'The economic and social effects of recession and depression on Greenock between the wars', *International Journal of Maritime History*, 18, 1: 281–306 (2006).

[8] *Glasgow Herald*, 27 Sep. 1927.

[9] I. MacDougall, *Voices from the Hunger Marches: Personal Recollections by Scottish Hunger Marchers of the 1920s and 1930s* (Edinburgh, 1990), 165–73.

[10] Clark, 'The Greenock labour movement and the General Strike', 3, 11.

potential constituency. In Greenock there was 'little evidence' that housing costs or conditions were catalysts of 'social agitation' which was a factor in women's political mobilisation in many areas of Scotland, as the next chapter will demonstrate. The Labour Party and the ILP benefited from the correlation between electoral success and the promotion of welfare issues, especially from the female electorate.[11] Nevertheless, while the Communist Party may have neglected issues of broader interest to women, it did involve females in protest against unemployment, recognising them as workers in their own right as well as wives who were supporting their unemployed husbands.

Mining districts were also very vulnerable to the effects of the recession and depression. In 1932 *Labour Women* suggested that Lanarkshire was 'a black area for unemployment' because 'unemployment in the mining and steel industries' had been 'exceptionally high for years'.[12] Mining areas endured the effects of the 1926 General Strike and the seven-month miners' lockout and this was often reflected in the political geography of these localities. Motherwell, like Greenock and Fife, had the most visibly thriving Communist Party support in Scotland, no doubt influenced by the high levels of unemployment and industrial strife acting as a catalyst to the growth of working-class awareness.[13] Mining regions, however, have been identified with overt gender discrimination against women in every area of life.[14] The Communist Party activist Marion Henery felt that Lanarkshire was a 'backward and depressing place for women'.[15] In many mining districts working-class women were largely excluded from formal political participation, as they apparently were in the textile town of Paisley, because unemployment took primacy over all other issues and unemployment was principally seen to affect men.[16] Thus, the nature of local socialist organisations, political mobilisation, the effects of recession and depression, along with the effects of General Strike of 1926 and the subsequent miners' lockout were all factors which could contribute to the development of class awareness and the success of the labour movement in a particular area of Scotland. Indeed, the ILP's success in penetrating local

---

[11] See J. Lawson, M. Savage and M. and A. Warde, 'Gender and local political struggles over welfare policies', in L. Murgatroyd et al. (eds), *Localities, Class and Gender* (London, 1996), 195–217.

[12] *Labour Women*, 15 May 1932, 63.

[13] In West Fife the Communist candidate Willie Gallacher won the Parliamentary seat in 1935 displacing the Labour Party MP, Willie Adamson. This was partly due to Adamson, the Fife County Union Miners' leader, advising striking workers to return to work and accept their employers' terms. Supported by the United Mine Workers of Scotland, Gallacher involved himself in pithead collections and organised feeding centres and the like, which helps explain his success. Knox, *Scottish Labour Leaders*, 118.

[14] See S. McIntyre, *Little Moscows* (London, 1980), 131–42.

[15] Interview with Joe and Marion Henery, William Gallagher Memorial Library, Glasgow Caledonian University, tape no. 7.

[16] For Paisley see Macdonald, *The Radical Thread*.

and national government between the wars in Scotland can be attributed to the party's extra-Parliamentary forms of protest that involved women and to the fact that it did not concentrate on male-centric policies, as the last chapter demonstrated.[17]

There is little to support the view that working-class women did not vote for left-wing parties. The studies of women's voting behaviour which do exist demonstrate that it was middle-class women who tended to support the Conservative Party rather than working-class women.[18] In Scotland the ILP offered what has been labelled a 'wives and weans' brand of socialism which linked the home, health and standards of living to the sphere of work via the effects of poor wages and unemployment.[19] This seems to have been a politics that appealed to many working-class women. Dundee had the most notable disproportionate number of women to men in Scotland but the ILP nevertheless commanded support in this area. For example, in 1922 the Labour MP E. D. Morel was elected in Dundee. In 1924 Dundee East elected the ILPer Tom Johnston. He was returned even though he had been identified as an advocate of 'class war'. He was vilified by the press as a 'socialist' aligned to the Communist Party of Dundee, whose members were encouraged to vote for him. He was also demonised by the Catholic Church, which 'counselled' Catholics to vote against him. By 1929 there were 16,735 more women than men on the electoral register in Dundee and at that point the Temperance candidate Ernest Scrymgeour, who was identified as a 'socialist', held his seat and was joined by another 'socialist' candidate, Mr Marcus.[20]

The west of Scotland was where the ILP had the strongest support. Because of this, if women were more inclined to vote against parties of the labour movement, then this region should reflect that position, especially after 1929 when women could vote on equal terms with men. As Table 3.1 highlights, in all of the Scottish constituencies selected from west central Scotland for this sample over 50 per cent of the potential female vote went to the labour movement, except in Govan, where there was a debacle over the candidate's selection, and in Greenock. The *Times* reported that the Labour candidate was not a significant threat to the Liberal candidate in Greenock because of the 'deadlock' between the Co-operative candidate and the Communist candidate which split the labour movement's vote.[21]

Yet it is also evident from the table that the more likely women were to turn out to the polls, the less well the labour movement did in a number of constituencies. Many women voted for the party of their parents or

---

[17] See also Smyth, *Labour in Glasgow* and W. W. Knox, *Industrial Nation: Work, Culture and Society in Scotland 1800–Present* (Edinburgh, 1999), 155–89.

[18] P. Thane, 'Women since 1945', in P. Johnson (ed.), *20th Century Britain: Economic, Social and Cultural Change* (London, 1994), 404.

[19] Findlay, 'The Labour party', 26.

[20] *Times*, 16 Nov. 1923 and *Scotsman*, 1 Jun. 1929.

[21] *Times*, 16 Nov. 1923.

Table 3.1 The 'women's' vote, 1929 election results in selected constituencies of west central Scotland.

Constituency	No. of new female voters	Increased no. of votes cast	Potential % of new female votes cast	Increased % swing of votes to the labour movement* over 1924 figures
Bridgeton	7,637	3,599	47%	116%
Camlachie	7,207	4,792	66%	66%
Gorbals	8,576	4,019	47%	140%
Govan	6,511	6,173	95%	36%
Greenock	8,695	8,193	94%	40%
Maryhill	7,994	6,781	85%	64%
Motherwell	6,151	4,141	67%	116%
Paisley	10,157	8,273	81%	65%
Partick	5,485	6,007	100%	58%
Shettleston	7,608	7,666	100%	90%
Springburn	7,646	4,511	59%	121%
Tradeston	6,744	5,715	85%	66%
St Rollox	7,367	3,146	43%	119%

Source: F. W. S. Craig, *British Parliamentary Election Results, Glasgow Herald*, 2, 10 and 15 May 1929. *Votes for the labour movement are the combined totals of votes for the ILP, the Labour Party and the Communist Party, where applicable.

their husbands' choice and one woman from Greenock went so far as to vote for the Conservative candidate because he was 'nice looking'.[22] Male ILP candidates also benefited from their popularity among women. The 'women's role in the 1929 campaigns in Bridgeton, Glasgow', it seems, 'was to hero worship Maxton, the ILP candidate'.[23] George Buchanan of the ILP was idolised in the Gorbals, where women who sung 'The Red Flag' and shouted 'We want Buchanan' heckled the Secretary of State for Scotland during the 1929 general election campaign. In the West Stirlingshire parliamentary constituency women heckled the sitting MP, Captain Fanshawe, in the run-up to the 1929 election. They offered to bet him a 'Top Hat' that Tom Johnston, the ILP candidate and editor of *Forward*, would take his seat. They then sung him 'The Reg Flag'. These women, moreover, were no doubt among the voters who ensured that Tom Johnston did take the seat.[24] It was in the more socially mixed constituencies such as Maryhill and Partick in Glasgow, and Greenock, Motherwell and Paisley that left-wing parties did least well rather than in those which were largely working-class, such as Bridgeton and the Gorbals in Glasgow.[25] In Aberdeen, Falkirk,

[22] SOHCA/019/022/Greenock, b. 1919.
[23] *Glasgow Herald*, 20 May 1929.
[24] *Glasgow Evening Times*, 22 May 1929.
[25] Smyth, *Labour in Glasgow*, 190–207.

Stirling and Fife the women's vote made no significant difference in 1929. However, Edinburgh witnessed the largest growth in women eligible to vote in Scotland and was regarded by the labour movement as difficult to penetrate. Yet in 1929 the labour movement held two of the five Edinburgh constituencies they had won in 1924 and increased their representation by taking the Edinburgh West constituency with the assistance of the 11,000 new women voters.[26] Thus, it would seem that working-class women, like working-class men, were just as likely to support parties of the left as they were to vote against them. Indeed, the rise in support for Labour in Scotland in the 1920s has been seen as evidence that class identities became more important than 'identities associated with ethnicity and religion'.[27]

However, it is also important to recognise that other forces continued to divide working-class communities and fractured class awareness. Inter-war housing developments and the relationship between these, respectability and, in Scotland, religion, were important in determining political identities in many neighbourhoods between the wars. In working-class neighbourhoods respectability was neither an overarching nor a fixed concept, but the main demarcations were between the 'respectable' working class and the 'roughs', those regarded as lower working class. The concept of 'rough' working-class was often associated with Catholicism due to the limited opportunities for social mobility amongst the Catholic community.[28] The divisions and hostilities that these demarcations created are still clearly visible in the narratives of respondents who lived through them. Mrs Ferguson recalled how notions of 'respectability' ensured that some people 'thought they were a cut above you'. Mrs Reid concurred and Mrs MacIntosh insisted that the respectable working class 'would have treated us like dirt if we would've allowed them'.[29] A marker of inter-war respectability and social mobility was home ownership, access to council housing or the ability to move from areas associated with the 'rough' and the 'poorer' working class. This was an aspiration and a signifier of self-improvement.[30] However, home ownership was impeded by economic, cultural and structural factors in Scotland.[31]

While 230,000 houses were built in Scotland by local authorities between the wars, by 1936 it was estimated that council accommodation housed only one in twenty Scottish families and few of these could be considered

---

[26] *Scotsman*, 22 Oct. 1931.

[27] Knox, *Industrial Nation*, 236.

[28] See I. Maver, 'The Catholic community', in Devine and Finlay, *Scotland in the Twentieth Century*, 260–1.

[29] SOHCA/019/07/Glasgow, b. 1911, SOHCA/019/019/Glasgow, b. 1907 and SOHCA/019/014/Glasgow b. 1911 respectively.

[30] P. Scott, 'Did owner-occupation lead to smaller families for interwar working-class families?', *Economic History Review*, 61, 1: 99–124.

[31] See J. Butt, 'Working-class housing in Glasgow 1900–1939', in I. MacDougall (ed.), *Essays in Scottish Labour History*, 143–69.

working-class.[32] When council houses were allocated in the Mosspark housing scheme, built in Glasgow in the 1920s, over 16 per cent were allocated to families from the 'professional' class, more than 30 per cent to the 'intermediate' class, almost 30 per cent to the 'skilled non-manual' class and only 18 per cent to skilled manual workers. Amongst the semi-skilled, unskilled and unemployed strata the numbers were negligible. In Glenlee, Hamilton, new houses were built in the early 1920s and the Council indicated that ex-servicemen and their families would be given priority, but the tax burden took precedence and to ensure rents could be paid the houses were allocated to professional and skilled workers.[33] Indeed, for many Scottish families the relationship between economic well-being, status, respectability and housing was summed up by the recollections of Mr Davidson:

> There were certain trades in Glasgow that always had a wee bit more in their wage packet than others, and they wanted the best. We used to call them respectable. They were that wee bit better off. They would stay up in what they called the wallie close, the tiled close. Well the likes of the lower class they had to contend with these black stone buildings.[34]

Housing issues had been a focal point of collective community politics during World War I and continued to be so between the wars, as Chapter eight will demonstrate, but demand for council housing also created cleavages amongst the working classes because there was an insufficient number of houses built to meet demand or to combat existing poor housing conditions and overcrowding. In 1929, the ILPer Patrick Dollan complained that 'according to official returns, 18,362 houses had been built in Glasgow', 13,362 of which had rents of between £26 10/- and £44 per annum, excluding the cost of rates. Dollan estimated that an income of between £300 and £400 per annum was required to pay the rents.[35] According to respondents in this study the wages of working men averaged between £120 and £200 per annum, an income well below that which Dollan determined was needed to afford to reside in the new 'garden cities'. Robert Adams, the sanitary inspector for Ayr, also insisted that inability to pay the higher rents commanded for new housing was the biggest impediment to housing mobility. He claimed that 'the new houses that had been erected since the war have done little more than meet the needs of population increase'. Edinburgh's Public Health Department agreed. In 1936 they argued that the 'average young working-class couple, although their combined incomes would suffice, feared to marry lest pregnancy halved their income

[32] *Govan Press*, 4 Jan. 1930 and *Scotsman*, 26 May 1936.
[33] M. Pacione, *Glasgow: the Socio-spatial Development of the City* (Chichester, 1995), 158 and Sinclair, '"Silenced, suppressed and passive"', 198–9.
[34] SOHCA/019/030/Glasgow, b. 1900.
[35] *Glasgow Herald*, 12 Nov. 1929.

and made it impossible for them to get suitable accommodation'.[36] Mr
Coyle, a teacher between the wars, declared that he was unable to afford
a council house in Greenock in the 1930s.[37] Inability to pay the higher
rents demanded for council accommodation may explain why, in 1932, the
Calton Improvement Scheme had to issue eviction orders to tenants who
lived in this area, even though they had been offered alternative housing.[38]
Mr Davidson recalled the Calton in Glasgow:

> You smelt the place even before you seen it and all outside toilets
> and even wash bowls were outside. You'd to go up wooden stairs to it.
> They were two apartments and some of them had seven or eight of a
> family, maybe more. There were an awful lot of people badly needing
> rehoused. The housing conditions, they were horrible, absolutely hor-
> rible! If they built a scheme and you were sent there, you were paying
> about four or five times more rent. The people couldn't do it.[39]

To eliminate these conditions, overcrowding and sub-standard housing
Glasgow Corporation estimated in 1937 that it would need to build 60,000
houses.[40] This was not unique to Glasgow. In Greenock the number of dwellings increased by 4,528 between 1911 and 1931, but the number of unoccu-
pied homes fell by 1,796, and by this time the number of families living more
than two people to a room rose from 47.2 per cent to 48.2 per cent. In 1927
a Rent Inquiry Committee was set up by Greenock Corporation. It found
that 'every second house in Greenock was sub-let and in some cases they
housed as many as three families'. Rat and bug infestation in Greenock's
town centre slums resulted in the Corporation holding a further enquiry
in 1931. In Market Street, out of six hundred and thirty homes, only two
had baths, no home had hot water and between seven and eight families
shared one outside toilet.[41] The area was redeveloped in the later 1930s, but
housing conditions such as these prevailed. A similar survey was conducted
in Aberdeen in 1935 which defined uninhabitable housing as homes with
excessive dampness, unsafe walls, roofs and stairs, congestion and lack of
ventilation. It found that 29 per cent of all housing was either unfit for habi-
tation, overcrowded or both and that 58 per cent of all housing stock was
without adequate sanitary arrangements.[42] Dundee's accommodation was
little better, especially the overcrowded and rat-infested slum areas like the
nine-storey tenement, labelled 'no mountain' and the 'Vault'.[43]

Newspaper accounts highlight the poor conditions of many of Scotland's

[36] *Glasgow Herald*, 11 May 1929 and *Scotsman*, 26 May 1936.

[37] SOHCA/019/046/Greenock, b. 1904.

[38] Glasgow City Council Minutes, 19 Oct. 1932.

[39] SOHCA/019030/Glasgow, b. 1900.

[40] *Scotsman*, 5 Oct. 1937.

[41] *Census*, 1921 and 1931, and *Scotsman*, 24 Oct. 1933.

[42] H. MacKenzie, *The Third Statistical Account of Scotland, The City of Aberdeen* (Edinburgh,
1953), 124–6.

[43] *Scotsman*, 12 Nov. 1929.

slums. The *Times* described the housing conditions in some areas of Scotland as 'notoriously bad'. Consider the report on the condition of housing in Anderston, Glasgow:

> The sunk flat houses even in a hot, dry summer remain damp and unwholesome. The stairs down to these houses are invariably dark so that only by feeling along the walls can one discover the doors. In all of these closes the stairs are evil smelling, water closets are constantly choked and foul water runs down the stairs . . . One close is known as 'The Coffin Close' so bad is its repute.[44]

For the majority of working-class families the price of social mobility through home ownership or the procurement of municipal housing was prohibitive. Indeed, many people found it increasingly difficult to pay the lower rents demanded by the private sector. Mr Gordon recalled how in Clydebank evictions 'were a common sight'.[45] Evictions due to non-payment of rents permeated throughout the 1920s. Between January and October 1929, 11,500 evictions took place in Glasgow. In February 1931, there were 13,973 new eviction cases brought before Glasgow's Rent Court and 13,181 re-enrolled cases. In 1932, 15,153 new cases were brought to court and 16,225 re-enrolments. Not all of these families lost their homes, but between 1931 and 1932, 9,876 evictions were granted.[46] In 1931 the Secretary of State for Scotland, Godfrey Collins, was challenged about the cost of council housing by the ILPer and MP for North Lanarkshire, Jennie Lee. She pointed out that 'the arrears are an indication that the general rental is higher than people can pay'.[47]

During the 1920s £5,200,000 was spent on council house building, but only £357,000 of this was used to clear slums, £1 for every £14 spent.[48] Moreover the price of rents for council housing and the allocation policies designed to ensure rents were paid by allocating the housing to high-income earners meant that many families displaced during the initial slum clearance moved to affordable housing in areas that had not yet been cleared, causing greater problems in these localities. However, by the 1930s legislative changes and the effects of the economic climate combined to ensure that slum clearances took precedence over the building of 'garden cities'. Slum clearance and the provision of cheaper state-subsidised council housing offered those on lower incomes access to better housing. In 1933 the Department of Health for Scotland issued instructions to housing corporations across the country which determined that 'the class of tenant occupying state subsidised housing' was to be 'income tested'. Those 'not in economic circumstances falling within the strict interpretation of working class' would not

44 *Times*, 21 Dec. 1925.
45 SOHCA/019/043/Clydebank, b. 1920.
46 *Glasgow Herald*, 22 Feb. 1933.
47 *Govan Press*, 20 Feb. 1931.
48 *Scotsman*, 24 Oct. 1933.

be eligible to apply for a house.[49] In 1938, faced with 6,600 housing applications, 'a number increasing every day', Dundee Corporation's Housing Committee acknowledged that for the last few years the Council had 'entirely concentrated on slum clearance and overcrowding' with the result that houses were not available for 'respectable applicants, people about to be married, married couples residing with parents or in lodgings'.[50] The policy of concentrating on slum clearance and overcrowding guaranteed that it was largely those on relatively low incomes with the largest families who were getting the opportunity to escape poor housing conditions, whilst those who could not afford to purchase their own home but who did not dwell in a 'slum' were denied access to better accommodation. Thus, the construction of more affordable council housing estates during the period of slum clearance in the 1930s caused considerable vying for decent accommodation and this fused with ideas about respectability and sectarianism in Scotland to fracture class cohesion.

Slum clearance took on implosive religious connotations because Catholics were highly represented amongst the lowest paid. Catholics also continued to have the largest families and were highly concentrated in some of the worst areas of Scotland; therefore they were at the forefront of slum clearance. Mr Davidson, a contemporary who worked for Glasgow City Council as a tram driver, was asked which areas of the city were considered Catholic areas. He replied 'the poorest of the poorest areas, that's where you got them'.[51] Looking at the number of Catholic children in Glasgow's school constituency also provides an indication of Catholic concentration; it seems that Glasgow's Catholic population was mainly located in a small radius from the city centre in many of the slum areas, as Table 3.2 indicates.

In Glasgow, corresponding with immigrant patterns, these areas included the Calton which bridged the constituencies of Bridgeton and Camlachie. There was a large concentration of Catholic families in Anderston, a rundown area of the largely middle-class constituency of Kelvingrove. Partick's east end in the Hillhead constituency had a significant number of Catholic families, as did Cowcaddens in the St Rollox constituency. Garngad, a working-class neighbourhood in the largely middle-class Central constituency of Glasgow, also had a large Catholic population. Outside the main regions of Catholic concentration, the Calton, Garngad, Cowcaddens, Anderston and the Gorbals, there were enclaves, labelled 'little Irelands' throughout Glasgow, in Springburn, Partick, Maryhill, Parkhead and Shettleston. However, with the exception of Kinning Park in the Tradeston constituency, Catholic penetration was marginal with only three Catholic schools accommodating around 2,500 children in the more affluent constituencies of Cathcart, Pollock and Tradeston.

---

[49] Glasgow City Council Minutes, 5 Apr. 1933.
[50] *Scotsman,* 19 Aug. 1938.
[51] SOHCA/019/030/Glasgow, b. 1900.

Table 3.2 Catholic school population as a percentage of the total public school capacity, Glasgow Council wards, 1930.

Constituency	Total school capacity	No. of Catholic children	Percentage of Catholic children in each constituency
All constituencies	218,681	43,740	20.0
Bridgeton	16,950	4,725	27.8
Camlachie	20,948	5,071	24.2
Cathcart	11,924	920	7.7
Central	10,339	3,017	28.6
Gorbals	17,136	4,903	28.6
Govan	14,205	3,501	24.6
Hillhead	11,035	3,132	28.3
Kelvingrove	15,146	2,170	14.3
Maryhill	14,795	1,964	13.2
Partick	8,542	620	7.2
Pollock	15,122	920	6.0
Shettleston	16,634	2,510	15.0
Springburn	15,378	3,416	22.2
St Rollox	15,926	4,949	31.0
Tradeston	14,401	1,922	13.3

Source: *Glasgow Education Diaries*, 1924 and 1930 and *Catholic Directory for Scotland*, 1924 and 1930.

Even in areas that seemed to have mixed religious communities, segregation within the neighbourhood existed, generally on a street-by-street basis. Certain streets in west Govan were known for their Catholic concentration and stigmatised as 'rough' because of this. Mrs Parsonage insisted that, 'Govan was more or less Protestant except Neptune Street and Nethan Street'. She also insisted that the Catholic community in Govan spent Saturday nights fighting and Sundays in St Anthony's Chapel.[52] Catholic concentration, along with the attitudes that this could give rise to, were replicated throughout the city of Glasgow:

> In Eastmuir there was more Catholics than anybody. Some of these women were always having babies. It was a shame. You used to see the kiddies round about with hardly any clothes on, just because drink and gambling had a strong hold. The men were too fond of drink and wanted more money and it was the wife and family they hurt.[53]

Whilst there was evidently some sympathy for the conditions endured by many Catholic families, there was also considerable stereotyping of this group of people. There was also a perception that Catholic families were

[52] SOHCA/019/026/Glasgow, b. 1917.
[53] SOHCA/019/0037/Glasgow, b. 1912.

receiving preferential treatment in housing allocation due to slum clearance policies based on such stereotyping. In Glasgow the inability of local residents to procure a home in the new Moorepark estate caused such animosity, with the new residents becoming targets of derogatory abuse. Mrs Duncan recalled how Moorepark came to be labelled the 'Wine Alley',

> It was promised to the Govan people. Instead of them getting it, it was given to Partick and Anderston people. So Govan people used to watch them going in and out the pub and that's when it got nicknamed the Wine Alley. When we got promised Vicarfield Street the Govan people called it the Promised Land because, well we all got houses.[54]

The signification of drunkenness and 'rough' behaviour was strongly associated with Irish Catholics and the poorer areas that Catholics resided in. Many of the new tenants were originally from Kinning Park, which was the more Catholic area of the Tradeston constituency. Other tenants came from Partick and Anderston, which had large Catholic populations. Ferguslie Park housing estate in Paisley suffered a similar stigma. Most of the families housed on this estate were from the slums in the centre of town. They were the families who were 'the poorest' and had the largest families, features associated with Catholicism.[55] Mrs Campbell recollected:

> There were thirteen of us in a room and kitchen and we were getting older. My mother was cramped. So my mother was fed up asking for a bigger house and it was a bath she wanted. We were always going to the baths so that was money all the time. She got us all together and took us up the High Street. She heard of people giving bungs [bribes] and getting houses, Irish people. My mother wasn't stupid. She said, 'This is my family. They were all born and bred in Glasgow. Why is there a Catholic community in Carntyne? They're coming off the Irish boat and waiting six weeks for a new house.'[56]

Glasgow City Council received complaints similar to Mrs Campbell's recollections. In 1932 and again in 1933 the Council entertained deputations representing constituents who accused housing officials of bribery and complained about the 'unfair allocation of houses'.[57] The Govan Municipal Ward Committee also complained on behalf of constituents who alleged that 'non-rate payers or those who have paid rates for a short time', in other words 'incomers', 'were obtaining Corporation houses'. The ILPer Jean Mann also asked for an inquiry into 'letting irregularities' in the Provan district of Glasgow.[58] The outcome of these inquiries was that

[54] SOHCA/01905/Glasgow, b. 1912 and S. Damer, 'Farewell to the Wine Alley', *Scottish Labour History Review*, 11: 9–11 (Winter 1997/Spring 1998).

[55] W. J. McKechin, *Politics: Paisley Pattern* (London, 1969), 21–2.

[56] SOHCA/019/04/Glasgow, b. 1910.

[57] Glasgow City Council Minutes, 5 Oct. 1932 and 5 Apr. 1933.

[58] *Times*, 23 Jun. 1933.

one employee was charged with corruption.[59] Nevertheless it is also clear that the discursive and structural forces surrounding housing pervaded the collective mentalities of many Protestant families and gave rise to the perception that Catholic families, especially Irish Catholic families, were being given preferential treatment in the allocation of housing often by means of bribery and deceit. This situation exacerbated divisions in working-class neighbourhoods based on religion and respectable status.

The divisive qualities of sectarianism were also aggravated by the belief that an individual's religious identity exerted considerable influence in the procurement of employment and not just in the better-documented heavy industries. Mrs McQueen maintained that her religion was important to her in Glasgow because 'in these days some factories you went to for a job asked, "What religion are you?" Now Mitchell's Tobacco work and Templeton's Carpet Factory wouldn't employ you if you weren't a Protestant. They were biased'.[60] Mrs Ferguson stated that, 'Sometimes it was pretty hard. You didn't get on. Sometimes people didn't treat you very well . . . if you were a Catholic you couldn't get a job, especially your father.' Indeed, Catholic employees continued 'to be faced with adverts in the job columns of the press saying that they need not apply'. This reinforces the strong suggestion of segregation in the structural labour market in the inter-war period.[61] Religious identity was much more than practising a particular faith in some parts of Scotland; for many individuals it was perceived as a birthright.[62] Indeed, Mrs Adams maintained that 'If you were Protestant you were supposed to be on the up and up.'[63] Thus, the economic climate, the potential threat from cheap unskilled Catholic labour, along with housing segregation based on religious denomination and the perception of preferential treatment being given to the Catholic community all combined to aggravate sectarianism.

Religious identity and Protestant religious anxieties were further heightened by the belief, often instigated by civic society, that Scotland was being over-run by Irish Catholics.[64] In 1923 a letter, signed 'Anxious', was sent to the editor of the *Glasgow Citizen* expressing these sentiments: 'It is with growing alarm that I notice the tremendous increase in Roman Catholics in Glasgow'. In 1929 the Joint Committee of the Scottish Presbyterian Churches expressed similar concern. It was suggested that Scotland was 'a decaying nation' because 'every year Scotland loses 50,000 people through

---

[59] *Glasgow Herald*, 1 Jul. 1932, Glasgow City Council Minutes, 22 Feb. and 5 Oct. 1933 and especially *Daily Record*, 6 Apr. 1933.

[60] SOHCA/019/018/Glasgow, b. 1909.

[61] SOHCA/019/07/Glasgow, b. 1911 and Knox, *Industrial Nation*, 200.

[62] SOHCA/019/07/Glasgow, b. 1911. See also Maver, 'The Catholic community', 269–84 and Campbell, *The Scottish Miners, Vol. One*.

[63] SOHCA/019/022/Greenock, b. 1919.

[64] Maver, 'The Catholic community' and G. Walker, 'Varieties of Scottish Protestant identity', in Devine and Finlay, *Scotland in the Twentieth Century*, 260–1.

emigration. This loss is not atoned for by the advent of an inferior type of immigrant from Ireland.'[65] This occurred at a time when many Protestant families, whilst having a profound desire to be 'on the up and up', were being opened to the possibilities of experiencing a sense of relative deprivation. For example, while there was no 'simple explanation' for the extreme sectarian conflict in Lanarkshire between the wars, there was 'some general correspondence with economic distress' and 'periods of falling wages'.[66] It seems that while sectarianism permeated society, inter-war economic distress aggravated pre-existing religious tensions and led to perceptions that Catholics were receiving preferential treatment not only in the allocation of council housing but also in employment. Mr Armstrong, who worked for Glasgow City Council, felt that there was 'a lot of Catholic workers in the municipal section', because 'there were a lot a Catholic councillors allied to the Labour Party'.[67]

The ILP's penetration of municipal politics in Scotland and the relationship between housing developments and the party's housing protests shored up linkages between the ILP and preferential treatment in access to employment and the provision of council housing for Catholics. It was seen as a strategy to command the Catholic vote. Such opinions opened many Protestant families to the anti-Catholic propaganda of the churches, the Scottish Protestant League and the Unionist Party that was disseminated in the press and filtered into popular mentalities.[68] Thus, religious affiliation was an important determining factor in voting behaviour and this was not limited to Protestant constituents. In the constituencies where the labour movement did best there were large Catholic populations. In some of the constituencies Catholics represented between 20 per cent and one-third of the electorate and they accounted for nearly 50 per cent of the Gorbals constituency of Glasgow.[69]

Yet many working-class females saw benefits from voting for a Conservative or Liberal candidate and these benefits included identification with respectability and expressing religious identity rather than anti-socialism and sectarianism as such. Indeed, Scottish Conservative MPs have been identified as the most liberal in Parliament and they were advocates of social policy, especially housing. Some, like Walter Elliot, had even flirted with socialism.[70] The Conservative Party, or rather the Unionist Party as it was known in Scotland, is seen to have attracted support because it challenged the Labour Party by offering a populist vision of class that was not

[65] *Citizen*, 6 Jan. 1923 and *Glasgow Herald*, 9 Apr. 1929. See also Knox, *Industrial Nation*, 201 and Smyth, *Labour in Glasgow*, 190–207.

[66] A. Campbell, *The Scottish Miners, 1874–1939, Vol. Two* (Aldershot, 2000), 317–31, 336.

[67] SOHCA/019/027/Glasgow, b. 1905.

[68] Walker, 'Protestant identity', 260–1.

[69] *Times*, 28 Dec. 1922.

[70] See J. F. McCaffrey, 'Political issues and developments', in W. H. Fraser and I. Maver (eds), *Glasgow Vol. II* (Manchester, 1996), 186–226 and Hutchison, 'Scottish issues', 82.

based on a society divided by income, wealth and status. The Conservatives emphasised unity, presenting themselves as the party of the nation, unlike the labour movement which was accused of putting sectional interests and 'greed and self interest' before the greater good of all.[71] Many women apparently embraced this vision of class and they may well have done so because women were expected to neglect their own needs for the greater good of family and community. There were women like Mrs Harris who had internalised the Unionist discourse that linked the ILP with sectional interests. She claimed that the ILP were 'Hot and Tots!' She 'wasn't impressed' by 'Labour folk' because she saw socialists as 'the greediest rascals under the sun. They wanted everything for nothing and that's what sickened me. It was grab grab grab.'[72]

However, gender, age and religion and the promotion of issues which strengthened the family, along with the creation of a culture which embraced women, but 'celebrated their subordination', ensured that a Conservative 'political tradition so little associated with the emancipation of women was so strongly rooted among women'.[73] Other factors were also important. Mrs Galbraith identified herself as a Unionist voter because she believed that she was 'slightly above working class'. That meant, 'You were just that wee bit more snobbish, at least you fancied yourself more and you wouldn't do things that some of the tougher ones would do', such as 'yelling and squealing out in the street, conducting yourself like a hooligan'. Mrs Galbraith voted for the Unionist Party because, 'We were always taught to behave ourselves and not to act like hooligans which most of them [socialists] did. You just had that feeling that the Conservatives were a better class and you did your best to try and copy them.' Mrs Galbraith believed that the Labour Party were 'rougher, just a different class' and that the Communist Party's membership were 'a rougher type of person'. She defined the Communist Party as 'really low. We would never be allowed to go near it. That was one thing we would not be allowed to do.'[74] These attitudes towards communists were not the preserve of women or those who voted against the ILP or the Labour Party. For many individuals such hostility was also due to significant differences in ideology which undermined a united front amongst the parties of the left. From the early 1920s, while the ILP may have moved to the left, the Labour Party opposed Communist Party affiliation. The ILP may have been divided over this issue but the party increasingly adopted the Labour Party's stance. Schism grew within the labour movement, especially in the years 1928 to 1934. In this period the ILP and the Labour Party's relationship was placed under stress due to the Labour Party's emphasis on Parliamentary gradualist reforms, whilst at the same time the Communist

---

[71] Cannadine, *Class in Britain*, 133–5.
[72] SOHCA/019/09/Glasgow, b. 1900.
[73] B. Campbell, *The Iron Ladies, Why do Women Vote Tory* (London, 1987), 3–7 and passim.
[74] SOHCA/019/08/Glasgow, b. 1916.

Party moved towards Stalinist social fascism under directives from Moscow, rejecting the gradualist approach and emphasising the use of extra-Parliamentary forms of protest. While this did not entirely stop individuals from the different branches from working together in protests, united campaigns were difficult at best until the Spanish Civil War.[75] Mr Troy voted for the ILP, but he thought the Communist Party was 'terrible', they were 'wicked'. He recalled how the Communists would stand at street corners and 'shout and bawl, vote for this and vote for that'. He added, 'they all just wanted to be rough working people'.[76]

The relationship between 'rough' and poverty influenced voting behaviour. Mrs Ingills maintained that the Labour Party was 'more or less treated as a lesser occupation'; Labour voters were identified as 'poorer people'.[77] Although it is acknowledged that poor and more affluent working-class people voted for the ILP, it is also clear that the ILP saw itself as the party of the respectable working class. Indeed, the ILP promoted 'teetotalism, pacifism and a Christian morality that was socially conservative'.[78] To distance itself from the association with poverty, the ILP tried to advance the idea that it was a respectable party, albeit not always advantageously. In 1926, the ILPer Mary Barbour stood as the municipal candidate for the Govan seat. In her address she stated that she represented the 'clean' and 'respectable' working-class people of that area. This was much to the annoyance of some of the constituents who waged a constant battle against the unsanitary conditions in which they were forced to live.[79] Nevertheless this was a pragmatic strategy because the signification that associated the ILP with the poor and the 'rough' guaranteed that certain 'respectable' women, and, for that matter, men, would refrain from voting for the labour movement. The link between the ILP and the poor was also enshrined in ideas about ability and educational levels, often seen amongst the working classes as the preserve of the elite. Mrs Parsonage claimed that she voted Conservative because,

> Well I always thought that they were the people who had the business brains. They were the people if they could run a business surely they could run the country, and that they had more up there, in the head, than Labour candidates.[80]

The association linking the ILP to the 'rough' working class was further entrenched to some extent because the ILP and the Communist Party often held public meetings which frequently involved raised voices and

[75] Campbell, *The Scottish Miners, Vol. Two,* 284–98 and 378–9, Knox, *Industrial Nation,* 236 and Smyth, *Labour in Glasgow,* 115–16.
[76] SOHCA/019/034/Glasgow, b. 1901.
[77] SOHCA/019/010/Glasgow, b. 1907.
[78] Knox, *Industrial Nation,* 237 and Smyth, *Labour in Glasgow,* 95–124.Knox, *Industrial Nation,* 237 and Smyth, *Labour in Glasgow,* 95–124.
[79] *Govan Press,* 9 Aug. 1929.
[80] SOHCA/019/026/Glasgow, b. 1917.

heckling, whilst police hostility, particularly towards the Communist Party, guaranteed that meetings were often disruptive. Moreover, although academic research may emphasise the growing schisms between the ILP and the Communist Party from the 1920s, these were not self-evident to ordinary working-class people. Respondents from both sides of the political divide associated the two parties with a broad inter-war 'socialism' that was not differentiated by theory and practice. This was partly due to media representation. With little or no differentiation, the Scottish press used the term 'socialist' to define male and female members of the ILP, the Labour Party, the Communist Party and the Co-operative Movement. The interconnection between the ILP and other left-wing parties was also signified in the ways in which these parties had worked together through community networks to promote and pursue their political discourses and their policies immediately before, during and in the wake of the First World War. Mr Ewart was a 'Labour man' by his own definition. He voted for Jimmy Maxton of the ILP, but stressed that 'it wasn't the Labour Party, it was the ILP and for years, they were treated as the Reds. If you voted ILP you were a communist.' Mrs Johnston, a Unionist voter, also labelled Maxton a communist. Mr Troy, a self-proclaimed 'Labour man' from Govan, an ILP constituency, stated, 'the ILP was half Communist. They were all mixed up.' Mrs Parsonage, a Unionist, concurred: 'they were communists or near enough'.[81] Mr Davidson, a self-defined socialist, voted for the ILP. He identified 'John Maclean, Jimmy Maxton, Manny Shinwell and John McGovern and another auld critter from Govan, Peter McIntyre' as strong leading lights of the party.[82] Indeed, only Maxton of this group was not a communist at some point in his political career, whilst John Maclean was a member of the British Socialist Party and a Bolshevik. Communism and communists were attacked by all other parties, the media and the churches and labelled deviant, and by association the ILP was also vilified in this way.

This aggravated the associations made between the ILP, the Labour Party and communists with Catholicism. Mrs Parsonage certainly felt that 'in our day you really found that a lot of the communists, they were Catholics. Ninety per cent of them had turned from Catholicism and a lot of them who hadn't turned from it were communists'.[83]Although prominent members of the ILP were Catholics, including John Wheatley and Patrick Dollan, the ILP attempted to dissociate itself from Catholicism. In 1922, the party categorically denied any links between Catholicism and socialism, emphasising that

> there are seven Labour members sitting on Glasgow's parish council. All seven are Protestant. Four are Elders in Protestant Churches, one is

---

[81] SOHCA/019/031/Glasgow, b.1908, SOHCA/019/025/Paisley, b.1914, SOHCA/019/034/Glasgow, b. 1901 and SOHCA/019/026/Glasgow b. 1917.

[82] SOHCA/019/030/Glasgow, b. 1900.

[83] SOHCA/019/026/Glasgow, b. 1917.

a Lay Preacher, and one is the daughter of a past Professor Of Divinity at the United Free College.

Nevertheless, by their own admission, the ILP acknowledged that their 'association with Catholicism alienated Protestants'.[84]

The growing strength of the ILP in Scotland also reinvigorated the other political parties and this corresponded with women's enfranchisement. Thus, these parties increasingly targeted the women's vote and at the same time the Unionist Party, in Scotland, Wales and Northern Ireland, although not in England, constructed its identity on nationalism and Protestantism. Women and the family unit were central to this representation of nation after World War I.[85] In 1923, the Duke of Sutherland expressed the view that 'from my knowledge of what is going on in Scotland to-day, it is very important that the Conservative Party's Women's Primrose League should be re-established there in an even stronger position than before' to oppose 'socialist doctrines' that might 'otherwise assert themselves'. He believed Edinburgh and Glasgow were 'especially worthy of attention'. This led to an increase in Scottish representation on the Grand Council of the League and in 1926 the Scottish Women Unionists' Conference was inaugurated, attended by 2,000 women. The Scottish Unionist Party was an extremely efficient organisation and has been identified, more than the Labour and Liberal parties, of 'managing to harness women'.[86] Women voters were also enticed to embrace a 'them and us' model of class based on their religious identity. In the aftermath of the 1926 General Strike, identified as 'an attempt at revolution', a 'new Scottish patriotic organisation' was inaugurated in Edinburgh, the Scottish Women Loyalists. Members were to 'Honour the King, Fear God' and avoid 'class hatred, disloyalty and sedition' in the form of socialism.[87] This populist agenda that was used by the Unionists was based on a 'loyalist message and fused with appeals of Empire, religion, Ulster and a definition of Scottishness derived to a large extent from Presbyterian mythology', which was fuelled by anti-Catholicism.[88] The links between Ireland and Scotland, king, country and religious denomination, combined with the strength of Protestant identity and the significance of the church in many Protestant women's lives to influence their images of class and their party political identity.

Ministers firmly supported the Unionist Party in Scotland. For example, almost one in twenty-four subscribers to the Scottish Conservative political fund in 1933 was a member of the cloth and of all Glasgow subscribers one in eight were listed as reverends.[89] Mr Davidson maintained that 'most

---

[84] *Forward*, 15 Apr. 1922. See also 4 Mar. 1923 and 16 May 1929.
[85] See P. Ward, *Unionism in the United Kingdom, 1918–1974* (Basingstoke, 2005), 45.
[86] *Times*, 4 May 1923. See also 22 Oct. 1924 and Hutchison, 'Scottish issues', 82–3.
[87] *Times*, 23 Oct. 1926.
[88] Walker, 'Protestant identity', 260–1.
[89] GRA, TD1373/DC83, Scottish Conservative Club Records: List of Subscribers to the Political Fund 1933.

church-goers didn't like the ILP. They thought they were out to do away with the churches.'[90] Others saw the labour movement, particularly the Communist Party, as a threat to the monarchy. Mrs Johnston was warned by her father to avoid Communists, 'to cross the street in case you get tainted'. Her father, a Unionist, 'couldn't stand anybody that was against the monarchy'. Women who voted ILP and Labour also rejected the Communist Party on the same grounds. It was widely believed that they were 'just making trouble. They wanted rid of the monarchy and all that.' Ms Anderson, who voted for the ILP, felt strongly about this issue, and read the communist discourse of class exploitation as a vilification of her class.

> Their ideas were too strong and people felt that they could never be safe with them. They were making out that you were downtrodden, everybody was walking over you, which wasn't true at all. I used to have an argument with a girl that worked in the next machine to me. She was a communist and she used to go on about the royal family. She was holding communism up to the sky, talking about our class, we were nothing, we were deprived people. Well a lot of Russians were deprived.[91]

Negative attitudes towards the Communist Party crossed the religious divide in Scotland with both ministers and the Catholic clergy contesting communist anti-clericalism. Coexisting with the labour movement's perceived accommodation of 'Rome', this gave greater currency to the Protestant churches' condemnation of 'socialism'. It also facilitated the Unionists' propaganda which 'gave political expression to the fears and prejudices of Protestant Scotland'.[92]

Religion proved a major obstacle to class unity and class politics, but divisions based on religion had a complex relationship with class and ethnic identities. Indeed, it has been shown that workplace issues, unemployment and class politics could provide the basis to transcend religious and ethnic identities. Irish Home Rule, Catholic education and the ILP's support for temperance may have plagued the relationship between the ILP and Catholic voters until at least 1922, but recent research highlights that many Catholics supported the ILP from its inception, although this support could be conditional. Significant numbers of Orangemen continued to vote Unionist in Scotland between the wars.[93] However, there was also a simultaneous growth of the Labour Party and the Orange Order at a time when the hierarchy of the Order linked socialism and Catholicism and demanded that its members did not ally themselves with the Labour Party. Many did, highlighting how working-class politics could transcend religious divisions and the tribalism and sense of community offered by

[90] SOHCA/019/030/Glasgow, b. 1900.
[91] SOHCA/019/025/Paisley, b. 1914 and SOHCA/019/02/Glasgow b. 1908.
[92] Walker, 'Protestant identity', 261.
[93] Campbell, *Scottish Miners*, 373.

religious organisations. The same conditions prevailed during the hunger marches when unemployed people who were members of the Orange Order walked alongside Catholics on a class issue even under the threat of being disaffiliated by their Order.[94] Religious identity and class awareness were not necessarily mutually exclusive, but under certain circumstances they could be. The links between Unionism and Protestant identity in Scotland were manifest in the success of the Scottish Protestant League. Glasgow had seven Scottish Protestant League councillors elected by 1933. Edinburgh elected nine Protestant Action Society councillors in 1936.[95] Many Unionist MPs had links with the Orange Order, such as Hugh Ferguson, Motherwell's Unionist candidate, who was elected in 1922 and again in 1923. Archibald Douglas MacInnes Shaw, a prominent Orangeman and Unionist candidate, was elected to the Paisley constituency in 1923 and has been identified as having 'activated the Order to a new political awareness' in this area despite the Order's split with Unionism.[96] On the other hand, Govan had the largest membership of the Orange Order with female members outnumbering men, but this constituency was retained throughout the inter-war years by the ILP. Yet, as it has been argued, if the workplace was the medium which undermined the tribalism of the community, then by implication working-class men and their organisations, because they marginalised or excluded women, contributed to the extent to which working-class women's political identity was influenced by community tribalism rather than it being a manifestation of socialist women's ignorance of the potential of the newly enfranchised women's vote.

In the wake of women being enfranchised community tribalism was heightened in Scotland by the formation of the Orange and Protestant Party in 1922, which emerged as a result of the 'Orange Order splitting with the Tories to form the new party'.[97] Following on from this, and coexisting with it, were the activities of a multiplicity of organisations representing Protestant religious identity. There were 'Protestant demonstrations held to discuss Romanism', which was perceived to be 'making inroads among Scotsmen'. In addition, there were 'attacks on Romanism by the Scottish Reformation Society', all of which was reported by the media.[98] There was also a growth of Protestant organisations such as the Scottish Protestant Evidence Guild which was formed in March 1932 to 'study all aspects of

[94] For the Catholic vote see Smyth, *Labour in Glasgow*, 124–54. For Protestant support see G. Walker, 'The Orange Order in Scotland between the wars', *International Review of Social History*, 37, 2: 177, 185–8 (1992) and passim and MacDougall, *Voices from the Hunger Marches*, 103, 134–6, 154–6, 161–5 and 185.

[95] *Scotsman*, 30 Nov. 1936 and Craig, *Parliamentary Election Results*, 634.

[96] Macdonald, *The Radical Thread*, 222 and Cairns, 'Women and the Clydeside labour movement', 73.

[97] *Glasgow Evening Times*, 12 Oct. 1922 and *Forward*, 4 Mar. 1922.

[98] *Glasgow Herald*, 15 Jun. and 20 Sep. 1927.

the Protestant faith, beliefs and doctrines'. By April this organisation was 'likening itself to the Scottish Protestant League'.[99]

Associational relationships were also cultivated in local communities to serve the anti-Labour alliance that existed in Scotland, and these exposed working-class constituents from relatively homogeneous communities to counter-class identities. They also offered status as well as a sense of purpose to women. Ministers and the upper echelons of society in particular areas participated in these associations so that the link between status, religious identity and Conservatism was formed. Mrs Kilpartick remembered

> We had Mrs Mackie, she bought the dairy, and she was an awful nice person – and her pal. Those two were great Unionists and I used to go to quite a lot of wee nights that they had up in the Orange Hall – all women. Mrs Mackie didn't work, well not with her hands, but when there was going to be an election in the area these two worked. They were Unionists and I worked with them as well, electioneering, and I liked it.[100]

Religious identity influenced images of class and correspondingly class politics. In response to the question 'which class do you belong to?', Mrs Harris, a resident of Kinning Park, an area which had a Scottish Protestant League councillor from 1931 to 1933, replied, 'How do you mean, Protestant?'[101] Between 1931 and 1935 the Dennistoun, Glasgow constituency also elected a candidate from this party. Mrs Ingills, who resided in this area, was asked what the local councillors were like. She replied

> It was more or less always on the Protestant side that I heard anything about them, because we didn't do much in the way of social work, the Labour. It was always Protestant to me. A Protestant company was a higher grade than a Labour.[102]

Mr Ewart claimed that in Partick, because of 'a big influx of Orangeman' who were 'Tories', 'if you were Labour you were ostracised, even the weans were pelted if they came out with a red rose on to celebrate May Day'.[103]

The Catholic clergy's influence on their parishioners and the direct involvement of priests in politics also created a situation whereby the links between church-going, religious identity and voting behaviour were formed. The *Daily Record* reported on a speech by the Archbishop of Glasgow in which he stated, 'no Catholic might or could give him or herself wholly to any party without departing from his or her status as a Catholic'.[104] However, it is clear that the Catholic vote could be given to individuals representing

[99] *Govan Press*, 11 Mar. and 8 Apr. 1932.
[100] SOHCA/019/012/Glasgow, b. 1907.
[101] SOHCA/019/009/Glasgow, b. 1900.
[102] SOHCA/019/010/Glasgow, b. 1907.
[103] SOHCA/019/031/Glasgow, b. 1908.
[104] *Daily Record*, 25 May 1931.

that particular faith. In 1928, twenty-eight Glasgow Parish Council seats were contested, five by Catholic Independent candidates. They were Dalmarnock, the Calton, Mile End, Provan and Cowcaddens, and all five candidates were elected. Two independent Catholic councillors were also elected onto the Govan Parish Council representing Hutchesontown and the Gorbals.[105] Mr Davidson recalled how priests tried to influence the way people voted, 'not by immediate say so, but by innuendo'.[106] Some priests were more direct, although not necessarily successful.

> Ma father-in-law became the election agent for the Labour member for the parish council and the priest saw him and said, 'What you doing here? I never thought one of my boys would turn on me like that'. Ma father-in-law said, 'It's my political party. It's the party I believe in, so that's the reason I'm doing this.[107]

While the clergy seems to have had less of an impact upon the political identities of men, Mrs Jones, who claimed 'priests were like policemen' in her community, recalled, 'they told us who to vote for. It was up to yourself, right enough, but they told us, no communists, the very opposite from communism, that won't interfere with the church.'[108] Significantly, this woman voted for the Conservative Party, the party regarded in Scotland as the very opposite of the Communist Party. She was the only Catholic female respondent interviewed to do so.

Religious identity was significant to many working-class people and thus the association which the labour movement had with Catholicism influenced their voting behaviour. In terms of Catholic women this was generally to the advantage of left-wing parties. The inverse is true of the female Protestant vote. Catholic women were more likely to vote for the ILP or the Labour Party than their Protestant male and female counterparts, but men, regardless of religious affiliation, were more supportive of left-wing parties than women. Of the female respondents who disclosed their voting behaviour, all but one Catholic woman voted Labour or ILP, whilst the Protestant women were more than twice as likely to vote Unionist, with some voting for militant Protestant political parties. By contrast, all Catholic men voted Labour or ILP and only one in three Protestant males stated that they voted Unionist.

Many working-class women voted for the labour movement in Scotland, but women's exclusion from work after marriage and the nature of their employment ensured that the local neighbourhood was an important force in shaping their political identities. While the effects of unemployment and adversarial relations between workers and employers as well as contact with local labour movement organisations and protests contributed to the

---

[105] *Govan Press*, 9 Aug. 1929.
[106] SOHCA/019/030/Glasgow, b. 1900.
[107] SOHCA/019/031/Glasgow, b. 1908.
[108] SOHCA/019/011/Glasgow, b. 1917.

class awareness of women, community tensions also fractured class unity. The adoption of the hierarchal model of class, although not fixed or static, along with developments in housing and the influence of religion, was reflected in voting behaviour amongst women more clearly than amongst men. However, if workplace experiences shaped class awareness and undermined the tribalism of the community then the labour movement contributed to a loss of a female constituency by its own making by depoliticising women in the sense of reducing working-class female support for trade unions and parties of the left. However, as the following chapter will demonstrate, experiences of gender and class discrimination in the workplace ensured that work was an important politicising force for working-class women regardless of the labour movement's neglect of this potential political constituency.

CHAPTER FOUR

'A Docile Workforce'? Women, Work and Political Identity

The expediency of the discourse used by employers, trade unionists and male workers that identified women workers as docile and politically apathetic has been bolstered by a historiography which argues that the nature of women's work between the wars meant that they were unlikely to be politicised by it. Domestic service, and office and retail jobs, the principal occupations of Scottish women, were not noted for their capacity to heighten class consciousness. In contrast to the expansion of blue-collar factory jobs employing men which resulted in greater levelling and possibilities for enhanced class awareness, women's work in domestic service, clerical occupations and shops was scattered, sidelined and in close proximity to employers. Seemingly, the nature of this work made it subject to paternalistic influences and capable of imbuing women with a false sense of status, which in turn constrained their class awareness.[1] Yet the extent of female activism and the varieties of women's militancy were as diverse as their work experiences. Many women expressed a consciousness of class membership that was shaped by their experiences of work. Thus, they responded to the effects of capitalism at the point of production both overtly and covertly using a range of strategies. Workplace oppression also created levels of gender awareness amongst women workers and led to the operation of gender-specific strategies to combat class and sex discrimination. However, because of their exclusion and marginalisation from institutional forms of militancy, working women also drew on older community-based tactics to contest exploitation in the workplace and in work-related disputes. Although these strategies did little to challenge the strengthening structural, cultural and ideological barriers that inhibited women's progress in the workplace, they empowered women psychologically at a time when many of their male counterparts were apparently experiencing levels of workplace 'rehabilitation'.

The female workforce was increasingly characterised by its close proximity to employers, in isolated and scattered jobs, but this did not necessarily ensure political passivity. Mrs MacIntosh was a domestic servant between the wars and she enjoyed her work. However, she was also a member of the Co-operative Women's Guild and the Labour Party, and when she lost

---

[1] See Savage and Miles, *The Remaking of the British Working Class*, 21–40.

her job she joined the Unemployed Workers' Movement.[2] In the mining districts of Scotland many domestic servants worked in the wealthier districts of Edinburgh and these women workers 'developed a sense of class antagonism during their pre-marital servile role'. They did so because of the 'glaring contrast' between the 'domestic comforts' of their employers' lives and those of their own families.[3] Thus, close proximity to employers could sharpen class awareness and paternalism was often a response to this. In the highly competitive retail sectors paternalism was not a strategy to offset the development of class awareness, but rather to mediate its effects. Paternalism was used to ensure a contented workforce that would guarantee good customer relations and moderate the agency of employees that was expressed through a very high turnover of workers.[4] Yet, by contrast, Paisley was monopolised by the Coats thread firm, a large, technologically advanced company that generated welfare policies.[5] Paternalism, to encourage workers to be loyal to the firm, was the employment strategy used by this company and it appears to have been relatively successful. There were no real efforts to develop trade unions and very little strife occurred between the wars, either in the Paisley mills or at their office in Glasgow. Ms Stewart, a Coats employee, recalled the reasons behind the comparative loyalty of workers. The owner, Mr Clark, apparently endeavoured to safeguard the employment of workers during the depression and only workers deemed 'badly behaved', who were 'always grumbling', lost their jobs.[6]

Coats also provided medical services, education, leisure facilities and a pension fund. It assumed that paternalism would ensure a cheap and deferential workforce. Ms Stewart claimed, 'Coats had a way of their own. When the girls were sixteen they took sixpence a week off their wages and gave them 10s a week 50 years later. Oh! The girls in Paisley were considered well off. They were in the money.' However, Ms Stewart also stated, 'if you got married you left or you were dismissed'.[7] Indeed, it was the comparative youth of workers, combined with the lack of support they received from the labour movement, that ensured that it was difficult for these workers to express an awareness of their exploitative working conditions.[8] This is not to suggest that every worker experienced these conditions in the same way. *Forward* reported on how, during periods of industrial action, Paisley's female textile workers were more likely to express their solidarity by financially assisting striking workers than their male counterparts were.[9]

[2] SOHCA/019/14/Glasgow, b. 1911.
[3] Campbell, *The Scottish Miners, Vol. One*, 232.
[4] Cushman, 'Negotiating the shop floor', 330.
[5] M. Blair, *The Paisley Thread Industry and the Men Who Created and Developed It* (Paisley, 1907), 79–83. See also Macdonald, *The Radical Thread*.
[6] SOHCA/019/020/Glasgow, b. 1895.
[7] SOHCA/019/020/Glasgow, b. 1895.
[8] Macdonald, *The Radical Thread*, 135–8.
[9] *Forward*, 18 Jul. 1929.

The complex dialectical relationship between class and gender consciousness and material reality in the context of women's day-to-day lives was an important influence on their political identity and was often manifest in supportive action based on empathy. This took many forms, including a considerable number of solidarity strikes involving women. Experiences were diverse.[10]

Women who worked in textiles were not sheltered from the impact of the adverse economic climate as retail workers were. They endured unemployment, reduced working hours and intensification, as well as the effects of the piece-rate systems designed to speed up work and undercut wages. For women, like the men so affected, work experiences at the point of production were catalysts for political activity, although this could differ by degree. Employers' strategies also varied not only by locality, but also from industry to industry and even from firm to firm. This obviously had an impact on women's work experiences. For example, paternalism was not the favoured managerial strategy of Paisley's Underwood Mill. Mary Neil worked at this mill between 1910 and 1914 until she transferred to munitions work during World War I. Claiming to prefer weaving to munitions work, she returned to this mill after the war, where she worked a twelve-hour day, operating one large loom and sometimes three to four small looms. There was no canteen and the toilet was a board over a pit of running water. Jessie Henderson did not take up employment with this mill until 1937. She too catalogued the poor conditions, particularly the 'wooden board' that substituted for a toilet and the rats which workers had to contend with. Alie Wright worked in the mill, initially as a warehouse girl before moving to the wages department. She recalled that if the weavers had a bad run of cloth their wages were cut, but they could get an advance on the next run. If they had too many bad runs and their work was behind they could get no more advances.[11] Between the wars, rather than investing in new technology, many textile firms used cheaper raw materials accompanied by wage cuts and work intensification to reduce running costs. In the textile sectors working conditions deteriorated along with wage levels. In Smith Brothers of Paisley, to maintain the company's 'competitiveness', wages were reduced and production speeded up.[12] Similarly, in the Ayrshire villages of Stewarton, Darvel and Newmilns workers were put on short time to reduce costs.[13]

Like men's experiences in heavy industries, many female textile workers suffered the effects of over-concentration and the re-emergence of foreign competition. They responded to this in a variety of ways. In the East End of

[10] Arnot, 'Women workers', 260–355.
[11] Old Paisley Society Transcripts, interviews with Mary Neil, born Paisley, Renfrewshire 1898, Alie Wright, born Paisley, Renfrewshire 1919 and Jessie McGregor, born Paisley, Renfrewshire 1926.
[12] *Forward*, 31 Jan. 1920.
[13] *Scotsman*, 13 Apr. and 3 Oct. 1923.

Glasgow, a female worker and trade unionist, who felt the need to remain anonymous, detailed how the introduction of the piece-rate system had been used to reduce wage levels. Initially wages were cut by 10 per cent to speed up work and, when the workers increased productivity to maintain wage levels, their incomes were reduced by a further 15 per cent.[14] The majority of strikes involving women were situated in the textile industries and many of these were a response to the introduction of quasi-scientific management strategies. In Dumfries in 1920, six hundred hosiery workers, mainly women, went on strike for six days to stop the introduction of a piece-rate system that would reduce their wages by 15 per cent. Dundee's jute industry experienced twenty-six strikes during the inter-war years to resist intensification and rationalisation and to ensure better wages and working conditions and in solidarity with other workers who were made redundant.[15]

The introduction of the piece-rate system created considerable animosity between employers and women workers. Ms Anderson defined the system in Templeton's Carpet Factory in Glasgow as 'tearing the life out of yourself'. Mrs Campbell worked in food production, which also experienced these conditions, and felt that 'you'd to knock your pan out to make a pound'. But experiences of the piece-rate system varied. Mrs Nicol, a lacemaker, recalled how she earned more than her father did when she was on piecework.[16] Mrs Patterson recollected the complex situation in the Co-operative shirt factory in Paisley,

> The shirt factory was always coming out on strike. They were striking because the girls at the machine could run the shirts up quicker than the women who did it by hand and they wanted piecework. But for the women sewing on buttons, piecework wasn't any good, because they couldn't sew enough buttons. There weren't a lot of strikes though. I don't know whether it was a company that owned it or not – maybe that had a lot to do with it.[17]

Although experiences varied, many women were well aware that their employers were exploiting them and these employers included those aligned to the labour movement, including the Paisley shirt factory and the Barrhead laundry, both of which exploited cheap female labour, and introduced scientific management and piece-rate systems in the 1930s intended to intensify work and reduce wages. Ms Anderson recalled, 'The rotten bit about it was, if you're on piece you actually work yourself out a job. It doesn't matter where you work if you're on piece-rates you've got to work dash hard.'[18] Rationalisation and routinisation were not employment

[14] *Forward*, 21 Jun 1919.
[15] Arnot, 'Women workers', 252–5, 300.
[16] SOHCA/019/02/Glasgow, b. 1908, SOHCA/019/011/Glasgow, b. 1917 and SOHCA/019/015/Glasgow, b. 1909.
[17] SOHCA/019/025/Paisley, b. 1914.
[18] SOHCA/019/02/Glasgow, b. 1908.

strategies that affected one sex only. Women workers also experienced the same anxieties as men over employers lengthening hours, and bringing in cheaper youth labour and new technology. For example, a machine was introduced into cigarette-making factories between the wars which displaced around 700 female workers.[19]

Men depended on trade unions to act as buffers against their employers but the adverse economic climate weakened the power of unions and therefore many men experienced levels of occupational 'rehabilitation'. The reduction of men's capacity to resist employers was partly linked to men's perceptions of themselves as the family breadwinner, which heightened their sense of responsibility, moderating their potential for militancy, especially when militants were being victimised by employers. Contemporary male workers such as Mr Troy, who was a baker between the wars, recalled what working conditions and employer-employee relations were like. He stated, 'Oh it was pretty bad at that time. It depended on the foreman. Some of them were pretty bad and you just spoke back to them and you got your books right away. It was hard at that time'. Mr Ewart, a docker, described his employers:

> Well the bosses at that time were bosses. They had to make money and they made sure they got it. It came out of your hide! They're like boots. Not all of them, a very faint number were really human. And then of course, you took the gaffer into the pub at night and put up a drink for him. By the time you did that you had very little money left.[20]

Mr Davidson, a foundry worker, maintained, 'You had to be very careful what you said to them. You couldn't give up cheek to your foreman or you'd to get your jacket on. You had to be very careful.' Shipyard workers also experienced a loss of traditional practices and workplace autonomy, reflected in their acceptance of dangerous conditions in the workplace.[21] However, there were also women who had dependants and this mediated their behaviour in work, but the secondary status applied to women's work and the idea that they were temporary workers until marriage contributed to a lesser degree of compliance to employers. Women had few promotional prospects, which might have ensured that they were reluctant to embark on industrial action or workplace militancy that may have jeopardised their advancement in work. Thus, women had a greater opportunity to reject the discourses that identified them as docile and attempted to moderate their awareness of their exploitation.

This permitted working-class women to respond to the challenges of modern capitalism. They were involved in a wide range of disputes and

---

[19] Tuckett, *Scottish Trades Union Congress*, 237–8.
[20] SOHCA/019/09/Glasgow, b. 1900, SOHCA/019/031/Glasgow, b. 1908.
[21] SOHCA/019/030/Glasgow, b. 1900 and McKinlay and Hampton, 'Making ships, making men', 24–5.

these went beyond contesting the effects of industrial over-concentration. Women participated, and some were injured, in the 1919 Forty Hours strike, one of the biggest strikes in Scotland. In the 1920s shop workers from Aberdeen and dairy workers from Edinburgh went on strike, as did catering workers from Glasgow. Like retail, catering was poorly unionised and workers were in close proximity to their employers, but these conditions did not mediate displays of class awareness or militancy. Tailoresses from Motherwell, Coatbridge and Airdrie, French polishers from Glasgow and Scottish female print workers and laundry workers were also on strike in the 1920s.[22] And these women were often extremely militant and aggressive, far from docile and politically apathetic. In 1921 a crowd of about a thousand people demonstrated on the streets to support 400 striking jute workers in Dundee. During the protest women were arrested for forming part of the 'disorderly crowd' and for using 'seditious language'.[23]

Women workers also used subversive forms of resistance. Mrs Galbraith recalled, 'I used to think that I got such an awful lot of work as an office girl. The rain would be pelting down and the secretary would say, "Just go out and get me something for lunch". I used to go up to the toilet and have a good swear and come back out again quite relieved.'[24] Between the wars 'swearing' was considered a gross transgression of the feminine and was hardly the behaviour expected of the 'aristocracy' of female labour, office workers. Strategies varied: there were women who were not averse to sabotage. Mrs Adams, a textile worker, remembered how she used to 'muck up the orders' and 'order things they didn't need and weren't expected to order'. Other women resorted to soldiering, an informal go-slow. 'They would watch him [the foreman] and they all downed tools when he went to the toilet.'[25] There was also worker solidarity and workplace political activism. Ms Anderson risked her employment and diminished the rewards of her own labour trying to safeguard the job of a fellow worker, a Communist Party activist, who spent a great deal of her working day trying to recruit co-employees for the party. Ms Anderson disagreed with her colleague's political views, but she maintained that 'she was so often away from her machine and we were expected to do a certain amount of work. I always knew my rota and stupid enough I'd go and do a lot of work for her.'[26] Margaret Quaile, a Co-operative laundry worker, recalled how women would help each other out when they fell behind with their work to maintain their wages and safeguard their jobs.[27]

Women also contested employers' attempts to subordinate them. Mrs MacIntosh worked as a print feeder in a well-unionised sector of female employment. She challenged her employer when he 'took a notion that

[22] Arnot, 'Women workers', 256–63.
[23] *Scotsman*, 15 Oct. 1921.
[24] SOHCA/019/08/Glasgow, b. 1916.
[25] SOHCA/019/022/Greenock, b. 1916 and SOHCA/019/012/Glasgow, b. 1907.
[26] SOHCA/019/02/Glasgow, b. 1908.
[27] The Barrhead People's Story Group, *It's Funny Whit Ye Remember*, 124.

he wouldn't give me my extra 4/- after serving my time'. Mrs MacIntosh lived in lodgings and feared the consequences of receiving '15/- a week off the Labour Exchange', but she remained defiant. 'On the Friday night before we finished work he said, "I'm sacking you." I said, "I'm taking the sack because I'm never going to break anybody's wages. I'll live on nothing rather than let you get away with it."' She was not dismissed and received her 4/-.[28] The capitulation of her employer and the ability of a young female worker to resist becoming cheap labour would have owed a great deal to the strength of the printing trade union and the possibility of a solidarity strike. However, it might also be suggested that Mrs MacIntosh exaggerated her response to her employer. Such exaggeration in the narratives highlights the 'hidden criticisms that formed part of the zone of struggle between subordinate and dominant groups'. Exaggeration can be construed as what the woman would have liked to have said had she been in a more powerful position to do so.[29] Defiance was used by women albeit often covertly. Mrs Harrison was a machinist and recalled being at the forefront of quasi-scientific management:

> He was a bugger to put it simple for output. Well I was singing from morning till night. Now by this time the firm was increasing, so they were opening a small factory. Mr Hamilton was a great one for getting slogans and putting them on the wall to help output. So this day him and I passed one another and as usual he says, 'You'll have to stop your singing.' Under my breath I'm saying to him, 'I'm bloody sure I don't.'[30]

Conflict against the introduction of quasi-Taylorist management and intensification was not always indirect. Mrs Jones remembered, 'The men's toilet was next door to the women's, so they put one of the men in charge. If we went to the toilet he took the time we went to the toilet.' The time that the women spent in the toilet was to be recorded by the male employee, and Mrs Jones took objection to this. After an argument with the man who was responsible for timing the women, she approached her employer. 'I said I wasn't letting him take the time I went to the toilet. I said, I'm not having that, so it was passed over.'[31] Margaret Quaile recalled how she was always getting into trouble for talking. She also remembered how the manager, Mr Brotherstone, desisted from chatting and

> brought in a rule that every set of machines had to press five dozen shirts an hour. So you couldn't blether and do five dozen shirts an hour, so we just done our bit. We got production Cards and after the first week, we were all called up to the office and Mr Brotherstone says, 'Congratulations, girls! We're all chuffed. But if I had got all the

[28] SOHCA/019/014/Glasgow, b. 1911.
[29] See Scott, *Domination and the Arts of Resistance*, 1–18.
[30] SOHCA/019/09/Glasgow, b. 1900.
[31] SOHCA/019/011/Glasgow, b. 1917.

shirts into the laundry that you have got down on your sheet, I'd need to open another laundry.' Because we just marked down five dozen whether we done five dozen or not.[32]

Women's responses to their working environment varied immensely but they do challenge the discourses that identified women with passivity and political apathy. Indeed, women's narratives are the antithesis of the fatalism reflected in those of male respondents. Male attitudes tended to mirror the dominant discourses of the inter-war years expressed by trade unions and Scottish Labour MPs on working conditions. Women's stories rejected this worldview from which they were largely excluded. They also provide evidence of a range of practices employed at the point of production, from criticism and defiance through to direct action and political activism that women participated in. Although strikes involving women abounded, women's resorting to informal strategies suggests that a considerable number were impeded from taking part in formal political struggle in the workplace because of the trade union neglect detailed in Chapter one.

Although working women were divided by age, marital status, ethnicity and religion and this could cause tensions between them in the workplace, women also developed gender-specific personal relationships and work cultures that formed part of a process by which they became politicised.[33] A major feature of women's work cultures was the development of self-definition, manifest in the ways in which women rejected male definitions of skill and created their own. Mrs Johnston practised this form of self-legitimisation. She was an office worker and while she may have been ranked at the lower end of this occupation by male standards, women so employed were regarded amongst their own sex, and regarded themselves, as the aristocracy of female labour. She stated, 'when I went to the office, oh I thought it was wonderful because you were mixing with a different class of people. People that worked in offices in my day were kind of better educated. Maybe that was snobbish, but I don't mean it snobbishly.' Women constructed 'skill', challenging the physiological aspects of their subordination, albeit unlike men, these strategies did not place them in a position to use exclusionary policies so that the construction of skill was reflected in status and pay. Nevertheless women displayed a pride in their work associated with skilled workers and at the same time legitimised their right to work, to status and to self-esteem. Mrs Galbraith recalled, 'I did treasury work, cash, I did invoicing, I did bookkeeping. I really did. I had a full round of office work I could do. It sounds awful smug saying I could do anything in an office, but I really did. I loved my job.'[34]

---

[32] The Barrhead People's Story Group, *It's Funny Whit Ye Remember*, 124.

[33] See C. Brown and J. Stephenson, 'The view from the workplace: Stirling women and work 1890–1950', in Breitenbach and Gordon, *Out of Bounds*, 7–27. This is not to suggest that there were not divisions among women. See Todd, *Young Women*.

[34] SOHCA/019/025/Paisley, b. 1914 and SOHCA/019/08/Glasgow, b. 1916.

This was not confined to office work. Rebecca Govan worked for a tailoring firm. She remembered being promoted to the cutting room and, 'I thought I was the cat's whiskers because the cutting room was a wee bit above the factory girls'.[35] Margaret Quaile, who worked in the Co-operative Laundry, maintained, 'You were one of the elite if you worked for the Co-operative whether it was a laundry or whatever.'[36] Mrs Reid, a hosiery worker, remembered, 'I started as a wee message girl but, with the meal over I would ask the girls could I get a shot at the machine. So I learned that and I went to the boss and said, "I would like to try a machine." He said, "Fair enough." I used to do that and I loved it!' In contrast, Nancy McLaughlin hated her first job in a shirt factory. She suggested that such jobs were 'the very bottom of the league' and that 'there was no furtherance for you'.[37] Thus, it is clear that women were interested in their jobs and that they created the same kind of occupational hierarchies, as men did, albeit less formally, and like men they used the construction of 'skill' to differentiate themselves from other workers. Although this was a form of empowerment, it did not provide grounds for coalition as it did for male skilled workers.

Women also relished the companionship of their colleagues and this moderated their sense of oppression. Margaret Quaile related how she worked in temperatures of up to 100°F and how workers 'were always getting burnt', but she also stated that 'it was hard, warm work, but the fun was good'.[38] Ms Anderson concurred that 'companionship' was the best aspect of her employment.[39] Female bonding has been seen as a form of feminine assertiveness and a political tactic. Like male bonding that was used in work to shore up masculinity and masculine privilege, female bonding was used to subvert attempts to ensure that women would identify with subservience. Women's work cultures involved games, rituals and traditions, 'feminine' behaviour that was identified as irrational and frowned upon by trade unionists, particularly when employed by women during strikes.[40] These forms of play drew men in and allowed women to display forms of assertiveness, enjoy relief from monotonous employment and feminise the public space of work that was deemed masculine.[41] Mrs Bruce recalled with much amusement how female workers passed the time in the confectionery factory where she was employed: 'what we did and it's laughable, some of us used to take in a skipping rope and we had the men jumping in and out of the ropes'.[42] Ms Anderson remembered how workers behaved when one of

---

[35] WEA, interview with Rebecca Govan, born Shettleston, Glasgow, 1909.
[36] The Barrhead People's Story Group, *It's Funny Whit Ye Remember*, 124.
[37] SOHCA/019/019/Glasgow, b. 1907 and The Barrhead People's Story Group, *It's Funny Whit Ye Remember*, 111.
[38] The Barrhead People's Story Group, *It's Funny Whit Ye Remember*, 124.
[39] SOHCA/019/02/Glasgow, b. 1908.
[40] See Gordon, *Women and the Labour Movement*.
[41] See Bruley, 'Women', 239.
[42] SOHCA/019/03/Glasgow, b. 1907.

the women was getting married. In Templeton's Carpet Factory 'they decorated the bride's loom and they went to awful lengths'.[43] These practices
were transplanted into the growing sectors of female employment between
the wars. Mrs Galbraith, an office-worker, stated

> I always remember the treasurer, he was getting married and it shows
> you the mentality we had. At that time it was bowler hats they wore. I
> remember getting the glue and putting it round his hat, then putting
> confetti all round. It was a great carry-on dressing him up. Some of
> them lost their temper with the banter and I don't blame them, but
> that was the sort of stupid carry-on that we had.[44]

Such behaviour allowed women to display forms of assertiveness over
men, even if only temporarily, and was conducted during working hours,
transferring free time from employers to workers. Popular culture was
used as a form of resistance to the effects of modern capitalism and men's
domination of workplaces.

Women continued to privilege informal organisation, rituals and games
because they were often marginalised or denied contact with the formal
structures of trade unionism. Yet women constantly challenged the effects
of capitalism and gender discrimination, overtly and covertly. They did not
see themselves as victims, but as agents in workplace struggles. Ultimately,
this provided a sense of class-gender awareness that could facilitate rough
forms of feminist behaviour. This was evident in the operation of women's
gender-specific popular culture in the workplace, which sustained self-
legitimisation and allowed women to contest the discursive constructions
of employers, working men and their organisations. These work cultures
allowed women to develop pride in their work, collectivity and camarade-
rie, and thereby the ability to reject the discourses designed to ensure their
exclusion from work or manageability in the workplace. Women's rejection
of their employers' discourse and the attitudes of trade unions towards
working women are evident in the conduct and experiences of women
during the 1926 General Strike. The dispute demonstrates that women
were neglected as a political constituency by the labour movement, but also
that they were more than capable of expressing a gendered class awareness
using the range of strategies that they employed in the workplace, as this
chapter and Chapter eight will highlight.

There is an extensive historiography on the General Strike in Britain
although little has been written about women's participation.[45] Recent
research has begun to highlight that in mining communities across
Britain women were actively involved in the General Strike and the subse-

---

[43] SOHCA/019/02/Glasgow, b. 1908.
[44] SOHCA/019/008/Glasgow, b. 1916.
[45] See K. Laybourn, *The General Strike: Day by Day* (Sutton, 1999). For Scotland see Campbell,
The Scottish Miners, Vol. Two, 232–42.

quent miners' lockout and that this influenced their political identities.[46] Nevertheless there remains a fundamental absence in the historiography regarding the involvement of working women who participated directly in the industrial action and the potential of contributing to the conflict to effect their class awareness. In spite of such omissions, women made a vital contribution to the General Strike and the miners' lock-out as industrial workers and also in the form of broader female intervention and agency during the disputes. In doing so, they linked the bureaucratic world of 'organised' trade unionism to the more traditional spontaneous and informal protests that marked women's work cultures and their industrial militancy.[47]

The General Strike was largely in support of the miners' strike to resist the imposition of lower wages and longer hours. However, it was also recognised that if the miners were forced to capitulate this might adversely affect the wages and working conditions of all workers. Thus, the General Strike involved an extraordinary number of workers from a range of industries including printing, transport, docks and metalworks. Indeed, the solidarity shown by 'male workers' and their 'brotherhood' was considered unprecedented. By contrast depictions of women's roles during periods of industrial action, as is the case of Scottish women's participation during the General Strike, stresses their 'steadfast loyalty' rather than their 'industrial militancy', and thereby denies women representation.[48] Indeed, Scottish women's contribution to the disputes of 1926 has been discursively written out of the labour movement's records in this way. Instead of accepting that women were militant in the sense that they were aggressive and vigorous in their support of the strike, women's role was documented as the 'unfailing' provision of encouragement that gave 'heart to the men'.[49] Scottish women were thanked by the labour movement for their 'sympathetic action' and for 'facing privation and hunger with a smile on their face', and in this way they provided 'encouragement to men during the strike'.[50] However, a reconsideration of the General Strike not only highlights the considerable participation of working women in the dispute but also demonstrates that working-class solidarity during the conflict was broader than has previously been detailed. It also shows how the male-dominated labour movement

---

[46] See Bruley, 'Women', 243; H. Barron, 'Women of the Durham coalfields and their reaction to the 1926 miners' lockout', *Historical Studies in Industrial Relations*, 22: 53–84 (2006); J. Gier-Viskovatoff and A. Porter, 'Women of the British coalfields on strike in 1926 and 1984: documenting lives using oral history and photography', *Frontiers: A Journal of Women's Studies*, 19: 190–230 (1998); Hall, 'Contrasting female identities', 107–33.

[47] See Gordon, *Women and the Labour Movement*, and N. Kirk, *Custom and Conflict in the 'Land of the Gael': Ballachulish, 1900–1910* (London, 2007).

[48] Nolan, 'The women were bloody marvellous', 127.

[49] GRA, Glasgow Trades and Labour Council, Miscellaneous Files and Papers [hereafter GTLC Files], Strike, 1926, *Scottish Worker*, 10 May 1926.

[50] GTLC Files, Strike, 1926, *Scottish Worker*, 10 May 1926.

undermined the potential of greater pan-class militancy by continuing to disregard women as a political constituency.[51]

The conduct of the trade union movement during the General Strike reflects the gendered languages of class to which it subscribed and which was signified through the male breadwinner and family wage ideals, both of which depended on women's exclusion from work and a commitment to traditional gender roles. Thus, women were expected to provide support for men during the strike and attempts were made by the trade union movement to deny women responsibility outside that regarded as 'women's work', fundraising and relief. The trade union movement in Scotland asked working-class women and 'socialist' women's organisations to provide recreational amenities for strikers and encouraged them to watch local food prices to subvert the possibility of retailers profiteering from the strike.[52] They also sidelined prominent women of the labour movement from the Strike Committees that organised the dispute locally.

In Scotland the Trades and Labour Councils, which had male and female representatives, were responsible for establishing strike committees to coordinate the strike. Yet women played no formal role on the Glasgow Strike Committee; all twenty-three officials were men.[53] This was contentious because there were many notable and able women on the executive of the Glasgow Trades Council who worked alongside Peter Kerrigan, the coordinator of the Glasgow Strike Committee. In 1926, the executive of the Glasgow Trades Council consisted of six men and six women.[54] The women on the executive comprised Miss Black, Miss Pettigrew, Mrs Alcook, Mrs Auld, Mrs Laird and Mrs Ross. These women, and in particular Mrs Laird, Mrs Auld and Miss Pettigrew, were pioneers of, and active in, the ILP. They were trade union activists and had worked on a number of Trade Council committees investigating a wide gamut of issues from unemployment to housing. In 1909, Miss Pettigrew became the first female member of the Trades Council. She was an active ILP platform speaker and 'became known throughout Scotland as part of a band of pioneers'. She maintained her commitment to Labour politics after her marriage, standing for, and winning, the seat of Springburn, Glasgow, after the death of the sitting candidate, her husband, George Hardie. Mrs Auld was President of the Glasgow Labour Advisory Council and went on to become Vice-President of the Scottish Council of the Labour Party.[55] Mrs Laird was an active member of the Glasgow Trades Council, President of the Glasgow Women's

[51] For the attitudes of the Scottish labour movement towards women in the nineteenth century see Gordon, *Women and the Labour Movement*.

[52] GTLC Files, Report of the Meeting called by the Trades Council, 5 May 1926, GRA, SCWG Central Council Minutes 1925–30, 5 May 1926; *Scotsman*, 3 May and 14 Jun. 1926, and Tuckett, *Scottish Trades Union Congress*, 212.

[53] GTLC, Executive Minutes 1925–7, 3 May 1926.

[54] GTLC, Executive Minutes 1925–7, 4, 11, 16 and 19 Feb. 1926.

[55] *Forward*, 8 Oct. 1921, Knox, *Scottish Labour Leaders*, 51, 136–7.

Housing Association and a member of the Glasgow Women's Labour League [WLL].[56] The WLL had strong links with the Federation of Women Workers and other trade unions. In 1915 the Glasgow WLL had 'played a prominent role in getting the shirtmakers and the women netmakers to join the Federation of Women Workers' and had 'nursed the Glasgow branch of the Domestic Workers Union into vigorous and healthy organisation'. Thus, inexperience can be ruled out as a factor in the exclusion of these women. Although women were excluded from formal participation on the strike committee they had no hesitation in sending deputations to the strike committees to represent the interests of women as wives and as workers.[57]

Moreover, the involvement in the strike by working women was significant irrespective of the labour movement's discourse which implied otherwise. Sources detailing women's activity during the strike may be profoundly limited, in part due to the gendered languages of class which sidelined women's involvement outside of 'support' for men, but trade union membership, census material, press reports and oral histories shed light on the potential number of women who worked in the industries involved in the strike and of women's conduct during the dispute. Workers from the printing industry were among the vanguard of workers called to strike in 1926 but by and large the historiography presents the print workers engaged in the strike as men, even though in some print-related jobs female employees outnumbered men by three to one.[58] In 1931, there were 9,163 women occupied in paper, printing, and publishing in Strathclyde.[59] Lanarkshire had 1,073 women registered in 1931 as working in either printing or a kindred trade and Glasgow had 7,647.[60] The Glasgow branch of the National Union of Print, Bookbinding and Paper Workers had 605 female members and 193 male members by the 1930s.[61] Indeed, the print trade was one of the three main occupations employing women in Edinburgh and an indication of the strength in numbers of female workers in this trade, and of women's trade union membership, was the appointment of women as delegates to the STUC. In 1925, at a special meeting called by the Scottish Printing and Kindred Trades Federation, four women were appointed as delegates to represent the interests of female paper workers and bookbinders.[62] It was also estimated by the

[56] *Forward*, 9 and 16 Jan. 1915.

[57] *Forward*, 31 Jan. 1915, Sinclair, '"Silenced, suppressed and passive"', 175–6.

[58] GRA, National Union of Paper, Bookbinding and Print Workers, Scottish District Council Minutes, 19 Mar. 1936.

[59] C. Lee, *British Regional Employment Statistics* (Cambridge, 1979).

[60] *Census*, 1931.

[61] GLA, Printing and Kindred Trades Federation, Glasgow Branch Manuscript Minutes Book, 1915–43, October 1931.

[62] GRA, Printing and Kindred Trades Federation, Scottish District Council Minutes, 17 Dec. 1925.

STUC that the number of men and women working in the print industry was equal, but that the number of women workers was increasing because of new technology.[63] Many of these women were involved in the strike: in Greenock all the 'men and women in printing and its kindred trades came out on strike'.[64] Mrs Ferguson was a bookbinder in the Mitchell Library in Glasgow and remembered being called to strike in 1926.[65] Other kindred trades were also on strike: the Glasgow Strike Committee refused J. Laird and Sons permission to continue printing paper bags. Caldwell's Paper Mill was also called out.[66] Of Glasgow's 4,543 paper and cardboard workers and bookbinders in 1921, 1,120 were men and 3,423 women.[67] The chairman of Inveresk Paper Mill reported that the company mills and all its associated mills except one 'were immediately closed down, without due notice owing to the withdrawal of their employees'.[68] Moreover, because of the inclusion of kindred trades, more women than men were likely to have been on strike in particular areas of Scotland.

Transport industries were also at the forefront of the strike and in 1931 there were 760 women employed in the railway industry in Glasgow, mainly in clerical positions. By this time the National Union of Railwaymen [NUR] enlisted women as members, while the Railway Clerks Association [RCA] – the strongest clerical union in Britain – was an all-grades union that accepted female members on equal terms with male members.[69] The Glasgow Southern Branch of the RCA also included at least two women amongst its collectors and auditors between 1921 and 1936, and women from this branch were being appointed as trade union delegates to the STUC. When women infiltrated the hierarchy of their unions this denoted that there was a significant number of female members; as did the Glasgow branch's report of a 'mass meeting' of women clerks, and in the unions' acceptance in 1925 of a proposal to set up a separate branch for its female members if the other Glasgow branches followed suit.[70] Scotland had 10,000 railway clerical and supervisory workers in 1921 and many of these workers were women: of these only 300 men and women blacklegged the strike. Moreover, correspondence between the RCA and the TUC shows that it was inspectors, generally men, rather than clerical and wages staff, who were often women, who blacklegged: 2,749 of the 2,917 Scottish wages staff were on strike compared to only 47 of the 121 inspectors. Scottish rail

---

[63] Tuckett, *Scottish Trades Union Congress*, 237, 269.
[64] GTLC Files, Strike, 1926, *Scottish Worker*, 10 May 1926.
[65] SOHCA/019/07/Glasgow, b. 1911.
[66] GTLC Files, Strike, 1926, Report of the Meeting called by the Trades Council, 5 May 1926.
[67] GTLC Files, 1926, Minutes of the Meeting of Building Groups, 7 May 1926, *Census*, 1921.
[68] *Scotsman*, 26 May 1926.
[69] Hamilton, *Trade Unionism*, 142–3.
[70] Hamilton, *Trade Unionism*, 142–3 and GRA, Railway Clerks Association, Glasgow Southern Branch Manuscript Minute Books, 1920–65, Book 1, 2 Feb. and 9 Mar. 1921 and Book 4, 4 May 1926; STUC, 33rd A/R, 1930, 77–8.

workers also experienced difficulties in obtaining their wages because the clerks were on strike.[71]

Other transport workers were also involved: in 1931 there were 1,301 women recorded as working in the transport industries in Lanarkshire, 464 in Dunbartonshire, 770 in Renfrewshire and 2,880 in Glasgow and most were conductresses. Apparently, had it not been for the participation of students and members of the government's Organisation for the Maintenance of Supplies, the trams in Glasgow and many other cities and towns across Scotland might have come to a standstill. As it was, it was reported that a service of only 200 out of over a thousand trams usually running were maintained in Glasgow.[72] In Greenock only 'three out of 100 tram drivers and conductresses blacklegged the strike'.[73] In Edinburgh it was reported that 'only 50 to 60 tramway cars were in operation' and all 'were manned by Corporation workers' but that a 'number of auxiliary workers' had to give 'assistance in collecting fares'. Men were drivers, and therefore those identified as blacklegs, women were conductresses, the employees who had to be replaced by 'auxiliary workers'.[74] Hence although not all of the 5,421 female transport workers in the Strathclyde area were involved in the strike, a significant number were, and many more were involved elsewhere in Scotland. Men including Mr Armstrong, a tram driver who was out on strike in 1926, and Mr Coyle from Greenock, who was a student strikebreaker, also indicated that a considerable number of women were involved in strike activity.[75]

The impact of the strike on transport services also affected production and resulted in workers being laid off during the strike, including Lerwick's fisher girls 'when work had to be abandoned due to the withdrawal of dock labour at Aberdeen Harbour'. This also affected workers in food production. Mrs Campbell was sixteen years old in 1926 and worked for the Camp Coffee work in Bridgeton, Glasgow; she remembered the strike 'as if it was today'. She stated, 'we had to go on strike because there were no workers to do the machines'.[76] Although Mrs Campbell's recollection suggests that women were compelled to strike and thus played a subsidiary role, the fact that she 'remembers' the strike as if it was 'today' intimates that it had an influence on her political identity, no doubt enhanced because she came from a family who supported trade unionism and the ILP.

Other working women supported the strike financially, including members of the National Union of Boot and Shoe Operatives and the

---

[71] GTLC Files, 1926, Official Bulletin of the Partick Area Strike, 11 May 1926. TUC History Online, Railway Clerks Association Statistics, 10 May 1926, http://www.unionhistory.info (accessed 6 Aug. 2008).

[72] Census 1931 and GTLC Files, 1926, *Scottish Worker*, 10 May 1926.

[73] *Scottish Worker*, 10 May 1926 and see also McLean, 'The 1926 strike in Lanarkshire', 10.

[74] *Scotsman*, 5 May 1926.

[75] Census 1931, SOHCA/019/027/Glasgow, b. 1905; SOHCA/019/046/Greenock, b. 1906.

[76] SOHCA/019/04/Bridgeton/Glasgow, b. 1910.

National Federation of Insurance Workers.[77] The Glasgow Branch of the Union of Post Office Workers, which had significant numbers of female employees, voted to assist strikers financially and threatened to come out in support of strikers.[78] In 1929 a Royal Committee Enquiry highlighted how women in the Post Office Service were becoming 'numerically predominant'.[79] There were 1,241 female Post Office workers in Glasgow registered in the 1931 census, many of whom, like the women in other industries, were made more aware of their class membership because of the strike. Some, like Miss House, the delegate of the Post Office Workers Union to the STUC, would become more actively political in trade union circles. She was a founding member of the STUC Organisation of Women's Committee in the wake of the strike, which suggested that the strike did influence the political identities of women.[80]

The TUC made 'quite inadequate plans' for the strike even though they had been cautioned to do so from within their own ranks.[81] This created confusion over which workers were to be called out on strike; many textile workers were called out although they should not have been.[82] In the wake of the strike the Bradford Dyers' Association Limited sued the Amalgamated Society of Dyers, Bleachers, Finishers and Kindred Trades, the National Union of Textile Workers and the General and Municipal Workers Union for breach of their 1914 contract in which the employers' association had agreed there would be no lockouts on condition that the unions would not call a strike without prior warning as they had done in the General Strike. In Scotland the trade unions affiliated to the STUC Organisation of Women Committee in 1929 represented 49,412 women. Of these 23,831 women were employed in textiles.[83] Many of them were involved in the strike, including textile workers from Partick in Glasgow. Employees of an Ayrshire textile factory were also locked out of their work-place.[84] Women workers from the tobacco trade were also involved in the strike: members of both the National Cigar and Tobacco Workers Union and the Tobacco Workers Union were called to strike – and significant numbers of women worked in this trade.[85]

Press reports also indicate the involvement of women workers on the

---

[77] TUC History Online, National Union of Boot and Shoe Operatives, letter, n.d., http://www.unionhistory.info (accessed 6 Aug. 2008) and National Federation of Insurance Workers, letter, n.d., http://www.unionhistory.info (accessed 6 Aug. 2008).

[78] GTLC Files, 1926, Official Strike Bulletin of the Partick Area Strike, 11 May 1926.

[79] *Scotsman*, 14 Dec. 1929.

[80] *Census*, 1931; *Glasgow Herald*, 8 Sep. 1926.

[81] E. Bevin, quoted in Tuckett, *Scottish Carter*, 173.

[82] K. Laybourn, *Britain on the Breadline: A Social and Political History of Britain Between the Wars* (London, 1990), 118.

[83] STUC, 32nd A/R, 1929, 70.

[84] GTLC Files, 1926, Official Strike Bulletin of the Partick Area Strike, 11 May 1926 and Arnot, 'Women workers', 276–7.

[85] TUC History Online, Tobacco Workers Union, letter, 19 May 1926 http://www.union

picket lines. In Falkirk three strikers from the transport industry were injured in what the *Scotsman* labelled a 'van driver's mistake'. A 'large number of the company's car and bus drivers and conductresses had arrived to collect arrears in wages due to them'. While waiting some of the strikers danced in the middle of the road and the van driver thought they were trying to impede his progress and drove into the crowd seriously injuring two men and a woman.[86] Clearly women transport workers were involved not only in the strike but, given the driver's reaction, also in picketing. Govan women wearing 'red rosettes', a symbol of left-wing support, also took to the streets and were 'standing at the stopping places on the car routes endeavouring to persuade members of the public not to use the cars'.[87] Dundee women were also involved in the strike; among these women was Jessie Latto, a spinner, who received a £3 fine when she was found guilty of intimidating the driver of a motor lorry by throwing a missile at him.[88]

However, although significant numbers of women were involved in the strike and in picketing, the strike did not endear women workers to the trade union movement'.[89] This may have been due to the women's conduct during periods of industrial unrest. The gendered nature of class formation meant that Scottish women were largely excluded from institutional protest and they therefore continued to engage in more informal, spontaneous and robust forms of industrial militancy. In this sense they acted as a linch-pin between two distinct forms of political protest, class-based industrial militancy and traditional radical protests that were 'exemplars' of women's potential in the 'elaboration of a class based ideology', but which also facili-tated the 'usurpation of gender norms'.[90] However, women's conduct was vilified as irrational by the labour movement because it was often aggressive. According to the *Scotsman*, 'A remarkable feature of the cases arising out of the strike disturbances heard at Glasgow Sheriff Court' was the significant involvement of women who were subsequently arrested, fined and impris-oned. These women included the twenty-six women who were prosecuted for attacking a blackleg bus driver in Govan and the women arrested in Glasgow for assaulting blackleg transport workers by throwing bags of flour in their faces. They also attacked police officers when they tried to inter-vene on behalf of the strikebreakers.[91] Such conduct diverged from the TUC's strike policies. The TUC reacted with anxiety over clashes between the protestors and authority because of the government's propaganda that

history.info (accessed 6 Aug. 2008) and National Cigar and Tobacco Union, letter, 6 May 1926 http://www.unionhistory.info (accessed 6 Aug. 2008).

[86] *Scotsman*, 8 May 1926.

[87] GTLC Files, 1926, *Emergency Press Special Edition*, 12 May 1926.

[88] Arnot, 'Women workers', 277 and *Scotsman*, 8 Jun. 1926.

[89] Arnot, 'Women workers', 276.

[90] C. M. M. Macdonald, 'Weak roots and branches: class, gender and the geography of indus-trial protest', *Scottish Labour History*, 33: 6–30 (1998).

[91] *Scotsman*, 12 May 1926.

the strike was political rather than industrial action. This was forcefully refuted by the TUC and to avert conflict or the potential that the strike might become political the TUC enlisted unions which they believed would be less militant and would follow orders. Indeed, for the RCA this strike was a 'baptism' – the first real call to cease work.[92] The TUC also insisted that 'conduct was to be exemplary'; pickets were to avoid 'obstruction' and to 'act in a constitutional manner'.[93]

Women clearly subverted these demands, the gendered language of class and trade union attempts to gender the General Strike. They entered the 'public' and 'masculine' arena of industrial militancy and acted in 'unwomanly' ways, engaging in violence and aggression associated not with the feminine but the masculine. Women also undermined the characterisation disseminated by employers and the trade union movement that they were politically apathetic. They joined the strike, participated in strike processions, attended strike meetings and picketed, but the ways in which they did this threatened the authority of the TUC. Indeed, this can be read as an open gesture of defiance and contempt, and a reassertion of women's dignity which held the capacity to provide them with 'personal release, satisfaction, pride and elation' and thereby mediated the 'frustration and the humiliation of reining in their agency'.[94] Thus, women were unlikely to have endeared themselves to the labour movement and so it was the supportive role of women that was historically recorded. Nevertheless, women expressed solidarity with the aims of the strike and actively supported it, and this heightened some women's political awareness. The rapidity of the formation of Women's Trade Union Guilds in the aftermath of the strike and the first Trade Union Women's Conference held in September 1926 highlights an increased awareness within the trade union movement of women's capabilities. It also points to a greater gendered awareness amongst the women themselves.[95]

Despite the marginalisation of women by the trade union movement, women's participation in the strike was important and it was hardly surprising that in the aftermath of the strike men and women were similarly affected. Relief that the strike was over was common, as was disillusionment with the leadership of the TUC for calling off the strike. Women workers who had been involved in the strike maintained, 'you got nowhere by striking' and 'we got nothing out of it'.[96] Discontentment with the leadership of the trade union movement was aggravated by the fact that the TUC failed to secure any assurances that those who participated in the strike would not be victimised. Employers were thereby in a position to punish workers

[92] TUC History Online, Railway Clerks Association Statistics, 10 May 1926, http://www. unionhistory.info (accessed 6 Aug. 2008).

[93] *Scotsman*, 6 May 1926.

[94] Scott, *Domination and the Arts of Resistance*, 208.

[95] *Scotsman*, 8 Sep. 1926, Tuckett, *Scottish Trades Union Congress*, 229.

[96] SOHCA/019/07/Glasgow, b. 1911, SOHCA/019/04/Glasgow, b. 1910.

for their involvement in the dispute and many did so. The victimisation endured by male workers who were involved in the General Strike and the miners' lockout is a common theme in the historiography, but what is less well documented is that women were also victimised as workers. Thus, the disgust and disillusionment that workers directed at the leadership of the industrial wing of the labour movement was not gender-specific.

Even before the strike commenced Edinburgh Corporation posted notices warning workers that 'in the event of any employees ceasing work without giving requisite notice, they will be considered as having resigned from their employment'.[97] The situation was similar in Glasgow and many Corporation transport workers lost their jobs, while others were demoted or denied promotion ensuring the infliction of lifetime victimisation.[98] The ILP Councillor, Patrick Dollan, was suspended from Glasgow City Council for protesting against a motion to have municipal workers sacked for their part in the strike.[99] Many female transport workers were only re-employed after accepting a pay cut of a ha'penny per hour.[100] Railway clerks in Edinburgh were also victimised: at a meeting, attended by thousands of male and female employees from two Edinburgh branches of the Railway Clerks Association, it was discussed that seventy-four of their members had yet to be reinstated while extra work was being imposed on those who had been allowed to return to work. The Glasgow branch of the RCA voted to remain on strike until all workers were allowed to return to work uncondi-tionally. Workers were also humiliated by employers as well as victimised.[101] This resulted in 'smouldering discontent' amongst the rank and file of the RCA. It was reported at the RCA conference in 1927 that men and women had been subjected to 'dismissal, short time work, humiliation and degrada-tion' for 'daring to strike' and that 'Scottish Companies were amongst the worst culprits'.[102]

Victimisation was not restricted to transport employees. One hundred female and twenty-eight male bookbinders in Edinburgh found themselves locked out of their firm after the strike. There were also dismissals at Singers in Clydebank, where significant numbers of women worked.[103] The General Strike had multiple effects on women, who played an important role in the disputes as pickets, protesters and fundraisers, and as striking workers. Many were victimised for their participation. Women also provided emotional and financial support for striking workers as Chapter eight will also show. Ultimately this had an effect on significant numbers of women's political identities. Some women became more actively involved in trade

[97] *Scotsman*, 4 May 1926.
[98] McLean, 'The 1926 strike in Lanarkshire', 13.
[99] GRA, Glasgow City Council Minutes, 26 Jul. 1926.
[100] Arnot, 'Women workers', 277.
[101] *Scotsman*, 14 May 1926.
[102] *Scotsman*, 24 May 1927.
[103] Arnot, 'Women workers', 277.

unionism, establishing the STUC Organisation of Women Committee. Others, such as the ILP MP for Lanarkshire, Jennie Lee, would go on to enter the world of politics.

Nor did the 'failure' of the General Strike 'rehabilitate' women workers by inhibiting them from becoming involved in further disputes between the wars. In Rutherglen, 800 women from Richmond Laundry came out on strike in 1935 demanding trade union recognition, two weeks' holiday with pay and a general increase in wages. As with the women involved in the General Strike they used a range of strategies including aggressive picketing and protesting, attacking blacklegs and holding demonstrations throughout the neighbourhood to garner support for their cause. Their efforts were rewarded and they gained recognition for their union, the National Union of Distributive and Allied Trades, and wage negotiations were opened between workers and employees. However, the cost of this for some of the women involved was high; four women workers, all from the same family, were prosecuted and two were convicted for their participation in the protests. Women were also involved in a variety of the principal disputes catalogued by the Ministry of Labour in the 1930s. In 1931 female textile workers from Paisley and Alexandria were among 1,800 workers participating in strike action. The same year Glasgow lace workers were among 2,200 workers on strike from this industry in Scotland.[104] Women responded in a variety of ways to modern capitalism and were far from acquiescent. As with men, women were frequently politicised at the point of production and responded to this with direct and indirect action.

Women responded to their oppression suggesting that men and the leadership of the industrial wing of the labour movement contributed to the subordination of females in paid work. Conflict involving women did not evaporate in the inter-war years. Women were not 'rehabilitated' by gender and class oppression. Rather, the form of working-class women's militancy was inhibited. Much of it remained within a traditional framework of informal action, which had been, and continued to be, a response to attempts by men, trade unions and employers to undervalue women in the world of work. To resist class and gender exploitation, women used this strategy in community and political protests throughout the period. Many feminists and women's representatives did little to address the situation, suggesting that they too perceived women's work in the formal economy to be largely temporary. Certainly many working-class women did. Thus, it was to the political arena that women of the labour movement and feminists looked to in order to address the demands of a constituency who would principally be defined, and define themselves, as wives and mothers, or 'the wives and mothers of tomorrow' and it is to this we now turn.

---

[104] HMSO, *Ministry of Labour Gazette*, 37, 12 (Dec. 1929); 38, 2 (Feb. 1930) and especially 39, 5 (May 1931) and 39,7 (Jul. 1932). See also *Forward*, 2 May 1931 and 27 Jun. 1931 and Sinclair, "'Silenced, suppressed and passive'", 142.

CHAPTER FIVE

Socialist Women, Feminists and Feminism

Many contemporary socialist men were antagonistic towards the first-wave feminist movement in Britain, believing that the women's movement 'deflected the minds of the people from socialist propaganda and socialist activities'.[1] Opinions such as these have led a number of labour and feminist historians to identify the British labour movement as male-dominated and hostile to feminism and the feminism movement.[2] Indeed, it seems that working men and men of the labour movement were so suspicious of the largely middle-class feminist movement and separate sex organisations which they regarded as undemocratic that they advocated a policy whereby socialist women were expected to avoid contact with such organisations to the detriment of feminism and potential coalitions.[3] However, feminism was not the preserve of middle-class women and formal feminist groups. There was a significant number of feminists within the labour movement in Scotland and among working-class women more generally. Although class issues may have remained more important than gender concerns within the labour movement, there were a variety of perspectives on feminism which allowed women to promote gender questions too. Furthermore, while feminists had to compete with anti-feminist ideas, most female activists within the labour movement were feminist in some form or another.[4] Attitudes towards feminism varied across the labour movement, within particular parties, at branch level and between individuals.[5] However, while the anti-feminism of the labour movement and the backlash against feminism were impediments that socialist women had to endure, in Scotland socialist-feminists were able to forge relationships with activists from the women's movement and with non-feminist women within and outside the labour movement. Some labour men were also sympathetic to feminist issues. Where they were not, many socialist-feminists adopted a range of strategies to forward their feminist aims and these included subversion and defiance of the male-dominated party line.

The fight for votes for women had acted as a framework for alliances between feminist women of different classes and political loyalties, but

---

[1] See J. Clayton, *The Rise and Decline of Socialism in Great Britain 1884–1926* (London, 1926), 154–8.
[2] See Hannam, 'Women and politics', 238.
[3] Pugh, *Women and the Women's Movement*, 134.
[4] Hannam, 'Women and politics', 237.
[5] See Law, *Suffrage and Power* and Holton, *Feminism and Democracy.*

the attainment of the franchise resulted in divisions amongst feminists. Feminists were unsure about the best way to employ women's votes and about the direction in which the movement itself should proceed.[6] They were also divided because some middle-class feminists assumed that all women were equal in their oppression without considering class and the everyday realities of working-class women's lives.[7] However, obstacles to unity were not merely based on class. Even feminist women of the labour movement were not united in their feminism, nor in their aims, objectives or strategies, although alliances could be forged on a temporary basis around particular issues.[8] The same is true of women in self-defined feminist societies. The first wave of feminism was infused by many traditions such as the social welfare tradition that gave rise to ideas about the moral superiority of women and insisted that women's 'unique qualities' could enhance citizenship. The Enlightenment tradition gave rise to egalitarian feminism and demands for equal political and civic rights with men.[9] Socialist traditions gave rise to a feminism which linked self-emancipation with social transformation. None of these traditions were mutually exclusive and feminists could and did draw from aspects of all three, especially where networks and alliances were formed amongst different groups of feminists. Feminism was part of a broader social movement for reforms in which there was a significant interlinking of ideas between feminist aims and other reform organisations including the labour movement. Fundamentally, the differences in aims, objectives and strategies used by self-defined feminists and those who sought alternative discourses to enhance women's position in society were based on the aspect of women's lives which activists chose to improve as their main objective. This was largely determined by the personal, social and economic circumstances of different women.[10] Thus, the political activity of feminists and 'non-feminists' cannot be divorced from the political, social and economic context of time and place and neither can their class or party loyalties. Feminist women also faced the problem that many women in political life endured: the choice between adopting a women-centred politics or embracing the party line. This dilemma was further aggravated by the gendered nature of citizenship that did not recognise the different experiences of men and women and subsumed women's experiences within a male-defined notion of citizenship.[11]

The gendered nature of citizenship and the strategies feminists adopted came to create tensions between the ILP and some feminists of the Glasgow and West of Scotland Suffrage Society [GWSS], straining relations between

---

[6] N. Cott, 'Feminist theory and feminist movements', in Mitchell and Oakley, *What is Feminism?*, 54–60.

[7] Law, *Suffrage and Power*, 176.

[8] Collette, *For Labour and for Women*, 62–75.

[9] Law, *Suffrage and Power*, 3–4 and R. Voet, *Feminism and Citizenship* (London, 1998), 21.

[10] Law, *Suffrage and Power*, 4–5, 176.

[11] See P. Hollis, *Ladies Elect: Women in English Local Government, 1895–1914* (Oxford, 1987).

them. The GWSS was affiliated to the National Union of Societies for Equal Citizenship that sought to promote the representation of women in political life irrespective of party allegiance. The GWSS may have shared these aims but it was unusual in its refusal to support female labour movement candidates. Indeed, the Edinburgh branch of this organisation was both willing and keen to support female Labour candidates.[12] Middle-class feminists who supported the Liberal and Conservative parties dominated the GWSS. Nevertheless, antagonism between women of feminist organisations and female working-class activists has not been attributed to the effects of the class and political loyalties of the self-defined feminists of organisations such as the GWSS, or the gendered nature of citizenship, but instead to the labour movement's 'extreme male-dominance'. In explorations of the relationship between feminists and the labour movement a woman's feminist identity has been privileged over that of class and political identities. This creates a one-dimensional analysis of the relationship between the labour movement and feminist organisations.

Relations between the GWSS and the ILP were poor before the interwar years because of the dominance of loyal Liberal Party workers in the GWSS.[13] Thus, the political and class loyalties of the GWSS were as much a factor as the male domination of the ILP in the hostilities which developed between both organisations and this was strained further in the context of acute working-class unrest in Scotland immediately after the First World War. Unlike the situation in the rest of Europe, the British women's movement undertook direct action and mobilised the support of working-class women because it did not believe this would undermine the existing social order.[14] This was complicated in Scotland because of class tensions. In Scotland from around 1910 until at least the 1920s class relations were increasingly strained by intense working-class militancy to such an extent that some contemporaries and a number of historians have suggested that the potential for revolution existed. Fear of political unrest in the wake of the Russian Revolution ensured that the conflict, much of which can be attributed to poor industrial relations and housing conditions, was perceived by many middle-class observers as political in nature, an 'attempt to smash the state'.[15] Furthermore, the effects of the adverse economic climate and the General Strike of 1926 aggravated class tensions. In 1926 the *Times* reported on a meeting of 2,000 Scottish women Unionists who were of the opinion that it was 'to be regretted' that the trade union movement

---

[12] See Smyth, *Labour in Glasgow*, 163–4.
[13] See Holton, *Feminism and Democracy*, 99–108 and K. Cowman, '"Incipient Toryism"? The women's social and political union and the Independent Labour Party, 1903–14', *History Workshop Journal*, 53: 129–48 (Spring 2002).
[14] Sowerwine, 'Feminism and the socialist women's movement', 376.
[15] See McLean, *The Legend of Red Clydeside* and McKay, 'Red Clydeside after 75 years: a reply to Iain McLean', *Scottish Labour History Society* 31: 87–8 (1996).

should permit its interests to be subordinated to political aims, by groups of ambitious men who make no secret that they take their instructions from a foreign country, and who were using their official positions as trade unionists as a means of enforcing the policy of those who would now openly advocate revolution in this country.[16]

The mentalities of middle-class women, whether feminist or not, may have been affected by this class conflict. The ILP was also associated with the political mobilisation of the unrest, a situation which is seen to have con-tributed to the party's electoral success in 1922. That year left-wing parties won two-thirds of Glasgow's Parliamentary seats and a further nine seats across the west of Scotland and they retained many of these throughout the inter-war years. Most of the new MPs were ILPers who were associated with working-class unrest in Scotland. Such were the fears that 'socialism was stalking the land' that an anti-Labour alliance developed, which the *Glasgow Evening Times* described as a 'pact between Conservatives and Liberals' that was 'more complete in Glasgow than elsewhere'.[17] Extreme forms of working-class militancy and the political and economic flux of the post-World War I years affected the mentalities of middle-class feminists. This intensified obstructions to alliances between the GWSS and the ILP. Middle-class members of the GWSS may have feared endangering the exist-ing social order. Hence the political environment contributed to tensions between feminists of different classes and political persuasions, as well as to the hostility between the GWSS and the ILP.

The ILP leader, Patrick Dollan, condemned feminists from the GWSS for refusing to support the female candidates put forward by the labour move-ment, while they nominated, financially supported and canvassed for women standing as Liberal and Unionist candidates.[18] The candidates supported by the GWSS stood in mainly middle-class wards like Kelvinside, Pollock, Cathcart, Sandyford and Park in Glasgow. The executive of the GWSS was also associated with the hierarchy of the Unionist Party and, as highlighted in Chapter three, the coalition between Liberals and Conservatives was intense in the west of Scotland. In 1920 Miss Alexander resigned her mem-bership on the executive of the GWSS to take up the post as Organiser to the Unionist Association.[19] The Unionist Party was not noted for its feminist sympathies, although women did play an active role in the party. However, as with current images of the female voter, it was believed that women were more inclined to vote Conservative. Putting forward and supporting female Unionist candidates could have been a political strategy by the GWSS to

---

[16] *Times*, 23 Oct. 1926.
[17] *Glasgow Evening Times*, 16 Nov. 1922.
[18] *Forward*, 13 Nov. 1920.
[19] Mitchell Library, SR157/891036/3, Glasgow Women's Suffrage Society, Manuscript Minutes, 1918–1924 [hereafter GWSS Manuscript Minutes], 17 Jan., 7 Feb. and 3 Mar. 1921, 27 Feb., 20 Sep., 4 Nov. and 7 Nov. 1922, 2 Oct., 16 Oct., 6 Nov. and 18 Dec. 1922.

attract the 'women's vote'. The Conservative and Liberal parties did well in a number of constituencies in Scotland, but so did the ILP, especially in the west of Scotland. The potential for electoral success did not entice the GWSS to support any of the ILP's female candidates, even those with feminist credentials. Such socialist women might have enhanced the cause of feminism by increasing the number of women in political positions. The reason why the GWSS desisted, unlike their Edinburgh sisters was that the ILP may have shared feminist aims but they opposed the political ideals of feminists from the GWSS. Moreover, neither the Conservative Party nor the Liberal Party held the mantle of championing women's causes that might have influenced the selection of candidates. Indeed, the Conservative Party was concerned about women's political emancipation because they identified the women's vote with socialism.[20]

Class and political loyalties undermined the potential for the GWSS to enlarge their political representation. The GWSS's political loyalties made them less attractive to women who did not identify with the Liberal or Conservative parties. Such women may have been influenced by a feminist candidate standing for the ILP. Political allegiances inhibited the GWSS's potential to create sympathetic alliances with others who were committed to enhancing the status of women. In addition, class was not an impediment to a feminist identity. In 1921 the GWSS had nearly 200 members in the Gorbals area of Glasgow, and almost 100 members in Possil, both predominantly working-class localities.[21] As Chapter two highlighted, these figures do not compare unfavourably with membership of labour movement organisations, even that of the more popular Women's Co-operative Guild. Furthermore, many female labour movement activists remained feminists throughout their political careers. Promoting women-centred policies or being recognised as a feminist was not an obstacle to being selected as a candidate for the labour movement. Thus, a lack of commitment to feminism fails to explain why the GWSS desisted from supporting socialist women.

By the 1930s uncertainties about women and their voting preferences or the ability of socialist women to overcome male labour movement hostility to feminism and gain selection and election had diminished. This led to a careful selection by feminists of the Glasgow Society for Equal Citizenship [GSEC], formerly the GWSS, of the seats that they would contest, in as much as they avoided working-class constituencies. The lack of success of feminists from the GSEC in working-class districts was summed up by one of their prominent activists, Helen Blair. She refused to stand in the ILP constituency of Springburn, stating that she would not stand again unless a more hopeful seat became available.[22] The GWSS were not successful in

---

[20] Law, *Suffrage and Power*, 227.
[21] GWSS Manuscript Minutes, 7 Feb. 1921.
[22] Mitchell Library, SR187/89101/36/36, Glasgow and West of Scotland Association for Women's Suffrage, Executive Manuscript Minutes, 1902–1933 [hereafter GSEC Executive Minutes], 15 Sep. and 20 Oct. 1930.

working-class seats because they continued to sponsor women standing as Liberal or Unionist candidates. This is contrary to the situation in other regions of Britain and within other branches of the women's movement. During her successful 1924 campaign for the Middlesbrough East constituency seat the Labour activist Ellen Wilkinson gained electoral support from the Women's Freedom League [WFL].[23] The WFL was an organisation that identified with the advancement of equal rights for women with men, unlike the NUWSS, which was more commonly associated with the promotion of welfare strategies to improve and enhance women's rights as women within society. Thus, in theory, if not in practice, branches of the NUWSS, as the GWSS was, had more in common, in terms of political aims, with the labour movement than the WFL did. Yet the WFL was prepared to form alliances with women of the labour movement: the GWSS was not.

After the extension of the franchise in 1928, many feminist societies began to concentrate on welfare reforms to enhance the lives of women, including the National Union of Societies for Equal Citizenship [NUSEC], formally the NUWSS.[24] The emphasis placed on 'welfare feminism' in the NUSEC did not exclude demands for equal rights that were more dominant in groups like the Six Points Group and the WFL. However, the emphasis on welfare feminism offered the potential for groups like the GSEC to form coalitions with the labour movement because both were committed, at least theoretically, to civic reform, even if the underlying aims differed. Nevertheless, feminists of the GSEC felt that to realise their aims they had to engage in electoral competition with the ILP. The GSEC may have had cause to doubt the ILP's claim that it was the 'Real Women's Party' and to assume that this was propaganda to attract women's votes. Although there were feminist women within the ILP, there were also many men and women hostile to feminism within the ranks of the party. There were socialists who maintained that promoting women-focused policies was anti-socialist as it privileged one group over others.[25] Some women, like the ILP feminist, Helen Gault, feared that by making women a 'special interest group' the cause of women's emancipation would be undermined.[26] Nevertheless, attempts to promote changes in social policy that would enhance women's lives were undertaken by many members of the ILP, men and women, feminist and non-feminist. The ILP was also known to work with organisations from the women's movement. In 1920, Eunice Murray, an organiser for the WFL, asked for the support of ILP members on Glasgow City Council to reject the recommendations of a Special Committee on Wage Conditions of Service. She objected to male tramway employees getting much higher war advances than female workers and to married women being ousted from work. Even

[23] Harrison, *Prudent Revolutionaries*, 134–5, 146.
[24] Holton, *Feminism and Democracy*, 229.
[25] Hannam and Hunt, *Socialist Women in Britain*, 149.
[26] *Forward*, 24 Apr. 1920.

though she had opposed a leading ILPer, James Maxton, in the 1918 general election, standing as a non-party candidate for the Bridgeton, Glasgow constituency, Eunice Murray nevertheless gained support on the issue of equal pay for women from prominent ILP men, including Patrick Dollan, leader of the Labour group in the Council, and George Buchanan, who went on to become MP for the Gorbals area of Glasgow. However, views were more mixed on the question of women's employment while pregnant and after the birth of a child. Some ILPers, male and female, supported a woman's right to work while pregnant and her right to return to work after childbirth, whilst others did not. Thus, Patrick Dollan decided that the ILP's executive should confer with its female membership before setting out its policy on the latter.[27] Thus, it was not merely feminist organisations that championed women's issues. There were grounds for coalitions and these were not merely on issues of civic reform.

The ILP's credentials for supporting women's rights were further heightened when in 1922, in line with the GWSS, it protested against the proposed expulsion of married women from local authority employment.[28] In the same year, the GWSS discussed whether it should support a married woman's right to work and expressed the view that 'although the question of married women working had nothing to do with unemployment, it would be inexpedient to take further action' because of the prevailing economic climate.[29] These pragmatic attitudes were not confined to equal rights issues, which were more difficult to attain, although the emphasis changed as the inter-war years progressed. Thus, it is apparent that the potential for rapprochement existed between the GWSS and the ILP. This was also evident in Helen Fraser's 1922 electoral campaign for the Parliamentary seat of Govan. Helen Fraser was a prominent member of the GWSS and was supported by the organisation to stand for election in the Govan seat on a Liberal manifesto. The seat was also targeted by the ILP. In an election address, Helen Fraser maintained that she felt aggrieved at what she referred to as 'the labour movement's appropriation of our feminist ideals and policies'. She was referring to the ILP's aim to establish widows' pensions. Many Liberals, feminist societies and feminists within the labour movement shared this goal along with the labour movement in general. Her claim against the labour movement was as much Liberal party political propaganda as it was condemnation from a feminist trying to infiltrate the male political citadel of Glasgow's politics. In addition, it was aimed at her opposition, Neil Maclean, who by the organisation's own admission, was the only man to sign the memorial for an equal franchise for women distributed by the GWSS.[30] Fraser gained little support in this ward. Neil Maclean won the constituency for the ILP.

---

[27] *Forward*, 24 Apr. 1920.
[28] GWSS Manuscript Minutes, 20 Dec. 1920 and 7 Nov. 1922, 3.
[29] GSEC Executive Minutes, 20 Jan. 1930 and 25 Apr. 1930.
[30] *Govan Press*, 3 Nov. 1922 and GWSS Manuscript Minutes, 21 Feb. 1921.

Divisions based on material conditions, class awareness and strategy under-mined the potential for coalitions, but these divisions were not merely the product of the male domination of the labour movement. In 1930, members of the GSEC illustrated their class and political loyalties in a letter sent to the *Women's Leader*, written by Mrs Bryson, Mrs Tucker and Miss Morrison of the executive on behalf of the organisation. They complained that the *Women's Leader* had become 'too socialist' in its 'tendencies'.[31] Class and political loyalties influenced the political priorities given to reforms that affected the lives of working-class women. Improving the working environment of house-wives and mothers was a priority of many branches of the NUSEC. Inter-war feminists, including those who were socialists, ensured that housing became a women's issue. Housing became part of a strategy amongst feminist women of the labour movement to redefine and revalue the housewife as a home worker, with workers' rights to decent working conditions.[32] This objective facilitated coalitions with non-feminist women and men of the ILP because improving housing conditions was not merely a feminist issue. Housing conditions concerned ILP activists, whether they were feminists or not, because it was part of a wider aim to produce improvements in social policy to enhance the standards of living of the working classes. Prominent female activists, including feminists of the ILP, waged constant campaigns to have the 'workshop' of the housewife improved. The Co-operative Women's Guild in Scotland consistently argued for better access to improved housing for working-class women, slum clearance and reasonable rents, petitioning the government and the Secretary of State for Scotland. The Guild not only advo-cated improved housing as a means of enhancing the workshop of women, but it also took the view that better housing would effect improvements in the health of women and the children that they were responsible for. The Guild linked housing improvements to the welfare of women and children and to maternal and child mortality, demonstrating the inter-relationship between these factors.[33] Other political women took direct action. The ILPer Agnes Paterson Hardie, the eldest daughter of Keir Hardie, in her role as Provost of Cumnock challenged and defeated the landowner, Lord Bute of Cumnock, to ensure the removal of slum dwellings from his land and their replacement with council housing. By 1945, three-quarters of Cumnock's population had been rehoused in council houses. *Labour Women* also commended the work of women from the labour movement in Kilsyth, where by 1935 nearly 50 per cent of the population lived in council housing.[34]

[31] GSEC Executive Minutes, 15 Dec. 1930.

[32] A. Hughes and K. Hunt, 'A culture transformed? Women's lives in Wythenshawe in the 1930s', in A. Davies and S. Fielding (eds), *Workers' Worlds: Culture and Communities in Manchester and Salford 1880–1939* (Manchester, 1992), 77 and Hannam and Hunt, *Socialist Women in Britain*, 149.

[33] See SCWG, 38th and 39th Annual Report and Statement and Central Council Minutes, 6 Feb. 1924.

[34] *Labour Women*, Nov. 1935, 169.

Many 'socialist' women regarded housing as a feminist issue because the home was the 'workshop' of the housewife and those who did not looked upon housing improvements as a political priority to improve the living conditions of their constituents. Thus, feminist and non-feminist socialist women continued to protest for improvements in housing conditions and over rental costs, as they had done with the support of working-class women during the 1915 rent strikes. This had led to the government's capitulation in the form of the Rent Restriction Act of that year. They also campaigned to ensure the continuation of this concession and against unfair rents, with socialist women from the ILP and Co-operative Women's Guild continuing to co-ordinate rent strikes.[35] In January 1926, the Glasgow Property Owners and Factors Association 'dubbed' Clydebank the 'spiritual home of anarchy', and they had good cause, given the level of rent strikes in this locality. By August 1927, rent strikes had commenced again in Clydebank.[36] In September 1929, Mary Barbour, the ILP councillor for Govan, along with Christine Moodie, another ILP councillor for Glasgow and president of the Glasgow Labour Housing Association, took a deputation to the Secretary of State for Scotland on behalf of Glasgow tenants. These women charged Glasgow's property owners with harsh and unfair treatment of their tenants and pointed out the monthly increases in evictions in the city, which stood at around 20,000 for the period September 1928 to September 1929, with 11,544 of the evictions taking place in the months between January and September 1929. The end result of the deputation was a request by the Secretary of State for Scotland that the Property Owners and House Factors Association should meet with him to try to resolve the situation.[37] While a solution was not reached, socialist women continued to protest and by June 1932, the National Federation of Property Owners and Factors of Scotland, and the Factors Association of Glasgow Ltd, presented a memorial to the Prime Minister, the Chancellor of the Exchequer and the Secretary of State for Scotland. It asked for the adoption of the English rating system and valuation system in the hope that this would reduce rents and ensure that occupiers knew definitively what the cost of services were, and that thereby friction between factor and tenant would be removed.[38] This request followed a mass meeting in Govan favouring rent strikes, where 'thousands rushed the doors and hundreds had to remain outside', as well as further rent strikes in Govan led by Barbour. These protests were significant because of the cuts in public expenditure in the 1930s.[39] In contrast, when the non-party Women's Constitutional Association proposed to 'urge the

---

[35] SCWG, Central Council Minutes, Feb., Aug. and Sep. 1920 and Aug. and Sep. 1929.
[36] *Govan Press*, 29 Jan. 1926 and *Forward*, 17 Aug. 1927.
[37] *Glasgow Herald*, 10 Sep. 1929.
[38] *Govan Press*, 17 Jun. 1932.
[39] *Govan Press*, 17 Jun., 29 Feb. 1932, *Forward*, 14 May 1932 and Glasgow City Council Minutes, 16 Mar. 1933.

government to give rent rebates when the family's income did not exceed £3 a week or 10s per head', the GSEC opposed the proposal.[40]

Housing was a reform that was embraced by the NUSEC, but on the issue of improving the living environment of housewives there was mixed support from the women's movement. In 1931 the GSEC stated, 'due to the level of taxation and the large number of unlet houses the building of Corporation housing should cease except for slum clearance'. The 'large' number of unlet houses in 1926 in Govan was two, in Fairfield four and in Kinning Park four. Scotland's housing shortage and housing conditions were amongst the worst in Britain.[41] The annual conference of the Scottish Council of Women Citizens' Association [SCWCA] was held in Kilmacolm in 1930. At this conference a proposal to abolish 'the present system of feu duties' [an annual levy to landowners for properties built on their land] was tabled. It was argued that this would 'encourage the middle class to build their own homes' which would 'incidentally relieve the housing problem' of the working-classes. The proposal was rejected because it was claimed that the feu system was 'too deeply rooted in Scottish social and economic life' and because it would 'amount to the confiscation of property'.[42] Concern with improving middle-class housing and only 'incidentally' the workshop of working-class women, as well as the over-riding anxiety to protect property rights, highlights the class bias of some feminists. In addition, the attitudes and behaviour of many Scottish feminists was the antithesis of the behaviour of feminists in Manchester from the same organisation who promoted the building of homes for working-class families and who involved themselves and working-class women in the design and construction.[43] Concern amongst feminists with the 'tax burden' mediated the promotion of 'welfare feminism' advanced by the NUSEC and negated possible alliances with the labour movement, feminists of the ILP and activists who advanced women-focused policies.

The GSEC's attitude to welfare spending was not confined to housing. In 1930, they discussed expenditure on social services, including maternity care, child welfare schemes and nurseries, all viewed as feminist issues by a significant number of members of the NUSEC and socialist feminists. Mrs Tucker, of the executive of the GSEC, nevertheless proposed that

> In view of the present financial condition of the Country and the great increase in unemployment we do not feel that it is the time to urge for any increases in social services which will mean increased taxation and a further burden on industry.[44]

---

[40] GSEC, Executive Minutes, 19 May 1930.
[41] GSEC, Executive Minutes, 2 Mar. and 18 May 1931, *Govan Press*, 15 Jan. 1926 and Butt, 'Working-class housing in Glasgow', 143–69.
[42] *Glasgow Herald*, 17 May 1930.
[43] Hughes and Hunt, 'A culture transformed', 74–101.
[44] GSEC, Executive Minutes, 17 Mar. 1931.

Clearly many middle-class feminists had little understanding of the conditions of life endured by the majority of working-class women in Scotland,
and their loyalties cohered around class rather than gender. The Women
Citizens' Association, affiliated to the NUSEC, was expected to 'educate
women as citizens, foster social contact between them, and promote the
skills and interests of women as housewives'.[45] In 1927, at the Annual
Conference of the SCWCA, the view was expressed that 'new modern conditions tend to make homes more habitable and healthy and make the lives
of the women who live in them less of a drudgery'.[46] However, while this was
regarded as a feminist cause because it educated women on the emancipat-
ing potential of new household technology, which middle-class women had
begun to enjoy, few working-class women in Scotland had access to these
or to electricity. For the majority of working-class women, life as a 'home-
maker' continued to be nothing short of drudgery. This would explain why
feminists in the ILP, and women who disavowed a feminist identity, argued
that all new houses should be equipped with labour-saving applications to
reduce household drudgery to a minimum. Such women also sought communal services to ensure wives and mothers could 'obtain the leisure to
enable them to take their proper share of the duties of citizenship'.[47]

Feminists of all political persuasions sought to emancipate women from
the drudgery of housework, but class and political loyalties often determined the strategies that they adopted in their efforts to effect change.
Opinions relating to the level of assistance that working-class mothers
should receive also diverged. The GSEC rejected any proposals to urge the
Council to establish nursery schools in congested areas under the education system because of the 'financial situation', while women of the ILP,
feminist and non-feminist, fought for this service.[48] For the feminists of the
ILP the provision of nursery schools was intended to emancipate women;
for non-feminists it would provide working-class women with the same
privileges as middle-class women. Nevertheless, regardless of the underlying reasons for advocating these policies, the shared aims did allow for
coalitions between feminists and activists within the ILP.

Class also prevented co-operation on the issue of family endowment, a
policy advanced by the NUSEC and its leader Eleanor Rathbone, identified
as the 'wise leader' of the GSEC. At no point in the 1930s did the GSEC
support family allowances and in 1921, they actually refused to support an
endowment for mothers. The Edinburgh branch of the movement did not
share this view and fully supported family allowances.[49] The GSEC's position was also the antithesis of the support given by women's groups who

---

[45] Pugh, 'Domesticity and the decline of feminism', 147.

[46] *Glasgow Herald*, 23 May 1927.

[47] *Forward*, 23 Apr. 1921 and 1 Jul. 1922.

[48] GSEC, Executive Minutes, 20 Jan. and 21 Oct. 1930 and *Forward*, 21 Feb. 1931, 4 Apr. 1931
and 8 Oct. 1932.

[49] *Scotsman*, 10 May 1929.

did not identify themselves as feminist.[50] Yet they were in line with the attitudes of the Women's National Liberal Federation as expressed in 1927 at their annual conference. A proposal was put forward to urge the Liberal Industrial Inquiry Committee to consider child allowances, but the motion was defeated.[51]

As Chapter two highlighted, the ILP advanced an endowment for mothers as part of the promotion of a 'family wage', and therefore not directly influenced by feminism.[52] In doing so the ILP challenged the orthodox objections of other branches of the labour movement that endowments would interfere with wages. It was not until 1930 that the STUC's Organisation of Women Committee showed support for family allowances because it would 'keep married women' out of the labour market. Trade union hostility prevailed and it was not until 1930, under pressure from the ILP, that the Labour Party added family endowment to its programme.[53] Women of the ILP who were feminists could support the party because an endowment was seen as a means of rewarding women for their roles as mothers and providing them with economic independence. Thus, socialist feminists campaigned incessantly for this resolution to be adopted, forming alliances with men and women of the ILP who promoted a family endowment as part of a wider aim to effect a redistribution of income and improve working-class standards of living.

Many GSEC feminists not only ignored issues which related to working-class women, but at times directly opposed their interests. When Edinburgh and Glasgow feminists met in 1932 to discuss married women's benefits, the diverging opinions of the two groups were clearly evident. Members of the Edinburgh Equal Citizenship Council, also affiliated to the Open Door Council, had conducted a study of the workings of unemployment and health insurance of women workers. They found that a 'vicious circle' existed whereby women's lower pay meant they contributed less towards health insurance benefits and thereby received less money when they were ill and unable to work. In addition married women faced more restrictions than single women because it was expected that their husbands would subsidise them when they were unable to work due to ill-health. Edinburgh feminists argued that 'the women worker had as much need of food, leisure and clothing as the male worker' so that it was unfair that men received 16/- sickness benefit, single women 12/- and married women 10/- per week. Mrs Hughes, from the Glasgow branch, conceded that 'there were many injustices', but she also thought they ought to take into account that

> The married women had got advantages that the unmarried woman had not. While they were sorry for her that she got only 10/- instead

[50] Beaumont, 'Citizens not feminists', 411–26.

[51] *Glasgow Herald*, 5 May 1927.

[52] ILP Women's Section, Minutes, 2 Mar. 1925 and 6 Sep. 1926, and *Forward*, 12 Apr. 1929.

[53] STUC 33rd A/R, 1930, 8 and Graves 'An experiment in women-centred socialism', 196.

of 12/-, were they not entitled to expect that she would get something from her husband? [54]

Clearly she had not considered married women's right to economic independence, or married women who worked to support unemployed husbands or to supplement the low wages of their partners. The attitudes of some feminists towards working women compounded this situation. At the Scottish Equal Citizenship Association's Summer School, Mrs White gave a talk on the 'Women Workers', She stated

> Women's work is monotonous, unintelligent and badly paid. They gain such employment because no man will do it. Such employment makes them stupid. They wear too much make-up and only think of clothes and boys, not real men. They need stimulation.[55]

Having read this, many working-class women were unlikely to feel disposed to view middle-class feminist organisations positively. Equally indicative of the attitudes of some feminists towards working-class women was the GSEC's proposal to reduce overheads. In 1931, it was decided to employ 'a younger female clerk'. As for the majority of working-class women out of work, they proposed that they should be trained to fill 'existing vacancies' and, almost certainly, domestic service would have been conspicuous on this list.[56] It could be argued that this viewpoint was feminist because it challenged the high levels of women's unemployment in this region and the signification that unemployment was a male problem.

Many feminist and socialist women's groups advocated schemes to train and provide work for unemployed women. The Council for Women's Trades under the secretary, Margaret Irwin, a prominent trade unionist, placed 1,000 unemployed young women into domestic service in farmhouses where 85 per cent remained. They also assisted the emigration of ninety-two young women from Glasgow to the colonies. As well as supporting birth control and better maternity benefits for women, the Industrial Women's Organisation created a scheme to train young women in domestic service with the aim of encouraging them to immigrate to the colonies to alleviate unemployment.[57] Female activists also believed that the introduction of training schemes for domestic service would enhance the status of this occupation and thereby the wages associated with it. However, this policy, like the GSEC's views on housing and welfare, also reflected the dominant political aims of the Conservative or Conservative-dominated governments between the wars to return women to 'women's work' as part of a broader attempt to reformulate traditional gender identities. The

---

[54] *Scotsman*, 10 Oct. 1932.
[55] *Glasgow Herald*, 7 Sep. 1928.
[56] GSEC Executive Minutes, 2 Mar. and 18 May 1931.
[57] *Glasgow Herald*, 13 Aug. 1924, 17 Dec. 1927 and 2 Oct. 1931.

support of such a policy by many middle-class feminists of the GSEC and trade unionists like Margaret Irwin highlights the problems which following a party line could pose. However, this policy was contested. The ILPer Mrs Laird demanded that the Glasgow Trades Council ensure that women could choose whatever employment training they thought appropriate, rather than having training foisted upon them.[58]

Domestic service had become unpopular as an occupation and this caused concern amongst middle-class women because domestic servants had been one source of their freedom, relieving them of the burdens of housewifery and allowing them leisure time and the time to exercise citizenship. In a letter to the editor of the *Glasgow Herald*, a Miss Jacobson expressed 'amazement mingled with indignation' that national funds were being used 'to train girls as domestic servants for the colonies'. Miss Jacobson stated, 'The average middle-class housewife finds it well nigh impossible to secure a really capable and reliable servant. Charity should begin at home. The result would be a blessing to many a harassed housewife.' Miss Jacobson went on to represent the 'harassed housewives' of her class by complaining that the 'new' type of servant prefers 'the fun and frivolity' of the dance halls. When employers had cause to reprimand their domestic servants, the employees just handed in their notice, 'those that is that had the courtesy to do so'. Such a situation was apparently creating an intolerable situation for many mistresses of the home.[59] Thus, the concern of many members of the GSEC to train women to fill existing vacancies might well have been less than altruistic. The combined effects of class and political loyalties ensured that, in reality, the attitudes of a significant number of the GSEC's membership towards working-class people were often closer to class exploitation than feminism. These views were unlikely to endear feminists to working-class women, the unemployed, young workers or the labour movement. The intended aim of the NUSEC was to promote issues that would benefit women and attract working-class women to the organisation. However, rather than fulfilling these aims, as the 1920s progressed, the GSEC seemed more concerned with the condition of the hockey pitch at Rouken Glen, a middle-class region of Glasgow, and the condition not of worn-out women, but of worn-out horses. These 'local' concerns certainly merited more attention than housing, maternal and child welfare, family endowment and nursery care.[60]

The GSEC was disbanded in 1933. This was attributed to the effects of the depression, competition from other women's organisations and 'an underlying lack of purpose', but as Chapter two demonstrated many socialist women's organisations faced similar problems.[61] Arguably, it was also

---

[58] GTLC Executive Minutes, 4 Feb. 1926.
[59] *Glasgow Herald*, 2 Oct. 1931.
[60] GSEC Executive Minutes, 16 Sep. 1929.
[61] Pugh, 'Domesticity and the decline of feminism', 147–8.

the feminism projected by the GSEC and their class loyalties that guaranteed that support from many working-class women was not forthcoming. Not all Scottish feminists behaved in this way. The Edinburgh branch of the movement consistently supported issues which would appeal to working-class women, including equal pay for women, equal moral standards for men and women and the introduction of information on birth control to be made available to working-class women.[62] However, the GSEC, as with many of their counterparts in Europe, were held back by their class backgrounds and found they were therefore 'unable to make contact with working-class women'.[63]

By the 1930s, an era of 'shrinking economic opportunities', male tolerance to female aspirations had diminished and hostility to feminism and feminist objectives had increased, exacerbating the divisions created by class.[64] In this aggressive environment, feminists of all political and class persuasions faced the difficulties posed by women's multiple identities, the gendered nature of citizenship and a choice of strategies to promote women's interests. However, although 'multiple identities did not always invalidate women's political agency', the admission of middle-class feminists into the bastions of political power ensured that working-class women's interests were undermined, except on occasion when the interests of working-class and middle-class women coincided. In addition, the antipathy of the GSEC to socialist groups, such as the ILP, ensured that men, and even women, who had 'good intentions', and who regarded themselves as women's representatives were 'treated as enemies'.[65] Class and political loyalties also influenced the men and women of the ILP so that reservations developed both ways. It was not merely the male dominance of the ILP that strained the potential for coalitions between them and the GSEC.

It is also the case that while socialist women could enlist the support of male ILPers, they often had to challenge the ILP's vision of womanhood to promote feminist objectives. The 'politics of the kitchen' was a discourse used by the male-dominated labour movement in an attempt to orchestrate women's political identity through a discursive construction that characterised their female constituency as essentially an 'interest group' and to fence female activists within the realm of domestic issues. In 1929, after the extension of the franchise to include all women over the age of twenty-one, this idea was promoted when the ILP asked the single woman to think of her future as a wife and to consider the price of pans and crockery when voting.[66] Although such a worldview could ensure that women's political demands were deemed secondary with the capacity to narrow women's

[62] *Scotsman*, 10 May 1929.

[63] Sowerwine, 'Feminism and the socialist women's movement', 383.

[64] Pugh, 'Domesticity and the decline of feminism', 147.

[65] See Voet, *Feminism and Citizenship*, 95.

[66] *Forward*, 28 Feb. 1925.

scope for equality with men, it also provided a foundation from which to mount a challenge to the male-defined conceptions of the 'politics of the kitchen'. This was what significant numbers of women did by exploiting the signifiers of gender norms and linking these to the ILP's promotion of municipal socialism and class-based propaganda. Socialist women adopted these strategies because they were under no illusion that their organisation was egalitarian. Kate Beaton openly confronted the male dominance of the labour movement:

> Some so called labour representatives are content to idle away their opportunities and sun themselves in the petty honours and privileges which the workers have placed in their grasp. Scrap the duds and replace them with females. Let us stand for the voicing and enforcing of demands which affect our homes and make our domestic econo-mies such a physical and mental burden. Let us have a federation of working females.[67]

Harry McShane, a contemporary socialist, maintains that nearly all the out-standing socialist women were in the ILP and that most were housewives who accepted the prevailing sexual division of labour just as their male counterparts did. Neither male nor female activists sought the 'abolition of family', and their attitude to sex was 'bourgeois'.[68] Certainly, the Scottish labour movement was more hostile to the issue of birth control than its English counterpart, but hostility was not uniform. In 1924, a number of prominent women of the labour movement sent a deputation to the ILPer and Labour Minister for Health, John Wheatley, to state the case for infor-mation on birth control to be made accessible to working-class women at clinics set up by local authorities. Wheatley rejected this and justified his objections thus, 'you might as well ask me why I don't eat beef on Fridays'.[69] Wheatley objected to birth control on religious grounds, but he was not unique in his hostility towards it. It was not until 1926 that *Forward* began to publicise the debate over birth control. At this time an article by Walton Newbold attacked the Motherwell MP, Reverend James Barr, for his

> superstitious and obscure speech on birth control, which deliberately closed the book of knowledge and forbade its opening by appealing to religious prejudices, even though the women of the labour move-ment had by majorities more overwhelming than they had shown on any other issue of a controversial character declared time and again in their conferences for legislation.

Wheatley argued that providing information on birth control was far too revolutionary.[70] Not one of the Scottish ILP MPs, who had gained 'revolu-

[67] *Forward*, 29 Mar. 1924.
[68] H. McShane and J. J. Smith, *No Mean Fighter* (London, 1978), 33–5.
[69] *Forward*, 29 Mar. 1924 and 17 Apr. 1926.
[70] *Forward*, 13 Mar. and 1 Apr. 1926.

tionary' reputations for their militant activities between 1910 and 1922 as well as their behaviour in Parliament, voted for the Birth Control Enabling Bill. The Bill would have merely made the dissemination of knowledge about birth control permissible. Yet there were various reasons for such behaviour. Support for birth control may have alienated the Catholic vote. In 1923, Father Henry Day gave an address on contraception to the congregation of St Aloysius' Church in Garnethill, Glasgow. He insisted that the results of the use of contraception were already 'too alarming' to allow the issue to be ignored. He added, 'this evil could only be counteracted by exposing it and by forming against it a sound public opinion based on Christian principles'.[71] These principles were 'unfolded in the moral teaching on the subject of the Catholic Church'. Dr Halliday Sutherland added to the debate at a meeting of the Knights of St Columbus in the City Hall in Glasgow in 1924, highlighting what he and many other objectors to birth control felt were the main dangers. Using the fear surrounding the climate of unrest in Europe, Dr Halliday Sutherland suggested that the use of contraception was 'sowing the seeds of revolution' because it would be unlikely that those who used birth control would 'place the interest of the state above their own comfort'.[72]

Places of worship and the media were used to disseminate the idea that Catholics who used contraception were selfish individuals who were disregarding the ethos of the Catholic Church. Individuals who used contraception were associated with 'political tendencies' that were a danger to Catholicism, namely communism. Even against such opposition the Birth Control Enabling Act was passed in 1930 and extended to Scotland in 1934, which made it permissible for married women, if their lives or the life of the unborn child was endangered, to receive information about birth control in local authority clinics. A Catholic priest responded to this, with the support of the Bishop of Glasgow, by organising opposition to a Women's Welfare Clinic in Paisley that issued birth control. Under pressure, the landlord, which was a Co-operative Society, asked the Scottish Federation of Mothers' Welfare Clinics to seek alternative accommodation. This was in spite of the support given to birth control by the females of the Scottish Co-operative Women's Guild.[73] Yet, opposition to birth control was not the preserve of the Catholic clergy. The ILPer James Barr, a United Free Church minister, was one of the most hostile critics of birth control. In fact, ministers from the Church of Scotland, unlike the Church of England, continued to regard the use of birth control as a 'mortal sin'.[74] Canon Laurie of Edinburgh maintained that the use of birth control 'attacked the moral and consciences of the people' who should in his opinion practise

[71] *Glasgow Herald*, 2 Oct. 1923.
[72] *Glasgow Herald*, 14 May and 22 Sep. 1924.
[73] GRA, Scottish Federation of Mothers' Welfare Clinics, Minute Book, 28 Feb. 1938.
[74] *Glasgow Herald*, 22 Sep. 1930.

'self control'. The Mothers' Union, influenced by these religious discourses on contraception, maintained that it was a women's duty to practise 'self control and train the next generation in self-discipline of body, mind and spirit'.[75]

In 1926, the socialist Dora Russell expressed the view in *Forward* that 'the shadow of threatened religious opposition blinds many Scottish members and organisers to the reality of possible support – great in numbers – passionate in belief' for birth control.[76] This was not exclusive to Scotland or men of the movement. The English activist Ellen Wilkinson was also hostile to the issue of birth control. She felt it was not a class issue, but the Catholic vote in her constituency has also been identified as a factor contributing to this position.[77] Many ILP members also perceived the use of birth control as irreligious, but other considerations were equally important. Organisations and individuals, including eugenicists, sexologists, the medical profession, politicians and the clergy, engaged in the debate over women's sexuality. The views expounded were often unlikely to gain the support of those who represented the working classes. Many supporters of eugenics saw birth control as a 'social remedy in the best interests of the race'.[78] In 1923, a feature appeared in the *Glasgow Herald* written by their medical correspondent, Dr Killock Millard. Millard advocated the use of birth control as a form of 'practicable eugenics' and signified quite clearly which class of people he felt should be using contraceptives: 'it appears undeniable that poverty, degradation, inefficiency, ignorance, over-crowding – almost everything in fact that in human judgement tends to disqualify for parenthood – are just the factors which too often exist within large families'.[79] The renowned 'social worker' Marjorie Spring Rice, at the National Liberal Federation argued that the use of birth control could increase the 'efficiency of the nation'.[80]

Many of the arguments for birth control also challenged the ILP's political rhetoric. When promoting municipalisation, the ILP consistently argued that poverty, poor living conditions, infant mortality and disease were by-products of the capitalist system. Large families were not the problem; capitalism was. Thus, the argument that birth control would reduce family size and thereby improve the standards of living of the working classes threatened the very premise of ILP propaganda. The birth control debate also gained in prominence following the debacle of the first Labour government in 1924. It then had to compete with concerns over the schisms between the Labour Party and the Communist Party that intensified in the mid-1920s, as well as the political upheaval caused by the 1926 General Strike. Thereafter, the recession, the failures of the second

---

[75] *Glasgow Herald*, 5 Oct. 1926 and *Scotsman*, 1 May 1930.

[76] *Forward*, 27 Mar. 1926.

[77] Harrison, *Prudent Revolutionaries*, 146.

[78] *Glasgow Herald*, 6 Feb. and 27 Nov. 1924.

[79] *Glasgow Herald*, 23 Apr. 1923.

[80] *Glasgow Herald*, 5 May 1927.

Labour government of 1929, the need for unity in the face of the reactionary forces in government in the 1930s, along with further splits within the
labour movement between the Labour Party and the ILP compounded
matters.[81] Thus, the issue of birth control was given little significance in the
wider gamut of labour movement politics. This was exacerbated as birth
control was sidelined because it could be identified with the personal and
the 'private' rather than a public political concern.

The birth control debate also divided ILP women: although in the minor-
ity, there were activists, including Jean Roberts, who held the view that birth
control was not a 'political question' which should be 'tacked' onto the
ILP's programme. Some female activists were also concerned that if contraceptives did not avert pregnancy then women would be held accountable
and possibly accused of adultery.[82] Religion was also a factor in determining women's stance on this issue. Yet, although there were Catholic women
who opposed contraception, many Catholic women did not adopt this
attitude, whilst others might have come to support the introduction of
birth control. Mrs Jones, a Catholic, felt that 'there's only one contracep-
tive and it's the word no! I didn't approve. I mean we weren't supposed to
have contraceptives – the religion.' However, she added, 'It was all right for
them, they weren't bringing up six kids on 10/- a week.'[83] Making a plea for
more voluntary welfare clinics, Dr Marwick, the honorary secretary of the
Edinburgh Mothers' Welfare Clinic, was emphatic that if local authorities
'took action' they could 'count on the support of working-class women'.[84]
Most Scottish socialist women agreed. They were also aware that the fight
for knowledge which would allow women to control their fertility would
have united and politicised significant numbers of women and this was
evident from the protests involving working-class women against the stance
taken by the male ILP MPs. In March 1926, a meeting of 600 voters, male
and female, took place in Motherwell. Only two people dissented from the
resolution passed to protest against Barr's decision not to support the Birth
Control Enabling Act, and to request that he 'reconsider his decision'.
There were ordinary working-class women, regardless of the influence of
religion, who thought women should have known about birth control and
that it should have been available to them. A further 300 people in Wishaw
and 400 women from Motherwell endorsed the cause of the female activists
of the labour movement by signing petitions demanding information on
birth control.[85]

Catholic and Protestant respondents also expressed the view that knowledge about birth control should have been available to them. This they

---

[81] Graves, 'An experiment in women-centred socialism', 189.
[82] *Forward*, 10 Apr. 1926 and 3 Apr. 1926.
[83] SOHCA/019/011/Glasgow, b. 1917.
[84] *Scotsman*, 26 May 1936.
[85] *Forward*, 27 Mar. 1926.

expressed personally and by way of the collective term 'women'. Mrs Johnson, a Protestant, affirmed 'of course they should've known. If I'd known I wouldn't have had six children. I got married and I'd never heard of condoms. When I didn't want any more I just didn't have any fun, let's put it that way.' Mrs MacIntosh, a Catholic, was a member of the Co-operative Women's Guild. She declared, 'A woman with a big family was a slave from morning till night. They'd nobody to help them. They were working, looking after children, cooking, cleaning, and the men in those days never helped them. It wasn't a man's place.'[86] This was a discourse shared by socialist women. Dora Russell challenged the prominent men of the ILP by subverting their reactionary and class-conscious reputations when she stated

> Women find our reactionary leaders shirking this, opposing it in defiance of decisions of the Women's conference. Our champions, profiting by women's votes, condemn women to suffering and ignorance as if they were a slave class.[87]

In line with the Labour Party and its leader Ramsay MacDonald, the ILP continued to consider the issue of birth control to have no 'economic or social value, whatever its individual and family virtues!'[88] In this, the party was out of touch with ordinary working-class women and men and thereby contributed to the fact that by the Second World War Scotland lagged significantly behind England in the provision of municipal birth control clinics. In 1936 there were one hundred and eighteen municipal clinics in England providing information on birth control and only two in Scotland, one in Aberdeen and one in Greenock.[89]

The ILP persisted in promoting socialism in ways that shored up existing gender norms. Women were identified as 'the Chancellors of the Exchequer of the home'. The home was to be their 'workshop'; 'the centre and pivot of human life'; 'the nursery of the child; the training ground of tomorrow's men and women; the cradle of the race' where women would produce citizens. Patrick Dollan could also state with comparative impunity that the issue of birth control should not undermine efforts to achieve direct labour schemes to tackle unemployment.[90] Dollan's attitude is representative of the shift in ILP policy, particularly noticeable as the 1920s progressed, to an emphasis on unemployment. The party linked unemployment to municipalisation. Poor environment and limited life chances were expressed through inability to procure a decent standard of living because of capitalism's exploitation of the 'breadwinner'. Scottish MPs were noted for their concern and agitation in relation to unemployment and its effects

---

[86] SOHCA/019/025/Paisley, b. 1914 and SOHCA/019/014/Glasgow, b. 1911.
[87] *Forward*, 27 Mar. 1926.
[88] *Forward*, 1 Oct. 1927.
[89] *Glasgow Herald*, 26 May 1936.
[90] *Forward*, 5 Nov. 1927.

on family life in Parliament and political circles. Yet this shift also symbol-
ised the inherent gendered context of the Scottish labour movement's
worldview which resulted in impediments for the women of the party.
Dollan's statement about birth control was a strategy to undermine any possibility that the issue of birth control would displace, or detract from, the
concerns about unemployment, a 'public' rather than a 'personal' political
question. Women's concerns were frequently conceptualised as 'personal',
subservient to the 'public' and thus sidelined.

Most of the male leadership of the labour movement refused to consider
promoting birth control. In response socialist women simply defied the
party line. The ILP activist Mrs Auld presided over the public opening
of Govan's branch of the Glasgow Women's Welfare and Advisory Clinic
and Mary Barbour was one of the main speakers. The latter wished the
organisers every success, and she referred to the great Labour involvement
in obtaining the objective for the establishment of the clinic. She was also
quite happy to work with the Moderate councillor, Mrs Bell, to realise her
objectives.[91] Barbour, by attributing the success of this local initiative to
the labour movement, negated condemnation of this defiant action that
she and Labour women like her took on behalf of their female working-
class constituents. By the late 1930s, the Glasgow branch of the Federation
of Mothers' Welfare Clinics was gaining as many as thirty new members
each week. Attendance was also increasing in Paisley. Many of these clinics
were aided by donations from town councils where women were politically influential. Branches of the Mothers' Welfare Clinics in Edinburgh,
Johnstone, Paisley and Renfrew all received council grants, whilst medical
officers employed by the councils often sent women to such clinics.[92] As
Chapter two demonstrated, local government was the arena of politics that
women had permeated in significant numbers in Scotland and it was also a
site where they voiced their aims. This is evident from the outrage of councillors, including Christine Muir, Laura McLean and Agnes Dollan, over
attempts by local authorities in Scotland to 'curtail expenditure' on maternal and child welfare where information on birth control was distributed.
Agnes Dollan, the wife of Patrick Dollan, insisted that women members had
to 'bring pressure on the local authorities to establish maternity hospitals
and homes and child welfare services'.[93]

Socialist women also contested the discursive context aimed at limiting
working-class women's access to contraception. In doing so they used the
signifiers of class to demand that working-class women should have the
same privileges as the 'rich', the right to control their fertility. They also
demanded that working-class women should have access to maternal and
child welfare services. Female activists linked these demands to the ILP's

[91] *Govan Press*, 13 Aug. 1926.
[92] GRA, HB77/1/1/1, Scottish Welfare Clinics, Minute Book, 28 Feb. 1938.
[93] *Scotsman*, 17 Oct. 1932.

promotion of social welfare and to general concerns about the health of the nation, and they were supported by women from the medical profession. Dr Jane Hawthorne insisted that 'women should be taught about matters so vital to themselves', a view endorsed by the Industrial Women's Organisation and Scottish socialist women who claimed that 'successive pregnancies harm women'.[94] The Scottish Co-operative Women's Guild established a Committee in 1931 to investigate the extent and causes of maternal mortality in Scotland. Based on the findings, members voted to support the dissemination of the 'instruction of constructive' birth control methods because they believed that the use of contraception would contribute to a decrease in maternal mortality.[95] This was clearly not the dominant opinion within the Labour Party or a reflection of the Labour Party's vision of womanhood, which it seems the Guild had embraced by the 1930s. Furthermore, the use of the language of their oppressors to legitimise demands, whether this was of the leaders of their own party or of the state, does not necessarily imply that women accepted the existing structures of society. This was a strategy not unique to women of the labour movement. The National Birth Control Association changed its name to the Federation of Mother's Welfare Clinics to 'convey a more constructive purpose'.[96]

Socialist women took educating and propaganda work seriously, but as far as birth control was concerned there appears to have been a quiet revolution in Scotland because of the impediments women faced. Marion Henery, a contemporary, recalled how she and other members of the Communist Party were aware of the Glasgow birth control clinic, but that it was 'very unusual' and a 'kind of keep quiet thing'. However, she attempted to interest, amongst other women in Lanarkshire, the wife of a Communist Party leader in birth control, whom, it might be noted, was horrified at the thought of using contraception.[97] Ignorance prevailed in Lanarkshire, as it did in Scotland more generally, but limited incomes also inhibited the use of contraceptives. The Federation of Mother's Welfare Clinics maintained that the principal cause of women failing to return to the clinics was their inability to pay the fees for consultation and contraceptives.[98] Male hostility also prevailed. One week before it became permissible to provide information on the availability of birth control to married women, George Buchanan, the ILP MP for the Gorbals, who had fought for equal pay for equal work, was still insisting that birth control was a middle-class ideal.[99] It seems that men's 'feminism' could be situational too! Buchanan's constitu-

[94]   *Glasgow Herald*, 16 Mar. 1925.
[95]   SCWG, Central Council Minutes, 7 Jan. and 4 Feb. 1931.
[96]   Scottish Welfare Clinics, Minute Book, 19 Oct. 1925.
[97]   William Gallagher Memorial Library, Glasgow Caledonian University, interview with Joe and Marion Henery, tape no. 7.
[98]   Scottish Welfare Clinics, Minute Book, 27 Sep. 1927.
[99]   *Forward*, 3 and 9 May 1930.

ency had a large Catholic population and this influenced how he broached the issue of birth control.

Women of the labour movement promoted and achieved their objectives, yet some were more successful than others. In west central Scotland by 1931 fifty day nurseries and child gardens were being maintained under maternal and child welfare schemes. Economic conditions resulted in closures, such as the Milton and Hutchesontown Day Nurseries in 1932, but women continued to fight for such provisions. Mrs McNab Shaw, at the behest of the ILP, fought for an 'experimental nursery in Ayrshire costing £1,000'.[100] Yet, economic considerations mediated the Scottish Co-operative Women's Guild's demands for a state-run maternity service to reduce maternal mortality.[101] The effects of the economy on considerations of women's issues were aggravated considerably in Scotland by the ILP's disaffiliation from the Labour Party in 1932. In 1925, when the ILP was at its strongest in terms of membership in Scotland, 25 per cent of Glasgow's councillors were women. However, although women maintained their presence, the proportion of women councillors declined immediately following the Labour Party's victory on Glasgow Council in 1933 and only rose above 10 per cent in 1938.[102] The ILP had acted as a think tank and a propaganda body for the Labour Party, linking the social to the political through its aims to effect municipal socialism, and this facilitated a space for women to advance their 'special interests'. This explains why it was 'under the auspices of the ILP that most of women's grass root activity took place'. It was also the ILP which challenged trade unions and the male-dominated Labour Party on issues relating to women, most notably over family endowment, widows' pensions and equal pay for equal work.

Male ILP activists promoted 'women's issues' and these were not always strictly contained within existing gender norms. Dollan and Buchanan contested married women's expulsion from work and advocated equal pay for equal work. Newbold supported the women of the party when they called for information on birth control to be made available to working-class women.[103] Kirkwood contested the Anomalies Act and the impact of unemployment on working-class women. Thus, the ILP not only provided scope for women of the ILP, the Labour Party and the Co-operative Women's Guild to work within a political framework with a tradition of accommodating diversity, but it did so with the support of many ILP men. ILP socialism also allowed women to exploit the broad ideals of municipal socialism in feminist ways. This many did, overtly and covertly, and at times in direct defiance of the attitudes of many of the men of the labour movement. However, not all women acted in this way. As highlighted in

[100] *Forward*, 21 Feb. 1931, 4 Apr. 1931 and 8 Oct. 1932.
[101] See SCWG, 37th A/R, 1930.
[102] Cairns, 'Women and the Clydeside labour movement', 106.
[103] *Forward*, 25 Sep. 1926.

Chapters two and three, Mary Sutherland and Eleanor Stewart were more accommodating of the dominant party line on women's issues. This may have owed something to their greater links with the more male-dominated areas of the labour movement as opposed to the ILP, the Labour Party in the case of Sutherland and the trade union movement in the case of Stewart. Nonetheless, in general, women of the labour movement captured the social agenda of politics and used the voting power of their constituents to advance gender-specific interests, especially at a local level. The ILP was extremely successful in urban Scotland, suggesting that there was a positive relationship between the politics of the community, women's predominance in such concerns and voting behaviour. Whilst women's acceptance of these gains within the existing division of labour may be perceived as passive, not only were the effects of the sexual division of labour challenged, but limited resources and pragmatism diminished what was obviously at times a very feminist agenda.

Women of the ILP and the Guild also argued against the imposition of marriage bars. They agitated to ensure that women who chose employment in the formal labour market should be entitled to equal pay for equal work and the right to choose the employment training they felt applicable rather than having training, especially in domestic service, foisted upon them. By contrast, the STUC demanded training schemes and suggested women be trained in 'plain cooking, mothercraft, hygiene and physical culture', evidently with the assumption that women should be confined to sex-typed occupations. Many ILP women, such as Ellen Wilkinson, also resented the assumption that women's work was a stopgap between girlhood and marriage. She pointed out that 'it is not true to say that 99 per cent of women wanted marriage and took their jobs in default of something better'.[104] Socialist women also demanded that 'the Trades Board Act should be strengthened to provide women in industry with more security'. Annie Maxton felt that the low level of wages received by husbands often compelled married women to work. Whilst she understood the hardship of the double burden she also recognised and supported women who chose to work in the formal labour market, arguing that they deserved equal pay for equal work.[105] However, the politics advanced by many women of the labour movement had a price. Equality of the sexes and the promotion of roles for men and women, which would be different but regarded as having equal value to society, limited women to either the home or the workplace. The continued necessity of married women's contribution to the family economy ensured that they endured the double burden of lower pay and benefit entitlements.

Equality of the sexes remained incompatible with demands for different but equal status for the roles of each sex when many men felt insecure.

---

[104] *Evening News*, 11 Oct. 1929 and Sinclair, '"Silenced, suppressed and passive"', 117.
[105] GTLC Executive Minutes, 4 Feb. 1926 and *Glasgow Herald*, 23 Sep. 1929.

These difficulties, although not insurmountable, were exacerbated by the attitudes and actions of the male-dominated industrial wing of the labour movement and by the links the Labour Party maintained with this wing. This ensured that women continued to be neglected as a political constituency. However, relative emancipation in the form of a redistribution of the social wage not only dispersed power but opened avenues which, because of the fixed gender roles, could be appropriated by women without direct confrontation and competition with male members who had greater resources and a tradition of activism to draw from. Despite this, women's practical politics, their 'muted language' and the symbolism of the 'personal', rather than the 'public', attached to working-class women's political agenda allowed it to be subverted and to some extent submerged beneath a politics personified as masculine. In turn, this diminished the possibilities of a more egalitarian political worldview. This was further exacerbated because of the declining influence of the ILP and its emphasis on the social aspects of the political as a significant area of concern, which ensured that socialist women were further inhibited in their aims to improve women's lives. The sense of righteousness, the zeal, the intimacy and the localism of the ILP and its promotion of social justice were replaced by the more authoritarian and bureaucratic approach of the Labour Party. This resulted in a decline of the radical tradition of populist politics that had facilitated the involvement of rank-and-file and political women in Labour politics.

Nevertheless, although women faced many obstacles and failed to achieve many of their aims, their political demands were unrelenting, even in the face of cutbacks in public spending in the 1930s. Their demands for welfare improvements, a social wage and women's right to make their own choices have largely been ignored by the male-centred historiography, which has given priority to men of the labour movement. However, these aims were vital and at times successful, and where they were not, female activists and their demands succeeded in keeping welfare at the centre of public attention. Regardless of this, the archaic vision of class advanced by the labour movement was increasingly used to sideline women's concerns and to avoid the issues they prioritised, including the effects of the sexual division of labour, birth control and female dependency. Economic conditions, social pessimism and internal vying for power within the labour movement combined to make this situation worse. In this context, women from the ILP, the Labour Party and the Co-operative Women's Guild were increasingly ill-equipped to promote a feminism that ensured that marriage and the breadwinner ideal did not 'subordinate and silence women'. Thus, working-class women had to find strategies to engage in the politics of marriage in inter-war Scotland where conflict and struggle within marriage was considerable, as the next chapter will demonstrate.

CHAPTER SIX

The Politics of Marriages of Conflict

The inter-war years were distinguished by marked changes that influenced gender relations not only in the spheres of work and politics but also within working-class families too. These years are seen to have offered women, particularly young single women, a 'new modernity', as employment opportunities extended the breadth of jobs open to them and the expansion of commercial leisure enhanced possibilities for pleasure.[1] Information on birth control and greater use of contraceptives also offered the potential to postpone marriage and reduce family size. Yet the new employment opportunities did little to alter the 'pin money' wages of women or women's economic dependency on marriage. As one contemporary unmarried woman recalled, custom and culture guaranteed that 'every girl was looking for a husband! They felt ashamed that they hadn't a man.'[2] Marriage and motherhood were actively promoted as the natural and fulfilling aspirations for women by the state, state agencies, the clergy, religious organisations and the media.[3] Ensuring the relative hegemony of this worldview was the way it saturated the pages of the press. Those who deviated from the traditional norm being promoted, especially young single women, were characterised as 'flappers' and demonised as party animals who would become future slatterns, poor wives and 'unfit' mothers.[4] The 'new' woman was identified as one who was so 'self-absorbed' that she would only 'make a good mother', when 'someone invented a combination cocktail-shaker and a cradle-rocker'.[5] Feminists and unmarried women were also presented as frigid women, lesbians and 'a danger to society, men and civilisation'.[6]

To encourage women to have more children attempts were made to propagate the 'companionate marriage' that identified a woman's role as different from her husband's, but of equal importance. Women were to be loved and respected, provided for and protected. Housing developments also helped facilitate the companionate marriage. As we saw in Chapter

---

[1] See Bingham, 'An era of domesticity?', 225–34.

[2] SOHCA/019/022/Glasgow, b. 1895.

[3] J. Bourke, *Working-Class Cultures in Britain* (London, 1994), 66.

[4] G. D. Nash, *The Crucial Era, The Great Depression and World War II, 1929–1945* (New York, 1992), 77.

[5] *Glasgow Herald*, 29 Nov. 1929.

[6] B. Brookes, 'The illegal operation: abortion, 1919–39', in London Feminist History Group (eds), *The Sexual Dynamics of History: Men's Power Women's Resistance* (London, 1983), 165–76.

three, council housing was not generally allocated to the very poor, at least until the later 1930s, but improved access to council housing in Britain nonetheless offered working-class families access to privacy and allowed the 'respectable family' to act 'as an intense domestic unit enclosed from the wider world'. This also contributed to male home-centredness which was embodied in the companionate marital ideal.[7] The marriage model became an aspiration amongst companionate sectors of the working class between the wars, but for many women it remained nothing more than an objective. Even in the decade after the Second World War few men were 'understanding' and many men 'resented the pressure' their wives put them under to achieve this ideal marriage.[8] Therefore, although there were women who gained access to new housing and who embraced the new marital ideals, many other women were denied access to the resources, economic and ideological, necessary to embrace change. For many of these women, conflict rather than companionship characterised their marriages between the wars.

The nature of work was instrumental in undermining the penetration of the companionate marriage in Scotland. According to Gittens, when men work in heavy industry and women's work is isolated in nature, as it was across much of Scotland, then a more rigid sexual division of labour develops. Women's restricted employment opportunities after marriage seemingly results in higher fertility. Scottish fertility rates did fall more slowly than was the norm in Britain between the wars. Moreover, isolated employment has been attributed to the lack of access women had to the spread of new ideas, such as those on contraception and marriage. In turn the traditional normative family ideal was replicated as defined by parents and by peers. Relationships were also more likely to be characterised by men and women participating in separate gendered tight-knit social groups and there was often an atmosphere of undeclared warfare between couples in which women faced real cruelty.[9] If this was the case, then Scottish wives may seem to compare less favourably than those in regions where the dual-income family model provided women with independence and status. In some textile regions it seems that marriages of conflict were less common and women enjoyed companionship and access to leisure with their spouses.[10]

However, Scotland too had areas where the dual-income family model prevailed, especially textile regions, where significant numbers of women were employed. Yet, women's economic contribution need not have mediated hegemonic forms of masculinity evident in areas dominated by heavy

[7] Hughes and Hunt, 'A culture transformed', 74–101.

[8] D. Gittins, *Fair Sex, Family Size and Structure, 1900–1939* (London, 1982), 40, 145 and J. Finch and P. Summerfield, 'Social reconstruction and the emergence of companionate marriage 1945–59', in D. Clark (ed.), *Marriage, Domestic Life and Social Change: Writings for Jacqueline Burgoyne (1944–88)* (London, 1991), 7–32.

[9] Gittins, *Fair Sex*, 79–80, 141–3.

[10] Roberts, *A Woman's Place*, 82–122.

industry. Many textile employers excluded married women from work, including the main textile employers in Paisley, where men worked predominantly in staple industries.[11] As Chapter two highlighted, married women were increasingly losing their jobs in textiles because of the economic climate and were therefore denied workplace resources, both economic and emotional, and information. These conditions ensured that younger women were employed in more isolated work, especially domestic service. Moreover, the nature of Scottish industrialisation, fuelled to some extent by the close proximity of natural resources, meant that many of Scotland's rural communities such as Ayrshire and Dunfermline embodied both textile and mining employment, and miners have not been noted for their egalitarian gender relations. In Dundee, which was labelled a women's town, many married women did work, but there was also significant male employment in heavy industry. Indeed, at the beginning of the twentieth century, before the effects of recession and depression reduced the number of jobs open to married women in textiles, a study highlighted that the number of male-headed households was almost double that of dual-income households in Dundee.[12] This situation appears to have mediated acceptance of companionship and shared leisure amongst working-class married men and women. In 1931, Dundee Court heard the deputations of a large number of religious and temperance bodies, and from the Dundee Trades and Labour Council, asking magistrates to reduce the opening hours of public houses on Saturdays. By doing so this group of delegates hoped to remove the temptation of male workers from the shipyards, jute mills and engineering shops to go to the public house with their wages rather than taking their earnings to where 'they ought to be delivered'. They demanded that public houses open later on Saturdays in the hope that this would address the 'frequent complaints' by wives that their husbands were getting home on Saturday 'in some instances with no pay', or 'considerably shortened amounts', because the husband had 'called at his favourite public-house on the way home, and liquidated debts which he had incurred in the previous week'.[13]

Studies have also shown that gender and poverty governed access to 'masculine republics', the main working-class male pursuits of alcohol consumption in public houses, gambling and football spectatorship between the wars. Although regulated by poverty, male expenditure on their pleasures provoked marital tensions. Spending could push a family below the poverty line and this created conflict between couples that frequently erupted into domestic violence.[14] However, deflationary policies reduced

---

[11] See Macdonald, *The Radical Thread*.

[12] See Campbell, *The Scottish Miners, Vol. One*, McIntyre, *Little Moscows* and S. Browne and J. Tomlinson, 'Dundee: A woman's town?' Paper presented at the Twentieth Century Conference, 26 Mar. 2009, University of Dundee.

[13] *Scotsman*, 15 Apr. 1931.

[14] A. Davies, 'Leisure in the "classic slum"', in Davies and Fielding, *Workers' Worlds*, 102–31.

the price of food, housing and consumer goods in the 1930s, raising real incomes. This meant that men's abuse of family wages could also affect women whose expectations were rising because of the potential for better standards of living, especially in families whose 'breadwinners' were in relatively well-paid and secure employment. Economic security was vital in providing access to 'respectable domesticity'. Thus, expenditure on male pursuits could prove detrimental and cause conflict in poorer and more affluent families. This situation was aggravated by men's inability or unwillingness to identify with companionship in marriage in contrast to women's embracing of the ideal.

Evidence from contemporary women indicates that their expectations of a 'good husband', although remaining mainly in terms of a provider, increasingly included demands for 'a caring sharing husband', not one who abused the wage or his wife. Women wanted help with childcare and shared leisure, a companion, not merely a provider. Mrs Lang sought 'a man that looked after his wife and family and took his wife out'. Mrs Jones defined a 'good man' as 'someone that handed in the pay packet, and took them to the pictures on a Saturday night'.[15] Men were aware of what was expected of the ideal husband. To be a good husband, according to Mr Coyle, 'you'd have to be loyal and true and loving and caring. My wife used one word: togetherness'. Mr Jamieson defined the 'caring sharing husband' as 'a husband that gave his wife a good allowance, took her out to the theatre or the music hall now 'n' again and gave her a holiday'. These particular men had the financial security to aspire to the companionate marriage. For many women, however, the ideal was not necessarily the reality. Mr Logan stated, 'there were plenty of good husbands. Them that didn't abuse their wives were good husbands.'[16]

Breadwinning placed an immense burden on men and it was a key component of masculinity and respectable identity.[17] However, women also carried this burden because they were responsible for keeping up the image of a respectable home life. Such a situation ensured that the economic and social priorities of both sexes could converge, but it also guaranteed that under particular economic circumstances, especially when men's ability to provide was undermined or vulnerable, that male identity could become fragile. Exacerbating these conditions was the fact that this was when working-class wives were most likely to become a 'reserve army of labour'. When they did, women competed with male workers and were seen as a threat with the potential to depreciate wages. Women's work in the informal economy also threatened the masculinity bound to the 'provider ideal' by impinging upon the male respectability linked to maintaining women

---

[15] SOHCA/019/013/Glasgow, b. 1907, SOHCA/019/011/Glasgow, b. 1917 and SOHCA/019/046/Greenock, b. 1906.

[16] SOHCA/019/036/Glasgow, b. 1895 and SOHCA/019/044/Lanarkshire, b. 1900.

[17] G. Stedman Jones quoted in S. O. Rose, 'Gender and labour history: the nineteenth century', *International Review of Social History*, 38: 205 (1993).

in the home. Hence such conditions could undermine male identity and strengthen the sense of male inability to combat social injustice, because 'respectability' in these conditions could not act as an alternative to wealth as it did in other circumstances.[18]

Prior to World War I a vast number of men worked in heavy industry; many were regarded as skilled workers and most took pride in their ability to endure hard physical toil. During the First World War there had also been a comparative social levelling between the different occupational groups of the working class. This gave semi-skilled and unskilled male workers an opportunity to express masculinity in terms of the provider ideal. The gains accrued were short-lived or precarious because of the nature of the economy, but they were there nonetheless. Masculine identity and a multiplicity of male privileges depended upon the breadwinner philosophy. Employment was an important medium from which men gained status, respect and masculine identity, but it also allowed them to accrue privileges as heads of households, especially pocket money, formal and informal leisure, and freedom from family and household responsibilities. However, there had to be a wage packet, which was no longer guaranteed because of the severity of unemployment that affected not only unskilled and semi-skilled workers, but also skilled workers, although in smaller numbers.[19] Exacerbating the situation was the expansion of 'women's work' and the necessity that compelled women to supplement their spouses' income between the wars. Intensification, deskilling and the threat and incidence of unemployment meant that many men had to accept that they were not sole breadwinners regardless of the identification of masculinity which deemed otherwise. Mr Ewart remembered that 'women kept half the houses going'. Mrs Campbell agreed. 'They all had part-time jobs, but they had to because labourers were only getting £2 a week and a tradesman was £3 6s. That was the wages.'[20]

Fluctuating wage levels, high levels of unemployment, benefit cuts and the introduction of the means test aggravated men's anxieties. Indeed, the 'devastating quality' of unemployment lay in the fact that it became 'an expectation, a way of life, not a singular misfortune'.[21] Mrs Johnson recalled the culture of apathy that existed:

> When they weren't working they just didn't bother. I don't know whether I'd say they were lazy, they just lay in bed half the day and played cards half the night, anybody that I knew. They were just idle so they just took it for granted the longer it went on.[22]

[18] G. Stedman Jones quoted in Rose, 'Gender and labour history', 205.
[19] GRA, TD1207/1-3 [170/1067E], Corporation of Glasgow Public Assistance Department Statistics: Abstracts of Cases [Heads of Households] Chargeable, 31 May. See Knox, *Industrial Nation*, 203–15.
[20] SOHCA/019/031/Glasgow, b. 1908 and SOHCA/019/04/Glasgow, b. 1910.
[21] T. C. Smout, *A History of the Scottish People 1830–1950* (Glasgow, 1990), 67–8, 117.
[22] SOHCA/019/025/Paisley, b. 1914.

Furthermore, many of those who found secure employment often had to accept that their wages were insufficient to maintain the family unit. As the 1930s progressed, wages in the sheltered industries were curbed and to some extent brought into line with those of other occupations. Although men's incomes often had to be supplemented, undermining masculine status based upon sole provision, women had had a long tradition of supplementing their husbands' incomes; this was not the preserve of unskilled workers.[23] The image of the female usurper discussed in Chapter one, therefore, indicates that it was the context that changed rather than the economic structure of the family unit. A combination of economic insecurity, the force of the reassertion of masculinity, as defined by the breadwinner ideal, and new economic, social and political opportunities for women, caused male insecurity, rather than men's inability to provide for and maintain a wife at home.

Inter-war masculinity is also seen to have been challenged by a sexual revolution that was aggravated by the public debate over female sexuality and which resulted in men internalising fears about their own sexuality. This corresponded with the introduction of contraception and the greater economic and leisure-based freedoms enjoyed by women. Combined with the coverage given to the notion of the sexually liberated woman by the clergy and the media, female sexuality gained widespread attention.[24] In addition, although working-class women remained relatively ignorant of the availability and growing social acceptance of contraceptives, knowledge and availability was increasing. The debate over birth control and the possibility that more working-class women could choose to limit family size could have contributed to men's insecurity, especially given the form which many working-class women were forced to adopt to control their fertility. For many women the only form of family limitation entailed 'having no more fun'. As already discussed in Chapter five Scotland lagged behind England in the provision of knowledge and availability of contraception and in the establishment of birth control clinics. In major cities like Glasgow fewer than ten women per week were examined in such clinics.[25] The situation had improved, if marginally by the later 1930s, but not dramatically enough to contribute to a 'sexual revolution'.

The physical and emotional scars of war, the sex imbalance in Scotland and the 'manliness' needed to endure and work in heavy industry by contrast could have resulted in women being attracted to an exaggerated masculinity just as the foundations of masculinity were being undermined by structural and ideological change. The Boer War followed in quick succession by the First World War caused an imbalance of the sexes and this was compounded by the visibility of 'ex-soldiers in bad shape mentally and

---

[23] See E. Ross, *Love and Toil: Motherhood in Outcast London 1870–1918* (Oxford, 1993).

[24] Adams, *A Woman's Place* (London, 1975), 84–6.

[25] SOHCA/019/025/Paisley, b. 1914 and Bourke, *Working-Class Cultures*, 55–6.

physically' such as those in Scotland who 'dragged themselves about, some on crutches with an empty trouser leg, or a sleeve crudely sewn up swinging in the wind'.[26] There is also evidence that the number of women exceeded that of men. In Glasgow boys under the age of 15 outnumbered girls by 732 in 1921, but by the age of 15 and over, females outnumbered males by 25,770. In textile areas the imbalance of the sexes tended to be greater at a time when women's employment opportunities and economic independence were being undermined by structural unemployment. This was exacerbated by male emigration: between 1920 and 1922, 390,000 more people left Scotland than entered it. From 1921 to 1926, 49,852 metalworkers and 23,193 engineers from Glasgow were amongst the skilled male workers who emigrated. Scotland also had a relatively high male mortality rate, a feature of heavy industrial occupations.[27] Thus, young widowhood was an ever-present possibility. Perhaps this explains Mrs Gallacher's sentiments. She had a 'good husband', who was, 'rough and ready and he liked his drink', but she remained 'a wee bit frightened of him' throughout her marriage. These factors may well also have underpinned a masculine self-image which was aggressive and synonymous with violence.

Structural, cultural and economic impediments destabilised masculinity and many men experienced vulnerability. However, working-class men could reassert their masculinity in alternative ways, using aspects of popular culture and control over the resources of the family unit. In this environment 'manly' recreational pursuits would provide a means of symbolically expressing masculinity, as well as acting as an arena from which to absorb male identity. Many of the respondents compared their husbands unfavourably with their fathers when discussing knowledge of men's wage levels, the handing over of unbroken pay packets, levels of male pocket money, abusive expenditure of family resources and levels of domestic violence. Indeed, the majority of the men interviewed perceived their wives not as exalted mothers and homemakers, but often as jailers who had the responsibility of 'keeping a good clean home and looking after you'.[28] Women's definition of their role highlights the expectations placed upon them. A good wife was 'a person that kept the house clean, looked after the food, looked after the children, and looked after the money, because she was always the poor soul that was left with the money'.[29] To fulfil this role and command respect, women had to control the family income. Although

---

[26] Adams, *A Woman's Place*, 84–6 and R. Glasser, *Growing Up in the Gorbals* (London, 1987), 48.

[27] *Census*, 1921. See also M. Anderson, 'Population and family life', in Dickson and Treble, *People and Society in Scotland, Vol. III*, 14, 17, 19.

[28] SOHCA/019/015/Glasgow, b. 1909. See also A. Davies, 'Youth gangs, masculinity and violence in late Victorian Manchester and Salford', *Journal of Social History*, 32, 2: 349–70 (1998) and Johnston and McIvor, 'Dangerous work, hard men and broken bodies', 135–51.

[29] SOHCA/019/044/Lanarkshire, b. 1900.

by no means confined to Scotland, this meant that the struggle over family resources and the practice of gender-specific spending priorities created conflict and marked gender relations.[30]

The pursuit of particular forms of leisure, from which women were culturally excluded, remained of immense consequence to many men between the wars and represented an arena of conflict for the control of family incomes. This was inconsistent with the ideals of the companionate marriage. Participation in aspects of popular culture continued to allow an expression of masculinity when the foundations of masculinity became insecure symbolically, if not quantitatively. Such expenditure impinged upon women's gender roles as household managers and was contested because it reduced women's power and inhibited their self-image. This ensured that sexual antagonism prevailed although the context changed. An article entitled 'The Docile Wife' appeared in the *Govan Press* in 1931 caricaturing conflict in marriage, and highlighting the perceived cultural changes that had occurred within marriage. The article questioned 'today's women' who were 'thumped' by their spouses. Yet it was not the husbands who 'amazed' the author, but the wives, because 'even the wife of a riveter who came home drunk in the olden days found the best way to put him to sleep and prevent him from going out for more drink was to hit him over the head with a ladle'. This gave wives 'the chance of going through pockets' to retrieve money that had been extracted from the wage. The article continued, 'truly the women of today are a tame lot'. Gone is the 'fun of a Saturday night' watching 'wives escort their "loving husbands" home when the pubs shut'. Gone also were the 'perennial Saturday night rows' that 'were a source of entertainment to the neighbours'. After all, 'without the pictures and wireless how would you expect poor working-class folk to enjoy themselves? All this fighting and quarrelling was only recreation.' The writer lamented, 'Alas for the jolly honest old times. There was certainly more drink consumed, but there were fewer divorces.'[31]

The 'docile wife' indicates that a cultural shift in women's responses to marital conflict, male drunkenness and violence occurred, with resultant transformations in the gendered power relations within marriages of conflict. Discourses that demonised female violence and idealised feminine dependency increasingly reduced women's capacity to respond to male violence, while doing nothing to alter an acceptance of wife-beating, especially if the alternative was a higher divorce rate that would undermine marriage and motherhood. However, the way that family violence in working-class neighbourhoods was ignored, representations of who the abusers were, and what drove them to violence correlates with discourses that permeated

[30] SOHCA/019/08/Glasgow, b. 1916.
[31] See P. Ayers and J. Lambertz, 'Marriage relations, money and domestic violence in working-class Liverpool 1919–39', in J. Lewis (ed.), *Labour and Love: Women's Experience of Home and Family, 1850–1940* (Oxford, 1986), 195–210.

British society from the late eighteenth century through to the inter-war years.[32] Wife-beating was identified with working-class marriages, caused by men's indulgence in aspects of working-class male popular culture, most notably alcohol consumption, gambling and sport, rather than individual deviance or particular forms of masculinity that depended on physical rather than moral control.

However, it has been argued that the discursive and legal contexts of domestic violence changed in the nineteenth century. Courts widened their definitions of violence and progressively found all forms of marital violence unacceptable, even against the most 'recalcitrant' wife. The penetration of a 'softer patriarchy' involving demonstrations of a more ordered, rational and non-violent masculinity ensured that men who failed to comply and acted violently towards women could expect harsh consequences from the criminal justice system. Although there was a considerable resistance to the attack on customary conceptions of masculinity by the end of the Victorian era, seemingly, a 'reasonable non-violent male' had emerged in all strata of society.[33] Such arguments ignore the distinctiveness of Scotland's legal, religious and cultural environment which mediated condemnation of violent men in the nineteenth and early twentieth centuries. For example a women's provocation continued to be widely accepted as extenuating circumstances in a defence, even in murder trials, and it was not until the end of the nineteenth century that a wife was considered a competent witness against her husband.[34]

Continuities in the discursive and legal contexts corresponded with a greater emphasis being placed on marriage after World War I and undermined the dissemination of alternative discourses that would challenge this dominant conception of wife-beating. Social scientists and social commentators chose to denigrate many areas of male popular culture, linking these to domestic conflict rather than tackling the problem head on. Dependence on a male breadwinner and the power of religion also fused to ensure that few women were ideologically equipped to leave an abusive relationship.[35] Women claimed to be trapped in marriages of conflict because 'It didn't matter what happened it was the women to blame' and due to the fact that, 'you'd nowhere to go. Your mother couldn't take you in because they all had big families, so it was impossible to run back to your

---

[32] *Govan Press*, 13 Feb. 1931.

[33] A. Hughes, 'Representations and counter-representations of domestic violence on Clydeside between the two World Wars', *Labour History Review*, 69, 2: 169–84 (2004).

[34] See M. Wiener, *Men of Blood: Violence, Manliness, and Criminal Justice in Victorian England* (Cambridge, 2004), 4–7 and passim, and J. A. Hammerton, *Cruelty and Companionship: Conflict in Nineteenth-Century Married Life* (London, 1995), 65.

[35] See C. A. Conley, 'Atonement and domestic homicide in late Victorian Scotland', in Richard McMahon (ed.), *Crime, Law and Popular Culture in Europe, 1500–1900* (Devon, 2008), Hughes, 'Representations' and L. Farmer, *Criminal Law, Tradition and Legal Order: Crime and the Genius of Scots Law, 1747 to the Present* (Cambridge, 1997), 73–4.

people' and 'your mother taught you, if you made your bed you lie in it. We were all told that.'[36]

Thus, the economic, ideological and recreational structures and the discursive context created an environment in which gender conflict thrived. Scottish women claimed that in the 1920s and 1930s 'it was a normal thing for a man to abuse his wife' and 'there really was a lot of wife-battering'. So common was sexual antagonism that respondents openly discussed experiences in the 1990s, often without resort to direct questioning. Mrs Gallacher recollected the neighbourliness of Springburn, Glasgow: 'All the people would have a sing-song. There were many people that fought and men that were bad to their wives. One man, he was awful bad to his wife. He'd take this stick and near kill her. That didn't make any difference to us. We'd take her in and watch her.'[37] In Scotland's mining communities a high level of wife-beating existed and even in the 1980s the saying that a good wife was one who could cook, clean and 'take a smack in the mouth' prevailed.[38] Lest such behaviour should be regarded as unrepresentative, Scottish wives are cited in inter-war publications highlighting family violence. Dr Robertson, a resident of Glasgow's Gorbals, was well acquainted with this area's inhabitants. In response to the Gorbals' 'No Mean City' image and in collaboration with the local beat policeman for the Gorbals between 1923 and 1930, he wrote, *Gorbals Doctor*. In this they argue:

> The most common kind of violence was wife-assault, particularly on a Friday or Saturday night between 11pm and 1am. Normally a child of between eight and fourteen years of age would come rushing into the Southern Division Police Station shouting: 'Ma faither's killin' ma mither.'[39]

High levels of wife-beating were exacerbated by various determinants which operated as constraints to married women.

By the twentieth century in Scotland although men were punished for wife abuse, they were rarely convicted for a first offence. Instead they were generally put on probation or cautioned if the offence was deemed less severe. For subsequent offences graduating fines were imposed before jail sentences were mandatory. Baillie Davidson, when 'imposing a monetary penalty' on Joseph Dickson, who beat his wife because he did not get his 'tea', stated, 'the proper thing to do is for you to go to prison', but he maintained that could not impose this sentence because it was the defendant's first appearance in court. In Kirkcaldy an unemployed labourer tortured his wife by filling her mouth with burning paper. He received his first jail sentence – twenty-one days' imprisonment. This was his fifth offence. In

---

[36] M. Tebbutt, *Making Ends Meet: Pawnbroking and Working-Class Credit* (Leicester, 1983), 38.

[37] SOHCA/019/014/Glasgow, b. 1911, SOHCA/019/018/Glasgow, b. 1909 and SOHCA/019/03/Glasgow, b. 1910, respectively.

[38] SOHCA/019/014/Glasgow, b. 1911.

[39] Campbell, *Scottish Miners*, 235.

Elgin a man hit his wife repeatedly over the head with a frying pan. He had thirteen previous convictions for assaulting her and received three months' imprisonment. On hearing the sentence this man turned to his wife and smiled before exclaiming, 'Three months, Elsie.' The threat was clear from his wife's response. The women fainted and had to be carried from the court.[40]

Contemporary women also believed that 'the police were never anxious to deal with domestic trouble'.[41] However, the police, courts and agencies of social welfare were aware of the penalties women incurred when they prosecuted abusive spouses. The Society of St Vincent De Paul took a four-year-old boy into their Rutherglen Children's Refuge in 1925 because his mother was 'existing on the charity of friends'. His father's whereabouts were unknown, but the child's mother was unable to apply for Parish Relief in case her husband was 'found and punished' for not maintaining his family. This had already occurred and she in return 'had received brutal treatment on his release'.[42] Scottish courts and social welfare agencies were also inclined to shore up marriage rather than prosecute abusive men. Thus, when Mrs McNeil took her husband to court for assaulting her, the magistrate lamented, 'It is unfortunate to see husband and wife living like cat and dog.' He asked the defendant and his victim, 'Are you willing to try to make a happier life?' He then went on to tell the husband, 'I will put you on probation for twelve months and see if you can come to some happier way of living.' By 1932, the Scottish Justices and Magistrates Association was calling for 'Family Courts' to deal with intimate domestic problems. They pointed out that there was more than 10,000 separation orders per annum in Britain because the courts were unable to go beyond the strictly legal definition of the case. In the proposed new Family Courts, where possible, reconciliation would be facilitated through the use of social workers.[43]

The ability to mend marriages was extended with the Probation of Offenders Act (Scotland) 1907. The Scottish probation service was used to rationalise punishment; in using leniency, some defendants were defined as 'deserving and others as undeserving of mercy'. The probation service was also part of the 'diagnosing of offending'. Thus, the defendant's age, social background, character and 'any extenuating circumstance' were significant in whether probation was regarded as an appropriate punishment.[44] Under this system wife-beaters could use a range of provocations available to them as 'extenuating circumstances' and they could exploit

---

[40] G. G. Robertson, *Gorbals Doctor* (London, 1975), 130–5. See also Spring Rice, *Working-class Wives*, 115–16, 141–2 and passim, and E. Rathbone, *The Disinherited Family, A Plea for Direct Provision for the Costs of Child Maintenance through Family Allowances* (London, 1927).

[41] *Govan Press*, 28 Sep. 1923 and *Scotsman*, 4 Oct. 1930 and 4 Jan. 1939.

[42] SOHCA/019/026/Glasgow, b. 1917.

[43] Society for St Vincent de Paul (Scotland) [hereafter SVDP], Annual Report, 1931.

[44] *Govan Press*, 28 Sep. 1923 and *Glasgow Herald*, 18 Oct. 1932.

Table 6.1 Adult men (over 21 years) as a percentage of all individuals given probation orders for assault, housebreaking and theft in Scotland, 1930–6.

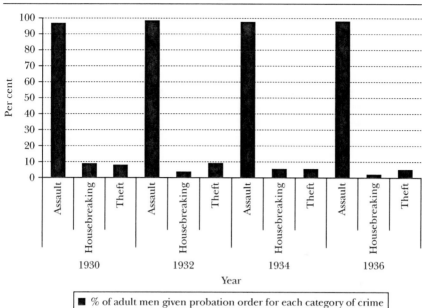

Source: Parliamentary Papers, *Report on Judicial Statistics of Scotland*, 1930, 1932, 1934 and 1936.

their work reputations to mediate the violent reputation being presented in court. Indeed, the Probation Act was extended in 1931, by which time probation was identified with marriage mending. Using probation men who had assaulted their wives were to be taught the 'privileges and responsibilities of being a husband' and the wives who had been assaulted were to be instructed in the 'arts of home-making'.[45] Clearly, the idea that wife-beating was a product of women's provocation was enshrined in this concept. Furthermore, Table 6.1 indicates how, in relation to other crimes, the adult men who were deemed most deserving of 'mercy' were men who committed assaults. Press reports indicate that these men were those who assaulted their wives.

In the role of marriage mending the courts often accepted a woman's lack of housekeeping skills as provocation. Men therefore were apt to vilify their spouse's home-making abilities as a justification for abusive behaviour and any personal trait that might undermine this role, especially drunkenness. Walter Parker was charged with locking his wife in a room,

[45] F. McNeill, 'Remembering probation in Scotland', *Probation Journal*, 52, 23: 23–32 (2005).

stripping her and 'thrashing' her with a buckled belt while his daughter stood outside listening to her mother's screams. He justified his behaviour by claiming that his wife was of 'drunken habits'. The *Daily Record* reported on how the bench 'posed a number of questions with a view to getting an admission' from Mrs Parker that she was of 'drunken habits'. She denied the allegation and asserted that her husband wanted 'to be rid of her' and therefore 'made her life unbearable'. On the victim's evidence and that of her daughter, the magistrate told Mrs Parker that he was prepared to imprison her husband, but only if she presented herself to a doctor to prove that she had been beaten. However, Mr Parker avoided prosecution because his wife refused to submit medical evidence of the beating and asked that her husband be put on probation because she had the welfare of her five children to consider.[46]

The general acceptance of wife abuse by the authorities and its visibility in working-class localities also created a situation whereby victims of male abuse could identify with the 'perfect personification of womanhood', the 'self-sacrificing long suffering wife'. The media endorsed this personification. The *Govan Press* reported on how Alexander Weir was given probation for assaulting his wife while he was 'mad with drink' because of the 'sympathy of the courts for a forgiving wife'.[47] This also highlights another problem facing victims who took their husbands to court: male drunkenness was seen to reduce a man's culpability. However, men's attempts to undermine women were often ineffective when their wives could show that they had transgressed the masculine ideal of protector and provider. Robert Wilkie, a Paisley labourer was sentenced to six months in prison for family violence. It was reported that he was addicted to drink, in contrast to his wife who was 'a most industrious woman' who was 'able, through hard work, when her husband was in the army, to build up a comfortable home. Since his return to civic life he had reduced it to a 'squalid, poverty-stricken dwelling'.[48]

Yet many working-class women also accepted the representation that linked male violence with aspects of popular culture. Not only were they victims constrained in violent marriages by economic and social impediments, but they were also constrained by gender pressures. By the twentieth century women were not expected to defend themselves physically in marriages of conflict. Those who did could expect little sympathy from the courts or the agencies of social welfare, and they could often expect to be ridiculed in their own communities. As a result of this, many women accepted some level of abuse as a fact of life, and internalised the discourse

---

[46] *Daily Record*, 25 and 26 May 1932.

[47] *Daily Record*, 9 Jan. 1924.

[48] *Govan Press*, 14 Sep. 1923 and J. Rowbotham, '"Only when drunk": the stereotyping of violence in England, c.1850–1900', in S. D'Cruze (ed.), *Everyday Violence in Britain, 1850–1950, Gender and Class* (Harlow, 2000), 155–69.

that wife-beating was caused by popular culture, not individual men. Thus, the general consensus of the women interviewed for this study was that 'the man getting over-loaded with drink' caused discord between married couples. Others maintained, 'Money was the one thing, because they didn't have it.'[49] Men's answers tended to be less composed but they supported the view that conflict over men's expenditure of the family income was considerable. Mr Gordon recalled that

> A lot of men didn't give their wife the wages that they should've. That caused arguments. Women wanted money to run the house and they didn't get it, while men were away drinking and gambling. These were some of the wrong things and, I'm not trying to make out I'm a great person. I've got faults like all the rest.

Indeed, the lack of composure and the assertion, 'I'm not trying to make out I'm a great person. I've got faults like all the rest', is a cultural admission of complicity in such behaviour. Thus, conflict over the wage ensured that a good husband was equally defined as 'a man who brought his pay home and didn't spend it in the pub on the road home'.[50] But many men did spend their wages in this way, so that disputes over money and male expenditure on leisure were a major source of tension between couples. Wives whose husbands did not behave in this way expressed the view that they were 'very lucky'.[51]

Conflict over men's spending between the wars might have been reduced by housing developments that involved the separation of work and living environments and offered opportunities for greater levels of male home-centredness. Some wives also benefited from the constraints that poverty placed on men's access to leisure. Clearly convictions for drunkenness fell along with the consumption of spirits and the licensing of public houses in Scotland.[52] Yet, as Table 6.2 highlights, the decline was not particularly significant in the 1920s.

By the 1930s, however, the consumption of alcohol had diminished to just over a quarter of that consumed in 1900 and no doubt this was influenced by the effects of the depression.[53] Many public houses were also closed as part of the slum clearance of the period and they were not replaced in the new housing estates. Greater restrictions were also placed on drinking hours and tax on alcohol increased. The *Glasgow Citizen* attributed the 'slump' in whisky drinking to 'heavy duties and light purses'.[54] However, although the statistical evidence suggests a decrease in consumption and

[49] *Daily Record*, 19 Oct. 1924.
[50] SOHCA/019/003/Glasgow, b. 1907, SOHCA/019/08/Glasgow, b. 1916, SOHCA/019/020/Glasgow, b. 1895 and SOHCA/019/043/Clydebank, b. 1920.
[51] SOHCA/019/06/Glasgow, b. 1907.
[52] Smout, *Scottish People*, 134–7.
[53] Knox, *Industrial Nation*, 197.
[54] *Citizen*, 9 Jan. 1923.

Table 6.2 Licensed premises and whisky consumption, Scotland, 1923–7.

Year	Number of public houses	Number of licensed grocers	Whisky consumed (gallons)
1923	5,933	2,784	2,757,190
1924	5,904	2,782	2,641,323
1925	5,827	2,698	2,532,494
1926	5,871	2,643	2,453,838
1927	5,832	2,642	2,099,235

Source: *Glasgow Herald*, 28 Feb. 1929.

drunkenness, men may have consumed much more alcohol than the figures imply. Legislation made it increasingly difficult for adolescents to consume alcohol and there is evidence to support the view that it was after the First World War that pubs became masculine domains in other areas of Britain.[55] Of the women interviewed for this book only one stated that she drank alcohol, except on special occasions when 'a sherry' was deemed respectable. Male respondents confirmed this. Mr Ewart was a barman between the wars. He stated, 'You couldn't turn round and say, "Get the hell out of here." You'd say, "Excuse me, you're not allowed to sell drink to a woman".' Mr Davidson actually believed that 'women were barred. They must've been barred because I never mind of seeing a woman.' In the mining district of Craigneuk, 'every public house bore the legend "No Women Allowed"'.[56] Women were never legally barred from public houses. Publicans created these 'masculine republics' because their male customers expected it of them. Further, not only were women culturally barred from public houses, but few females were employed there either. By 1931, entertainment and leisure was the fastest-growing industry in Glasgow, but at this time there were only 238 barmaids as opposed to 3,173 barmen and most of the barmaids worked in hotels. Paisley had 18 barmaids and 150 barmen, whilst Greenock had 6 barmaids and 164 barmen.[57]

Not only do the statistics fail to provide any indication of who was consuming alcohol, but they also underestimate how much alcohol was being consumed because illicit drinking in shebeens prevailed. Amongst the illegal stills discovered by the police were those in a dance hall in Budhill, in the outskirts of Glasgow, and another in an Airdrie home. Anthony Simons was fined £10 for 'trafficking exciseable liquor' from a hairdressing and tobacconist premises.[58] Shebeens were discovered in the 1920s in

[55] See E. Ross, 'Survival networks: women's neighbourhood sharing in London before World War 1', *History Workshop*, 15: 4–27 (1983).

[56] SOHCA/019/031/Glasgow, b. 1908, SOHCA/019/030/Glasgow, b. 1900 and Campbell, *Scottish Miners*, 239.

[57] *Census*, 1931.

[58] *Govan Press*, 29 Jan. and 11 May 1923, *Daily Record*, 21 May 1932.

regions across Scotland from Paisley to Wick. Methylated spirit was also used to make alcoholic beverages.[59]

Poverty may have regulated expenditure, but it did not ensure sobriety, while price rises ensured that men drank 'greater quantities of beer to supplement the more expensive spirits'. The Amulree Report stressed that this was often at the expense of family necessities.[60] Unemployed Neil Robertson of Dalmuir, a father of five children, was fined 20/- for attacking his wife while drunk. At his trial it was reported that his Parish Relief had been stopped because he spent the family's income on alcohol. In lieu of his benefit, his wife received vouchers to obtain necessities from local shops. Mr Robertson's response was to strip his home of anything the pawn would accept for money for alcohol.[61] Mrs Jones remembered that 'there was a pub on the corner and the unemployed used to go into it and it was jungle juice they called it. See when they got a glass of jungle juice, God they were in the jungle'.[62]

However, men did not have to drink excessively to act aggressively, as behaviour is situational. It was not drunkenness that caused aggression, but rather it was the 'expectation of aggressive behaviour' or the 'provocation to aggress'.[63] The home was the terrain in which the struggle over resources took place so that the expectation and provocation to behave aggressively, as perceived by many husbands, was a wife's challenge to his 'right' to spend 'his' wage on alcohol. And there were many women who did challenge such expenditure through their expectations of a good husband and directly, because it disempowered them if they did not. There were women who determined that 'if a man came into me drunk, by God he would've went out quicker than he came in!' Mrs Galbraith stated, 'I don't know what other men did, but my man and my father always gave over the pay packet. That kept the peace.' Some women 'would go straight to the work and ask' how much their husbands earned.[64] Other women were subject to violence when 'desperation of unpaid bills and hungry children' sent them into public houses to 'drag out their poor foolish husbands with the remnants of their pay packets'. Others were 'battered in public houses for having the temerity to demand a share of a man's wage'.[65] The identification of the poor husband with drunkenness and violence ensured that men's guilt could compound the situation, because they knew what was expected of a good husband. He was 'a man that went home and took

[59] Glasgow University Archives, DC19/4/2/2, Records of the Scottish Temperance Movement and 'The Story Writes Itself, Crime, 1925–1929', Press Cuttings, *Dundee Courier*, 14 Jan. 1926.

[60] J. Levy, *Drink: An Economic And Social Study* (London, 1951), 6, 30–1, 69–71.

[61] *Evening News*, 8 Jan. 1929.

[62] SOHCA/019/011/Glasgow, b. 1917.

[63] B. D. Hore, 'Alcohol And Crime', *Alcohol And Alcoholism*, 6: 435–9 (1988).

[64] SOHCA/019/08/Glasgow, b. 1916, SOHCA/019/019/Glasgow, b. 1907 and SOHCA/019/ 07/Glasgow, b. 1911.

[65] Campbell, *Scottish Miners*, 235 and Knox, *Industrial Nation*, 197.

out his pay poke unopened, "Here you are darling. There you are." She'd open it and give him his pocket money.' He was also 'one that stayed out the pub'.[66]

However, many men resorted to secret spending which entailed denying wives knowledge of how much they earned.[67] Mr Gordon's recollections signify how this operated. In answer to the question, did men let their wives know how much they earned, he replied, 'Oh no! That would have been terrible, your wife knowing that!' He stated that men would take as much 'pocket money' as they could. Mr Davidson related how 'some men would get their pay packet' and after giving their wives their housekeeping, 'he'd have as much in his pocket'.[68] This inhibited women from identifying with respectability by reducing their resources and it also imposed an incredible burden upon them.

> You never knew what your man earned. You got your housekeeper's money and that was it. You'd £2 10/-. You did what you wanted . . . He never asked, what about his rent book, but he knew what I was capable of doing. There were others who couldn't pay the rents. People hadn't the coppers.[69]

Mrs O'Neil stated that her husband, a skilled tradesman, 'went off the rails sometimes'. She recalled, 'His wages were three pounds. I got two pounds and he got one pound. I couldn't tell you much he earned when the wages got bigger. They varied, I suppose.' Describing the difficulties of being a wife, she maintained, 'money was a big problem. We used to say to ourselves, how can I make ends meet with this money? My husband was a tradesman and still the biggest wage he came home with was three pounds.'[70]

Concealing and controlling the true level of the wage allowed many men secret spending on masculine recreation in Scotland, where a 'strong correlation between manliness and the ability to consume a great deal of alcohol' existed and where 'cultural constraints restricted male affiliation' but alcohol allowed its manifestation.[71] The pub, therefore, was an 'institution where men increasingly had their masculinity recognised and reinforced', and where they 'learned they were entitled to power' and 'how to keep it'.[72] Pub culture was associated with manliness and permitted a means of expression and absorption of manly identity at a time when men's identities were insecure. However, it was not excessive alcohol consumption that

---

[66] SOHCA/019/030/Glasgow, b. 1900 and SOHCA/019/042/Glasgow, b. 1915.

[67] Davies, 'Leisure in the "classic slum"', 105.

[68] SOHCA/019/043/Clydebank, b. 1902 and SOHCA/019/030/Glasgow, b. 1900 respectively.

[69] SOHCA/019/05/Glasgow, b. 1912.

[70] SOHCA/019/016/Glasgow, b. 1905.

[71] L. Tiger, *Men in Groups* (London, 1969), 184–5.

[72] V. Hey, *Patriarchy and Pub Culture* (London, 1986), 10.

caused wife-beating, contrary to popular perceptions of men's pastimes, but this discourse allowed men access to disavowal. Having catalogued how his frequent drunkenness had a terrible effect upon his family, Mr Scott responded rather vaguely to the question, 'Did you hit your wife?' by answering, 'To the best of my knowledge, no.'[73] The need for interview composure contributed to his response, but this was a form of disavowal practised by many husbands. Rather than acknowledging aberrant behaviour, disavowal under the guise of impaired memory, due to excessive alcohol consumption, allowed men the power of expenditure regardless of the consequences to their families, reinforced by the threat and incidence of violence.

Street gambling was also represented as catalytic to the incidence of gender conflict. Victorian moralists perceived gambling as an excessive vice, contributing to the poverty, misery and brutality of working-class family life. These views contributed to the introduction of legislation, culminating in the Gambling Act of 1906 that prohibited working-class gambling, but allowed the upper classes to continue to participate unabated. That it did so detracts from a predilection to view gambling as a symptom of poverty. What it does imply is that although gambling is synonymous with a dream of instant wealth, it is much more than this. In fact, given the rise in the propensity to gamble between the wars in Scotland, gambling could be read as part of the shift in working-class mentalities from a belief in 'notions of progress, solidarity and religious faith' to belief in 'luck, chance and fate', reflecting a process of 'individuation, atomisation or anomie'.[74] The adverse economic climate undermined notions of progress and moderated trade union solidarity, whilst, as will be highlighted, men were, to a much greater extent than women, turning from religion. Yet, the lure of a flutter was also a means of establishing 'character', the main qualities of which were 'gameness, gallantry, courage, integrity, composure and presence of mind', many of the attributes associated with the employment under threat between the wars. In this context gambling provided 'the possibility of effecting reputation in a society which had all but arranged action out of everyday life'.[75]

Gambling was also enhanced by the element of deviance and offered the participants the status of rebel, winner and even a good loser. Mrs Lang remembered, 'My man, he'd have pawned the shirt off his back. He put a lot of money on, because when he won he won.' Mrs Reid's husband 'loved to gamble'. It was 'his only vice. His whole pocket money went back, although somebody told me he was quite a lucky winner.' It is also clear that some women were denied knowledge not only of wages, but of other sources of men's income too. Mrs McQueen recalled, 'he'd have emptied your purse in a minute. I'd to hide all my money. He was a good loser right

[73] SOHCA/019/042/Glasgow, b. 1915.
[74] Gittins, *Fair Sex*, 57.
[75] D. M. Downes et al., *Gambling, Work and Leisure* (London, 1976), 27–40.

enough and he didn't win very often.'[76] Men recalled how a win felt: 'oh you felt like a millionaire. A couple a bob was a lot of money too. A pint of beer cost you 4d at that time.'[77] Gambling had strong links with Scotland's pub culture. Mr Armstrong recalled:

> You used to get the *Topical Times*, and my father picked some horses . . . and they all won. He sent me along with the line. He said, 'It comes to nearly two pound ten.' So I went along and brought the money back. He gave me a dollar and oh he was down the pub with all his mates and they were all drunk for days.[78]

This heightened the potential for gambling to contribute to gender conflict because some men would 'do without food to keep the money for gambling'. Mrs MacIntosh was a victim of wife-beating. She also worked to supplement her husband's unemployment benefit. She recollected how her husband and his gambling associates would stand at the street corner and 'they'd all a drink in them. I turned and said, "What's left for eating? Have you had your pals up?"' When her husband returned home he was annoyed that she had challenged him in front of his acquaintances and his 'pals' used to say, 'I wouldn't take that off her.' These men felt the need to defuse the threat to masculinity through violence that was 'ever present if not indulged', which characterised marriages of conflict rather than companionship.[79]

However, it has been suggested that working-class gambling was not excessive and was relative to income with stakes ranging from 6d to 2/6.[80] Measurements of gambling relative to income could be gender-specific. Mrs Gallacher catalogued how a family of eleven could be fed 'for near three days on 2/6'.[81] For many families bets of 2/6 could represent the difference between living on the margins or below the poverty line, while more excessive gambling could also mean the difference between average and comfortable living conditions for more affluent families. In 1926, excluding those who escaped, 131 men were arrested after the police raided a Glasgow tenement backcourt that was being used for the purposes of organised pitch-and-toss gambling. The magistrate read out a letter from a wife, who asked to remain anonymous for fear of reprisals. She had appealed to the authorities to 'raid the gambling hell' because her

---

[76] SOHCA/019/019/Glasgow, b. 1907, SOHCA/019/08/Glasgow, b. 1916 and SOHCA/019/014/Glasgow, b. 1911 respectively.

[77] SOHCA/019/030/Glasgow, b. 1900.

[78] SOHCA/019/027/Glasgow, b. 1905.

[79] SOHCA/019/014/Glasgow, b. 1909 and J. Hammerton, 'The targets of rough music: respectability and domestic violence in Victorian England', *Gender and History*, 3, 1: 36 (1991).

[80] M. Clapson, *A Bit of a Flutter: Popular Gambling and English Society, c1823–1961* (Manchester, 1992), 10, 27, 48, 210.

[81] SOHCA/019/015/Glasgow, b. 1909.

husband was 'gambling the money he gets from the Parish, leaving me and my children wanting'. Her letter was signed 'One of the many sufferers'.[82]

There exists a substantial body of evidence to refute the assertion that gambling was relative to income. The amount spent at dog tracks in Britain rose from £10,000,000 to £75,300,000 per annum between 1927 and 1938. At the oldest of the three greyhound tracks in the city of Edinburgh, Powderhall, it was estimated that average daily attendance was 5,000, with about £500 placed on bets per night. On a Saturday night £1,200 was spent at only one of the totalisator machines.[83] Street gambling also escalated, particularly in working-class communities where it was associated with sport. Ms Stewart maintained that the working class were 'running after the bookies'. Ms Stewart's assertion may reflect the dominant discourses on gambling but Croy, in Lanarkshire, with a population of around 'two hundred people', had three bookies.[84] Indeed, the ILP estimated that there were between 10,000 and 20,000 bookmakers in Scotland in 1920 and that the working classes spent around £5,000,000 per annum on betting. In 1929, *Forward* reported that a bookmaker responsible for 148 closes in Plantation Street in Glasgow took £35 per day prior to 1914. By 1923 he was making an estimated £300 each day in the flat season.[85]

There also existed the propensity to gamble in different ways, some of which are unquantifiable. Betting on horses, dogs, football coupons, pitch-and-toss, and card playing were among the variety of ways to gamble, as was betting on cock-fighting, for which twelve men were convicted in April 1933. Mrs Gallacher's husband was a bookmaker's runner. She recollected how 'what the men used to do if anybody was in trouble or if anybody needed their rent paid, they used to say, "Can we have a game of cards in your house?" Each winner contributed a penny towards the rent arrears.'[86] Gambling provided a source of employment for working-class people and some women could gain from this, although often at the expense of someone else's family. One son recalled how his father 'took horse bets, dog bets, football bets and boxing bets, but when he got that done he'd drink the winnings. He didn't know when to stop because it went to his head.'[87] Rather than being relative to income, gambling was often intrin-sically linked to the pursuit of masculinity, exacerbating marital tension. Gambling held the capacity to push many families to the margins or below

[82] *Glasgow Herald*, 12 Jul. 1926.

[83] A. Howkins and J. Lowerson, *Trends In Leisure 1919–1939* (London, 1976), 36 and *Scotsman*, 3 Dec. 1932.

[84] SOHCA/019/020/Glasgow, b. 1895 and SOHCA/019/044/Lanarkshire, b. 1900 respec-tively. See C. Brown, 'Sport and the Scottish Office in the twentieth century: the control of a social problem', *The European Sports History Review*, 1: 171–2 (1999).

[85] *Forward*, 20 Nov. 1920 and 4 Oct. 1929.

[86] *Daily Record*, 10 Apr. 1933 and SOHCA/019/015/Glasgow, b. 1909.

[87] See Hughes, 'Popular pastimes and wife assault in inter-war Glasgow', B.A. dissertation (University of Strathclyde, 1976), 30.

the poverty line. It also eroded the potential of families to enjoy improved living standards. Women also gambled, but seemingly not with the same frequency as men. In their narratives women offered a representation that correlated to the idea of gambling as a form of working-class saving or a 'dream of instant wealth' and this wealth could exclude the 'breadwinner'. Mrs Campbell remembered, 'If they had a shilling, try your luck and see if you can win something. If you won you could take five weans and yourself to the pictures.'[88] Male gambling, by contrast, like pub culture, was a means of male bonding and a source of masculine identity, as well as a source of marital conflict; where it was profitable it would seem that winnings were rarely shared.

The final area of Scotland's 'three cornerstones' of male working-class culture was football. In Scotland the game became synonymous with men and 'machismo', drinking, gambling and crowd misconduct. Using the signifiers 'rough, Irish Catholic and working-class', the Scottish Office, the police and the media demonised football as the sport of the 'urban heathens'. The vilification of football was counterproductive. Many men 'ate, slept, drank and lived football seven days a week'. Football, the game, spectatorship and discussion, facilitated male bonding and masculine competitiveness, and were tied to gambling and the pub. Moreover, support for Scotland's most prominent football clubs, Celtic and Rangers, grew at a phenomenal rate from 1914, reflecting the sectarian schisms of inter-war Scottish society.[89] The religious and sectarian identities that were vital to the growth of these teams were associated with particular occupations in Scotland. Celtic Football Club drew their support principally from unskilled Catholic workers. Rangers Football Club's support was predominantly drawn from skilled Protestant workers. Being a Protestant was almost a prerequisite for employment in the skilled work of Scotland's heavy industries that were being undermined by the economic conditions of the inter-war years. This period also witnessed an intensification of sectarianism in Scotland and these clubs provided an alternative outlet for the expression of a sectarian identity, especially in the face of male secularisation discussed in the next chapter. The transference of work-related sectarian identities into aspects of popular culture, manifest in the bigotry associated with supporting Rangers and Celtic, was not restricted to these teams or Glasgow. Similar conflict existed between rival teams, albeit to a lesser extent, across Scotland.[90] Thus, the growth of football clubs, and the sectarianism associated with them, is a reflection of more than the commercialisation of leisure at this time; it was also a way for men to express masculine and religious identities.

The inter-war years were a period of economic North–South divide and

---

[88] SOHCA/019/04/Glasgow, b. 1910.

[89] Brown, 'The control of a social problem', 172–4 and B. Murray, *The Old Firm: Sectarianism, Sport and Society in Scotland* (Edinburgh, 1990), 7.

[90] Brown, 'The control of a social problem', 103. See also Knox, *Industrial Nation*, 198–9.

a time when the myth of the working-class hero, the poor tenement boy who overcomes the obstacles of poverty to make good through footballing skills, emerged. This was seemingly 'endemic of the fatalism engendered by relative deprivation'. The myth was also the allegorical equivalent of the skilled occupations of Scotland's heavy industries, encompassing 'skills of precision, quality and expertise – rare craftsmanship passed in the blood'. In addition, football support provided a vicarious outlet for the expression of 'competitiveness, aggression and instrumentality'.[91] In this respect, a team's defeat could be internalised as a personal challenge to masculine identity. Mr Bruce certainly 'didn't feel very well when Celtic was defeated', because being a 'Celtic man' meant 'something worthwhile'. On the other hand, Mr Ewart stated that a man's football team meant 'the pub. It can lead you to it.' Thus, 'many a poor woman was frightened for the match being finished and the man coming home'.[92] As masculinity was drawn from such identification, football and its links with gambling and the pub culture could prove a volatile cocktail when contested by wives. Gender conflict in this context can be read as a physical manifestation of masculine insecurity, which some men resolved via the pursuit of pastimes that could cause poverty or undermine the aspirations of more affluent women. Not all men behaved this way. There were different ideals of masculinity to identify with and also a variety of 'propensities for male bonding and aggression' which were influenced by different 'socialisations'. [93] However, recreational pursuits are agents of socialisation which reflect and reinforce the wider society, and hold significance and meanings for the participants. The pub, like gambling and football, was significant to many men in inter-war Scotland. For those men, such behaviour proved a pragmatic narcotic against adverse economic and social forces, which ensured that the construction of a working-class society centred on gender conflict. There existed a clear sexual division of labour in the home and leisure spheres and little demonstration of compromise or the companionate marriage.

Nevertheless, individually and as a group, there were also women who would contest male power and privilege, often fiercely, and even in the face of social condemnation from other women. Mrs Adams from Greenock recalled how her neighbour discovered her husband was secretly concealing money from her and because of this she attacked her spouse. Mrs Adams maintained, 'she hit the high heavens about it. She was a bad

[91] J. J. Moorhouse, 'Shooting stars: footballers and working-class culture in twentieth-century Scotland', in R. Holt (ed.), *Sport and the Working Class in Modern Britain* (Manchester, 1990), 183–5, J. Grayson, '"But it's more than a game it's an institution": feminist perspectives on sport', *Feminist Review*, 13: 5–17 (1983).

[92] SOHCA/019/028/Glasgow, b. 1905, SOHCA/019/030/Glasgow, b. 1908 and Hughes, 'Popular pastimes and wife assault', 31 respectively.

[93] Tiger, *Men in Groups*, 189.

bitch.'[94] As with the women of the urban poor in England, not all Scottish wives were 'ladylike or deferential'; not all women called their husbands 'master'.[95] Of those interviewed only one person actually admitted using violence against their partner; that individual was a woman. Mrs Lang assaulted her husband because

> He tried to lift his hand to me. He was in the boozers and I was setting the fire and he came and he shoved me. I lifted a shovel and hit him over the head with it. That's the only time in his life that he ever lifted his hands to me.[96]

Women assaulted their husbands, but female violence, verbal or physical, was not considered legitimate in the popular discourses of the period.[97] However, women escaped criticism when men transgressed gender roles by assaulting their wives, even in retaliation, after excessive abuse of the family income. Moreover, women who indulged in violence against their partners rejected the discourses that maligned them and exploited gender representations to present themselves as good wives. Women represented their violence as a challenge to men who threatened them or their status as good household managers. If men withheld money, or 'squandered it on drink', women could gain some sympathy and justify their abhorrent behaviour, mediating the negative influence this might have on their womanly identities. In 1928, to applause from the public gallery, a 'popular verdict' of justifiable homicide was passed on a twenty-eight-year-old mother who had stabbed her husband to death. Witnesses for the defence included female neighbours and the deceased's mother. These women bore testimony to the years of abuse and terror the defendant had endured at the hands of her husband, who was 'violent in drink' and spent the family income on alcohol and gambling.[98] The discursive relationship between working-class men's abuse of the family, and the family's income, offered women ways to challenge the discourse that identified them as unwomanly when they embarked on violence to 'safeguard' themselves or their families.

Women also provided support for each other against violent men. A seventy-eight- year-old woman had her breast bone broken when she challenged a man for attacking his wife. Mrs Nicol recalled providing aid because 'I knew if that husband came in and there was no bread she would get hit'. Mrs Gallacher stitched her neighbour's head, after the woman's husband had beaten her with a stick, because the victim 'wouldn't go near the doctor because she knew she'd need to tell'.[99] Doctors were expected

---

94 SOHCA/019/022/Greenock, b. 1919.
95 See Chinn, *They Worked All Their Lives*, 164.
96 SOHCA/019/013/Glasgow, b. 1902.
97 Rowbotham, 'Only when drunk', 155–69.
98 *Glasgow Herald*, 28 Aug. 1928.
99 *Scotsman*, 24 Feb. 1915, SOHCA/019/014/Glasgow, b. 1911 and SOHCA/019/015/Glasgow, b. 1909.

to report such assault to the police and therefore this victim feared the potential repercussions should she seek medical attention. Many women were subjected to further abuse when abusers were prosecuted and if the breadwinner was convicted or fined wives suffered economic hardship. Aid in this context was vital. Other women sought shelter: 'We used to go next door. It's not the first time I've been lying under Mrs Cavanagh's bed when he's come in, "Is my Helen here?".' Some women were more forceful. According to Mrs Jones, 'Women ganged up on men. They had to.'[100] However, amongst the more affluent sections of the working classes the idea that 'a lot of men go out for a drink, but it's their wives' fault because they drive them to it' and that 'beating wives and beating children was mostly among the Irish community' meant that domestic abuse was often cloaked behind the need to uphold appearances.[101] Corresponding with the growing currency given to privacy amongst the more affluent this increased the incidence of invisible crime.

Women challenged this worldview that female provocation caused marital violence and confronted male domination as expressed in men's abuse of 'family wages, 'manly' drinking and family violence. They did this directly and through their participation in organisations that also brought them into contact with feminists and feminism. One of the most significant of these organisations was the British Women's Temperance Association [BWTA]. One in five Scottish women were members of the BWTA in the early 1920s and although the number of women involved diminished between the wars, as Table 6.3 highlights, it nonetheless maintained a significant membership. Moreover, the majority of its members were working class from the industrial heartlands of Scotland.[102] Indeed, so significant was the membership of the largely working-class region of Greenock that this branch of the BWTA consistently had a disproportionate representation on the Scottish Executive of the Association, with two of its members selected throughout the 1920s.[103] In 1926, Glasgow's Whiteinch, a residential area, had a branch with 71 members, but the Motherwell branch had 730 members. Highlighting the significance of the BWTA's membership in Motherwell is the fact that in 1926 the Motherwell branch of the Women's Co-operative Guild feared closure because of its vast membership loss as a result of the miners' lockout in this coal-mining town. While women's membership of some organisations lapsed because of the economic circumstances at this time, other organisations apparently did not fare as badly.[104]

[100] SOHCA/019/011/Glasgow, b. 1917 and SOHCA/019/011/Glasgow, b. 1917.

[101] Hughes, 'Popular pastimes and wife assault', 37.

[102] Mitchell Library, British Women's Temperance Association [hereafter BWTA], Greenock Branch, Manuscript Minutes, 1 Oct. 1925 and *Scotsman*, 2 Apr. 1923 and 2 Apr. 1925.

[103] See BWTA, Greenock Branch, Manuscript Minutes, 1914–39 and Alexandria Branch, Secretary's Book, Manuscript Minutes, 1922–39.

[104] BWTA, Manuscript Minutes, Alexandria Branch, Secretary's Book, 23 Nov. 1926.

Table 6.3 British Women's Temperance Association (Scottish Christian Union) membership and branches, 1920–33.

Year	Membership	Number of branches
1920	67,523	405
1924	62,101	543
1928	55,555	510
1930	54,113	493
1933	48,963	470

Source: *Scotsman*, Reports of Annual Meetings, 14 Apr. 1920, 2 Apr. 1924, 18 Apr. 1928, 28 Mar. 1930 and 5 Apr. 1933.

Like many other women's groups, the BWTA did not identify itself as feminist but used the concept of citizenship to argue for reforms which mirrored those of socialist-feminist and formal feminist organisations.[105] It regarded the vote for women as a vehicle to effect social change and the organisation worked with feminists to these ends. After the extension of the franchise in 1918 that allowed most women over thirty years of age to vote, the BWTA inaugurated the National Citizens Council and Citizens' Departments to enrol and educate women voters. It actively encouraged women to 'take a greater part in public life'.[106]

The BWTA saw itself as 'an immense sisterhood' and engaged in a wide range of what were clearly feminist campaigns. After the extension of the franchise to women in 1918, along with the Women Citizens' Association, the Society for Equal Citizenship and the Women's Freedom League, the BWTA sent out questionnaires to prospective and sitting MPs. Its main question was whether the individual concerned would support temperance. However, in a similar way to the socialist-feminist demands highlighted in Chapter five, the BWTA also enquired as to whether there would be improvements in housing and the home, which was seen as the workshop of the wife, identified by the organisation as its constituents. The organisation also demanded equality of moral standards for men and women, 'real equality in the law and legislation', equal pay for women and equal access to public and political life. It also demanded an equal franchise for women. In 1924 it pointed out that 'women are coming to terms of equality with men in civic and industrial power', and that 'it was high time the government fulfilled its promise and implemented the franchise without delay for all women over twenty-one years of age'. The BTWA argued it was 'unjust and untenable' not to pass a measure giving women equal rights to men. When the franchise was conceded they referred to this as 'the latest political act of justice towards women in this country'.[107] In addition, the BWTA

[105] See Beaumont, 'Citizens not feminists', 413–26.
[106] *Scotsman*, 12 Apr. and 6 Dec. 1918.
[107] *Scotsman*, 11 Apr. 1923, 3 and 8 May 1927 and 20 Mar. 1929; *Forward*, 24 Apr. 1924.

provided women with a political platform. It also offered sociability and a venue to express shared values which included contesting men's abuse of wives and family incomes.

For the BWTA the 'most urgent problem' facing society was 'the home life of the land' and they maintained that women should be instrumental in addressing this question, especially as housewives and mothers. Members were informed that the effects of alcohol were 'cruellest on the children of the country'. The Association maintained that women 'could not have decent homes, could not be loving mothers or rear healthy children' whilst the 'curse of alcohol devastated cities' and while men, 'who could not tell the difference between running a home and making a home', took drink to escape from their environment.[108] Thus, the BWTA provided its female members with a discourse to challenge male abuse of family incomes for self-expenditure on alcohol consumption which adversely affected many women's roles and identities, and contributed to conflict in their homes. In doing so, the BWTA also allowed women to contest the worldview that women caused or contributed to the incidence of male intemperance or that it was a woman's provocation which led to wife-beating.

The compatibility between the discourses offered by the BWTA and the worldview of working-class women was reflected not only in membership figures but also in the women's contribution to the unity campaign in 1920 to have the Temperance (Scotland) Act 1913 enacted. The Act allowed the Scottish electorate of local wards, parishes and burghs a vote on whether the area should be made 'dry' by withdrawing the licences for public houses, whether to limit licences or whether to remain 'wet' and refrain from withdrawing licences. However, the campaign in support of a 'dry' Scotland was identified as a 'woman's battle' that was 'essentially about family politics'[109] Indeed, according to the *Scotsman* the vote to go dry was strongest in areas with a large female population, especially the textile areas of Ayrshire, Perthshire and Airdrie. Moreover, during the campaign women from the BWTA brought the issue of domestic violence to public attention and this was part of a broader strategy of using 'guilt tactics' aimed at men. Floats, decorated lorries and tableaux were used to depict the home of the drunkard which in some cases presented his 'wife' battered and bruised. Rallies were held outside pubs and factory gates to draw attention to this issue.[110]

Moreover, support for this campaign has been under-estimated and under-reported. Almost 78 per cent of the Scottish electorate voted on whether to support or reject the Act and, of those who voted, 42 per cent

---

[108] BWTA, Greenock Branch, Manuscript Minutes, 8 Oct. 1925 and *Scotsman*, 3 Apr. 1924, 8 Apr. 1927 and 21 Mar. 1929.

[109] J. Black, 'An assessment of the impact of the Temperance (Scotland) Act 1913', B.A. independent study project (University of Strathclyde, 1999), 33.

[110] J. Black, 'An assessment of the impact of the Temperance (Scotland) Act 1913', B.A. independent study project (University of Strathclyde, 1999), 34–5.

favoured the no-licence clause. What defeated the issue in many areas of Scotland was the clause stipulating that for an area to go 'dry' a 55 per cent majority of the votes cast was needed. Nevertheless, such was the strength of the BWTA in Greenock that the largely working-class eighth ward did go dry. Wards in Motherwell also voted to abolish public houses.[111]Other areas that voted to abolish public houses included Kilsyth and the Ayrshire villages of Darvel, Newmilns and Stewarton, Auchterarder in Perthshire and Dornoch in the Highlands. Significant numbers of women from these areas were also directly involved in the unity campaign, forming processions and carrying banners with the legend 'If you want a happy home vote No Licence'.[112]

In Scotland 436 licences were withdrawn, 13 of them from Stewarton. It was estimated that £500 per week was spent on alcohol in this small village. Women from this area claimed that withdrawing the licences was a 'boon to them' as they were apparently able to save an extra 7/- per week for household purposes. In Auchterarder it was reported that the women stated unanimously that they would have their village 'as it is' rather than 'as it was'. Women from Greenock also insisted that their economic position had improved since licences had been withdrawn.[113] The BWTA also argued against gambling on horses and football on the basis that it undermined 'home life' and took the food from the mouths of children.[114] Their consistent argument that expenditure on alcohol and gambling was the curse of family life offered women a collective discourse to challenge men's behaviour which undermined women's resources and their power.

However, although women challenged men's abuse of their wives and family incomes, women did so at a time when many men found it difficult to face the insecurity and vulnerability stemming from the precarious economic climate, perceptions of a female usurper and the concessions to women embedded in the companionate marital ideal. Women's aspirations of the companionate marriage model, whilst working-class men were unable or unwilling to participate, ensured that intense gender antagonism marked gender relations. In addition, the fragility of work and its associated masculine privileges guaranteed that many men resorted to popular culture as a means of expressing and developing a masculine identity. The pillars of male working-class leisure had a long tradition as centres of male power, privilege and identity and these were amplified between the wars, if not always quantitatively, at least symbolically. Gender antagonism and marriages of conflict, which had marked Scotland from at least the eight-

---

[111] J. Black, 'An assessment of the impact of the Temperance (Scotland) Act 1913', B.A. independent study project (University of Strathclyde, 1999), 44–6 and *Scotsman*, 3 Nov. 1920.

[112] BWTA, Alexandria Branch, Secretary's Book, 1926, *Times*, 15 Oct. 1919 and *Scotsman*, 13 Apr. 1923 and 20 Oct. 1933.

[113] *Scotsman*, 13 Apr. 1923 and BWTA, Greenock Branch, Manuscript Minutes, 1 Oct. 1925.

[114] *Scotsman*, 16 Oct. 1923 and 2 Apr. 1924.

eenth century, prevailed, if in a modified form. This influenced women's political identities and was expressed in both the private and public spheres in women's challenges against men's abuse of power and men's violent subordination of them. Such behaviour may have been a reflection of empathy due to the level of sexual antagonism and the comparatively shared material and the cultural circumstances woman endured, but it was nonetheless political and at times feminist. It also allowed women to reject the demonisations that implied that they were responsible for the gender conflict, a discourse often used to justify men's violent behaviour towards women. Women used a range of strategies to resist men's domination in the private sphere and, as the following chapter will highlight, this included making men dependent on them.

CHAPTER SEVEN

Marriage, Mothering and Political Identity

Women challenged their unequal positions in the worlds of work, politics and marriage but changes in the inter-war years threatened to reshape gender relations by transforming women's roles in ways that could undermine their autonomy and reduce their access to support. Not only did the state, state agencies, the clergy, religious organisations and the media actively promote marriage and mothering as the natural and fulfilling aspirations for women, but this was reinforced by greater state supervision of housewives and mothers. In addition, increased access to home ownership and municipal housing placed greater expectations on women's domestic role and mothering skills. Inter-war working-class aspirations to respectability required smaller families and a more intense focus on the domestic unit as well as 'conspicuous consumption' of domestic goods as markers of this respectability. It has been suggested that as a result of these changes the inter-war years witnessed a shift from a community-orientated working class to a family-orientated one which heralded the apogee of domesticity for working-class women.[1] Yet restricted access to home ownership and municipal housing for working-class families, along with relatively slower rates of family reduction than was the British norm, low wages, high levels of poverty and unemployment mediated change in Scotland and ensured continuities as well as changes in both ideologies and experiences. Working-class women had aspirations and enjoyed some improvements in material culture. However, the collective memories of women in this period present a picture of a shared culture of deprivation alleviated by women's networks, the influence of 'reciprocity and sympathy' and working-class religious concepts of neighbourliness and charity that revolved around their roles as mothers and housewives. Indeed, there were Scottish women who felt that 'we were closer to one another because everybody was in the one boat. There were none of us had much more than another and it made us understand one another.'[2] These sentiments reflect older traditions in which women's networks operated to mediate financial insecurity, the burdens of household managing and mothering, and men's abuse of the family and the 'family wage'.

The institution of marriage offered women an important identity and a specified space to define as their own, the 'private sphere'. Marriage was

---

[1] Scott, 'Did owner-occupation lead to smaller families', 99–124.
[2] SOHCA/019/07/Glasgow, b. 1911.

an expectation with young women being trained in housewifery skills from an early age. Mrs Ingills stated, 'My mother had three girls and as each left school, you weren't asked to go and look for work – you had to stay in the house for at least two years to give you a knowledge of what your true work would be. You learned everything there was to be done.'[3] Marriage was not only an expectation, it was also an aspiration in which for working-class women love meant being a family.[4] Rebecca West recollected, 'Engagements were lucky and you took your ring into work and all the girls took a wish off it by turning it on their finger three times, and I suppose hoping for their turn to come.'[5]

Being a housewife was a burden, but it provided women with a sense of pride and achievement. Mrs Galbraith stated, 'women were really slaves', but it still allowed her to feel, 'very smug, very smug. I could do everything.' Mrs Edwards recalled

> Oh I felt great seeing the results, and when your man came in on a Friday night from work you'd to have a nice tea going, ready for him with his wage. They were great nights and they enjoyed it too. I'd a neighbour, we'd say, 'A man was brought into this world to be the breadwinner. No wife unless it's necessary should be out working. She should be at home attending to him and the children.' I think that's right. There were some poor widows that had to take a job to look after their children. That was different, that was an emergency.[6]

Household management required a great deal of skill and thereby offered opportunities for pride and a sense of satisfaction, but it was also the means by which women could make 'men dependent' upon them in the 'process of negotiating power within the family'.[7] Indeed, according to the contemporary Scottish feminist, Miss Muir, of the Edinburgh branch of the Women Citizens' Association, men were 'ill-equipped to take on the responsibility of running a home'. It was women who 'had a higher function', which men could not 'perform'.[8] Most women denied men the opportunity of assisting in the home to ensure their dependency. In mining districts women's control of the domestic sphere provided them with some 'autonomy and respect in a male-dominated world'. 'Being treated like little kings when they were at home' fulfilled an 'almost childlike need for nurture, born out of the dangers and hardship which miners faced'. It also made them feel powerful and 'so compensated for their oppressive work conditions', but they could not enjoy this without dependency on women.[9]

[3] SOHCA/019/04/Glasgow, b. 1912.
[4] Bourke, *Working-Class Cultures*, 62.
[5] WEA, interview with Rebecca West, born Shettleston, Glasgow 1918.
[6] SOHCA/019/08/Glasgow, b. 1916 and SOHCA/019/06/Glasgow, b. 1907.
[7] Bourke, *Working-Class Cultures*, 66.
[8] *Scotsman*, 18 Jan. 1935.
[9] Hall, 'Contrasting female identities', 109–14.

Men acknowledged this dependency: 'My wife has looked after me so well that I could never repay her. When I was working I always had my meals ready – not that I wanted it that way. She kept me decently dressed and never had any debt.'[10]

However, not all women could fulfil the ideal that they rely on a bread-winner and serve a higher 'function' of housewifery without contributing to the family economy. Many married women had to carry the double burden of housewifery and paid work. Mrs Lang remembered, 'I got married and of course I discovered I still had to go out and work. I worked harder than ever.'[11] Nevertheless, undertaking the double burden of work and housewifery, although difficult, did not act as a major obstacle to women's identification with the signifiers of respectable womanhood. Female respondents who had worked between the wars did not identify themselves as workers. It was only when they were asked whether they did anything to earn extra income that significant numbers of the women acknowledged that they had earned money through charring, childcare services and homework. Mrs Parsonage recalled how her 'father was one of the old type that didn't think that wives should work'. She maintained that 'most men didn't approve of their wives working. My mother once mentioned working and my father nearly blew his top.' Yet Mrs Parsonage's mother was a paid childminder and her husband had no objection to this.[12] Income-generating activities were presented as an extension of a woman's role in the private sphere rather than linked with the more public and mas-culine role of production. This allowed women to sustain their identities as good household managers and mothers whilst avoiding conflict with their spouses and the disparagement working married women faced. Even the Dundee trade union movement accused the working mothers of Dundee of being 'ill-trained' for womanhood.[13]

Women could command respect for their economic contribution and for the centrality of their roles in the family and the neighbourhood, but to do so often involved the support of other women. Studies of women's networks highlight how they were vital in helping women cope with the double burden of work and household responsibilities. They were also important in assisting women to deal with financial insecurity and to cope with 'the worst excesses of male abuse', especially domestic violence and men's excessive expenditure of family incomes. Women's networks also provided a 'site of play, gossip and social interaction which cemented social relations and consolidated vital support for women'.[14] This is not to suggest that women's networks were an 'empowering sisterhood' because they were

[10] SOHCA/019/043/Clydebank, b. 1920.
[11] SOHCA/019/012/Glasgow, b. 1907.
[12] SOHCA/019/026/Glasgow, b. 1917.
[13] *Scotsman*, 2 May 1923.
[14] E. Ross, 'Survival networks', 6–14. See also Chinn, *They Worked All Their Lives*, 156–65 and Roberts, *A Woman's Place*, 82–122.

used by women to provide for the entire family, men included. Women's networks provided women with 'a sense of belonging and safety against those who might wield power' and they were also used to 'sustain behaviours expected and necessary for them to be identified as a good woman'.[15] However, not only did the identity of 'good womanhood' offer avenues of power to women, but there were also times when they were needed to provide safety against a husband's misuse of power. This was particularly the case where sexual antagonism and the struggle for control of family resources was manifestly evident, as it was in Scotland and thus women's networks were important in shaping political identities.

Social relations in the home could 'legitimise some women's subordination' but it also afforded other women 'opportunities for dominance'.[16]An economic contribution helped women overcome powerlessness, but where women could not command status from an economic role they used alternative strategies. While marriage was an aspiration and could be a form of empowerment women had to work to enhance their position in the home and resist men's 'unlawful power over them'. This involved concessions whereby women gave up independence but made men dependent upon them.[17] Bessie Laycock recalled how her 'mother was very much the head of the household'. 'My mother was the boss. My father went out and worked and handed in the money, but she ran the house and the children. She was boss.' Elizabeth Wheeler insisted that her grandmother ran everything and that her grandfather 'just went along with her' and that her mother saw her husband as the 'provider' and 'expected nothing else from him'.[18]

However, the desire for respectable domesticity and privacy that was facilitated by increased owner occupation and the expansion of municipal housing along with increased working-class mobility is seen to have reduced the geographical spread of women's kinship networks that helped women make men reliant upon them. Yet, in Scotland the conditions that underpinned change were impeded, as Chapter three highlighted. Home ownership and access to council housing was obstructed to such an extent that by 1936 only one-fifth of the population resided in municipal accommodation. Nor did social mobility necessarily give rise to a shift from a community-orientated working class to an aspirational one in which women's networks abated. During the slum clearance schemes of the 1930s that did provide greater access to municipal housing for working-class families, entire neighbourhoods were transplanted into replacement tenement structure housing. For example, the Glasgow Housing and General Town Improvement Committee agreed to the erection of Possil in Glasgow

[15] S. D'Cruze, 'Women and the Family', in Purvis, *Women's History*, 91–2.

[16] J. Giles, *Women, Identity and Private Life in Britain* (London, 1995), 12–17, 179.

[17] Bourke, *Working-Class Cultures*, 63–6.

[18] WEA, interview with Bessie Laycock, born Dennistoun, Glasgow 1910, SOHCA/019/08/ Glasgow, b. 1916 and Wheeler, *Cowie*, 5.

to clear a nearby slum. Houses were erected in Possil, to transplant entire neighbourhoods into what was a reproduction of the tenements they replaced rather than 'garden suburbs' that facilitated privacy. Mrs Laird, President of the Glasgow Labour Party Housing Association, complained that 'Scotland should not be content with a lower standard of housing than that aimed at in England where demand for cottages was common'.[19]

It was not just building structure that guaranteed that neighbourhood cultures would be transplanted into the new estates. Local residents' attitudes towards 'slum dwellers' being rehoused in their area contributed to continuities in neighbourhood cultures. In 1932, Glasgow's Sub-Committee on Sites and Buildings received a deputation from the tenants of Govanhill protesting against the proposed erection of houses in Dixon Street and Allison Street aimed at clearing slums.[20] Indeed, continuities can be ascertained from the Conference on Housing and Town Planning, held in 1932. At this venue female Labour Party activists argued that there was a need to coopt women onto housing sub-committees because it was 'evident that men [did] not understand that when slum clearing, the people should be scattered, so that they really get away from their old associations'.[21] In these circumstances prevailing cultures were transplanted rather than transformed, mediating access to the ideals of respectable domesticity, privacy and home-centred leisure and because of this survival networks prevailed to a greater extent in Scotland ensuring their decline was more drawn out than in other regions of Britain. They were further embedded because of high levels of poverty and unemployment. Recession and the structural weaknesses of the economy between the wars did little to alleviate the poverty and close proximity of tenement life, while the risk and reality of poverty, and the persistence of male privilege and power combined to ensure that networks remained vitally important to women.

Women's networks were used to shore up and protect the institution of marriage and 'women's talk', or what is commonly demonised as gossip, was the medium through which this filtered. Marriage provided access to economic security and a significant womanly identity. Whether there was companionship or conflict in marriage (and companionship itself is a psychological resource), and regardless of the level of a family's income, the breadwinner was an economic and emotional resource. As an economic resource, the breadwinner's wage was of immense significance and had to be protected from the threat of family breakdown. Thus, gossip was also used to challenge all forms of deviance by women, as well as men, that might undermine women's economic and social security as a group. Mrs Jones recalled how 'there was one woman beside us and she took men in. It might have been quite innocent, I don't know, but the rest of the women

[19] *Glasgow Herald*, 23 Mar. and 27 Mar. 1922.
[20] Glasgow City Council Minutes, 5 Aug. 1932.
[21] *Labour Women*, Jun. 1932, 94.

ganged up on her, so she must've been doing something. They called her names, some of them; some didn't speak to her.'[22] Sexual deviance, particularly adultery, separation and divorce, along with alcohol abuse and 'rough' behaviour were condemned through gossip. In this way gossip reflected the shared values of women, bound networks together and allowed women to determine what was acceptable and what was not in their neighbourhoods.

This clearly had an opportunity cost for many women, especially those whose marriages had broken down and who were thereby seen as a threat to the security of other married women. Gossip reflected and reinforced the idealisation of marriage in ways which were exclusive and condemnatory of those who did not conform to the ideal. Women who were divorced were often 'condemned by the general public'. Mrs Nicol stated, 'At one time if anybody passed you and you knew, you'd say, "Look at her, she's nothing but a slut."' Ms Anderson recalled, 'divorce was a scandal. People would talk as though it really is a big issue.'[23] When the Stirling Councillor, Reverend Buchanan, contested a proposal to use Poor Law provisions to assist the poor to divorce, he claimed that many 'rate-payers considered divorce as much a breach of moral law as burglary'.[24] He was not necessarily overstating his case in relation to the worldview expressed by Scottish inter-war women. Separation was also condemned, although it was more common than divorce due to the costs of the latter, economically and culturally. Mrs Galbraith maintained that separation 'was the most awful thing to happen. You really were bad then.'[25]

While gossip was used to punish or chastise, it was also part of the creation of a relatively safe and autonomous public realm of criticism. Because of this, gossip offered women a means to challenge men's power. It was employed to dispute what women deemed aberrant forms of male behaviour. Where this did not alter men's conduct, it did mediate community condemnation of women. Gossip was used to ensure that inability to cope if men abused the family wage was not identified as bad household management by a 'slovenly wife'.[26] In his autobiography, *Growing Up in the Gorbals*, Glasser depicts the potency of gossip, and men's awareness of gossip's power and their attitudes towards it. He is uncomplimentary about female neighbours who, through gossip, condemned his father's gambling addiction and attributed his mother's early death to his father's conduct. He argues that these women were unaware of the true relationship between his parents.[27] Yet he misinterprets the context of the criticism. Many wives were aware of how men's spending inhibited them from fulfilling their

---

[22] SOHCA/019/011/Glasgow, b. 1917.
[23] SOHCA/019/06/Glasgow, b. 1907 and SOHCA/019/015/Glasgow, b. 1909.
[24] *Scotsman*, 29 Nov. 1935.
[25] SOHCA/019/08/Glasgow, b. 1916.
[26] See Scott, *Domination and the Arts of Resistance*, 26–7, 131–2 and M. Tebbutt, *'Women's Talk?' Gossip and Women's Words in Working-class Communities 1880–1939* (Manchester, 1992), 49.
[27] Glasser, *Growing Up in the Gorbals*, 138–9.

roles of managers and mothers. They also understood the burdens women endured when men misused the family's resources and the ways in which domestic conflict resulted from contesting male expenditure. Gossip was a means of participating in vicarious condemnation of their own real or potential circumstances in a bid to avoid direct conflict with their husbands. At the same time it allowed women to use the power of community criticism to undermine a man's right to excessive self-expenditure. In other words, gossip was a safe and relatively anonymous direct articulation of verbal aggression and hostility that acknowledged, communicated and carried effective meaning which addressed women's mutual experiences.

Gossip allowed women to condemn men's behaviour indirectly, thereby imposing guilt on men, whilst at the same time vindicating women's inability to cope when men abused the 'family wage'. It was a psychological resource which they shared collectively, but it was also part of a wider linguistic power struggle involving men and women for control of resources within the neighbourhood and family, both economic and ideological. Men demonised gossip as a form of disobedience because it provided women with access to a language and skills that they could use against men in the contest for scarce resources within the family. Indeed, wife-beaters often cited this as a form of provocation when women used these skills to contest men's abuse of family resources.[28]

Gossip also provided women with a forum to release their confusion and despair and this safety valve often took dramatic and exaggerated forms.[29] Yet as much as it was a comfort in that it reduced women's sense of isolation, 'women's talk' often moderated condemnation of unacceptable behaviour by providing a social measure by which wives might judge their own experiences. Mrs McQueen recalled, 'The only time my husband hit me, we were arguing about something and I was standing on the rug and I was pregnant at the time. He got angry. He pulled the rug and I fell on my behind. He was more alarmed than me.' Mrs McQueen may have been less alarmed because she could measure her experience through gossip. Recalling the frequency of domestic violence, she stated, 'We used to stand at the corner with our babies in their shawls. One came down she'd have a black eye; another would say her man burnt her stockings.'[30] In this environment women's networks were particularly important if they were to contest male power and privilege and make men dependent on them.

Scottish oral histories and autobiographies are permeated with representations of the mutual support that helped women sustain their command of the family and cope with the day to day struggles to survive and with the strategies women used to make ends meet. This is in stark contrast to the argument that a 'new' working class was emerging as a result of changing

[28] Tebbutt, *Women's Talk*, 51–3.
[29] Tebbutt, *Women's Talk*, 51.
[30] SOHCA/019/018/Glasgow, b. 1909.

patterns of consumption and 'status competition' associated with moves to the new suburbia. Whilst there is evidence that some families were in a position to buy a greater range of consumer goods, including radios, gramophones and clothing, much of this was on hire purchase. Yet what shaped the narratives of Scottish women was not the 'new' consumerism, but rather the community-based buttress which reflected long-standing traditions of working-class women's mutual support in the face of financial insecurities and material hardship.

An indication of this hardship is the continuing importance of pawnbroking in Scottish working-class neighbourhoods. The high point of pawnbroking in Britain was between 1900 and 1913, but licence figures for pawnbroking in Glasgow in 1938 exceeded those of the earlier period. Furthermore, while pledging items of clothing declined in significance, as it did in Britain as a whole, indicating growing prosperity, clothing was pledged more frequently in the north, where low-value pledges were of greater relative importance.[31] Mrs Lang recalled how 'the women next door used to come and get a loan of my dad's suit to put in the pawn. My father used to go off his head. He used to say he was a tradesman. They shouldn't do that. They didn't need to do that.' Mrs Gallacher's husband objected to her borrowing sums of money from other women and the reciprocity of lending in return. He attributed this to poor household management and told his wife that he 'was handing in enough money' and that his 'pocket money had nothing to do with her'. He also informed her that 'you get the wages and if you can't make them work you shouldn't be here'. Mrs Gallacher was twenty years of age and had four children. She stated that she felt 'hurt' and 'frightened' and that she then realised that she would have to look for work. She found employment as a cleaner. However, she recalled later in the interview how

> There was a mother stayed upstairs from me and she'd two married daughters. One of the sisters, her man was out of work for a long while, and she used to come to me and she'd get a loan of a half a crown. She'd go up and give her sister a shilling. I'd get it back on Friday. Nobody knew about it. You're the first, and you know it was great. Nobody ever said anything about it. It was really good.[32]

Apparently, many women felt that mutually supportive networks served their needs better than obedience to their husbands. The above quote also illustrates that this support could be based on subversive forms of knowledge, defiance and courage that constituted a forum of gender consciousness. Evidence abounds of such support. Mrs Davidson recalled how her mother worked seasonally on a farm. Her neighbours looked after her children and she dispersed the food she got as part payment for her labour. Mrs Davidson emphasised that

---

[31] Tebbutt, *Making Ends Meet*, 137,151–95.
[32] SOHCA/019/013/Glasgow, b. 1907 and SOHCA/019/015/Glasgow, b. 1909.

My mum had good neighbours. If you were in a hole they were in a hole. I mean they'd made a big pot of soup and if you'd nothing they took you soup. My mum used to give them potatoes and turnip. She was having the same. They all helped one another.[33]

Mrs Reid recollected that

My mother got a job as a scrubber in a warehouse and she only got 4/-. It was only at certain times that they got that work, but I remember my aunt saying, 'I'll be glad whenever your mother says, will you come down and give me a hand at the warehouse.' It got our supper in. She used to give my auntie 2/- and she got 2/-. They were the lucky ones.[34]

Women's support networks could also enhance their physical and psychological resources that empowered them in their neighbourhoods, in the family and in their relations with men. Mrs Kilpatrick's husband was a moulder to trade. He was laid off six months after completing his apprenticeship. She recalled,

He couldn't get a job because there wasn't such a thing then. I said, 'I was speaking to Helen this morning. She says there's a job in the Cleansing.' 'Cleansing! Oh! The very thought of that! Me going into that! Oh no no!' I said, 'Remember it's honest and if you don't take it your not going to be here. I'm not going to be here to do all the work to keep you, so you'll just go.' He worked there right up till he got another job.[35]

Poverty and misfortune were not generally censured because women appreciated that they too might find themselves in a similar situation. Thus, they generally adhered to the principle that 'if we knew that there was a woman in want then we clubbed in and helped her'.[36]

Women also gained assistance from their networks to facilitate their mothering skills in which they took pride and which gave them status in their communities. Mrs MacIntosh was unable to have children but she observed that 'there were not many that were not good mothers in the working class because all they did was love their kids. They had nowhere to go but to look after those children, and they gave them the best attention they possibly could. The majority of working-class women were really kind to their kids.'[37] However, from the late nineteenth century the surveillance of working-class mothers and the promotion of scientific motherhood had been growing in significance. Policy makers influenced by concerns over national efficiency, rising foreign and military competition, and

---

[33] SOHCA/019/05/Glasgow, b. 1912.
[34] SOHCA/019/019/Glasgow, b. 1907.
[35] SOHCA/019/019/Glasgow, b. 1907.
[36] SOHCA/019/016/Glasgow, b. 1911.
[37] SOHCA/019/016/Glasgow, b. 1911.

Table 7.1 Infant mortality per 1,000 live births, 1907–27.

	1907–16	*1917–27*
England and Wales	110	70
Scotland	110	89
Glasgow	129	108
Greenock	262	103
Motherwell	108	83
Paisley	113	94
Port Glasgow	113	89

Source: *Evening News*, 18 Jan. 1929.

the declining birth rate shifted their attention towards the future of the race, children, and by association mothers. World War I accelerated this trend, so that by the inter-war years not only was scientific motherhood being endorsed, but working-class women were increasingly overseen by a multiplicity of state organisations.

Increased state supervision over mothers is evident in the promotion of education on mothering by professionals. Events such as 'Baby Week', when 'all manner of societies and individuals engaged in teaching working-class mothers drew together for mutual encouragement and the work they saw as of national importance' were not uncommon.[38] State supervision over mothers also manifested itself in the growth of maternal and child welfare clinics. There were 2,054 clinics in Britain in 1920, 1,061 run by local authorities. In 1938 there were 4,585 clinics, of which local authorities ran 2,752.[39] High infant mortality rates were a driving force behind the dissemination of scientific knowledge of child-rearing practices and although declining, Scotland had the highest infant mortality rates in Britain.

Moreover, by the 1930s infant mortality rates across Scotland were rising, although some women were affected more than others. When the causes of the high sickness rates amongst working married women in Dundee were discussed by the sub-committee of the General Federation of Trade Unions Approved Society, it was shown that eleven women had given birth to seventy-eight babies between them and of these forty-nine had died – an infant mortality rate of 62 per cent. Infant mortality rates were also extremely high in mining areas.[40] Fertility rates were also higher than the national average in mining districts like Lanarkshire, as were stillbirth rates, which between the wars were 25 per cent higher than the national average. This was due to pollution, poor housing, more pregnancies and the heavy burden expected of household managers.[41] Infant mortality rates

---

[38] Rathbone, *The Disinherited Family*, 102.
[39] Gittins, *Fair Sex*, 51.
[40] *Scotsman*, 13 Feb. 1935.
[41] Hall, 'Contrasting female identities', 112–14.

were also high in Scotland's city slum areas. In 1928, in Glasgow it was 107 per 1,000 live births, but the Calton area, a run-down slum, had 161 deaths per 1,000 live births.[42]

Concerns to reduce the infant mortality and child death rate, to 'rescue future citizens', drew on a number of discourses. There were liberal and radical reformers and labour movement activists who used the discourse of national efficiency and child 'wastage' to demand reforms including improvements in housing and medical attention, the provision of family endowments and birth control. Others linked infant mortality to a discourse on maternal inefficiency to undermine arguments that the death of children was a reflection on the economy and living environments of Scotland. The Medical Research Council undertook a study, funded by the Carnegie Trust, which examined the differences between the health, well-being and weight of over 5,000 children in relation to family income per person per week. Children from rural and mining localities were compared with those from the slums of Glasgow, Edinburgh and Dundee. The main findings of the research were published in 1926 in the wake of the General Strike and during the subsequent miners' lockout and it was concluded that children from rural and mining areas were healthier and heavier than slum children. It was conceded that cottage-style housing was a positive factor in the mining areas. However, no consideration was given to the high level of poor health amongst slum-dwelling mothers which in Glasgow was around 25 per cent of the cohort. In Dundee 40 per cent of the women were in 'indifferent health'. Whilst these conditions were noted, there were no links made between maternal ill-health and children's health. The report also excluded poverty as a factor, except to suggest that it was self-induced because of alcohol consumption. Thus, it was decided that 'the saying that what is the matter with the poor is poverty' was 'not substantiated' and that it was 'the efficiency of the mother which was the factor most definitely related to the growth and nutrition of the child'. Slum mothers were demonised as being 'shamelessly lazy and negligent' or not having 'the heart to struggle against the difficulties in their way'. They were deemed inefficient because they failed to prepare regular meals and have regular bedtimes and did not keep their homes and children 'scrupulously clean'. These women were accused of rearing a 'pale pinched undersized little mortal' that grew up 'almost uncared for in a confined and sunless atmosphere'.[43] Investigations such as these ensured that 'professionals' were increasingly advised to 'educate women on how to keep a strict account of their household budgets', something the average women apparently did not do.[44] In 1936, when one in every fourteen people in Scotland was on the Poor Roll, a Scottish Ministry of Health Report stated that

[42] *Forward*, 13 Jul. 1929.
[43] *Scotsman*, 24 Jun. and 30 Jul. 1926.
[44] *Glasgow Herald*, 4 Jan. 1926.

While no doubt there are many cases where there are financial reasons for the lack of proper feeding, there are undoubtedly a large number of mothers who cannot be bothered to prepare a proper meal, and with whom knowledge of how to fry and brew a pot of tea forms the bulk of their culinary equipment. In these unsatisfactory homes tinned milk, bread and margarine and fried foods, with soups perhaps once a week, form the staple diet.[45]

Throughout the period under discussion attempts were made to educate mothers on how food should be purchased and cooked. In 1931, Professor Finlay, ex-Superintendent of the Royal Sick Children's Hospital in Glasgow, addressed a conference held for health visitors, sanitary inspectors and Scottish nurses. He emphasised the work of supervision and care and expressed the view that the declining incidence of infant mortality was due to mothers receiving a better education on the benefits of a good diet. Findlay argued that previously 'in part due to custom and fashion' working-class women had been guilty of 'bad buying and bad cooking'. He went on to stress that more had to be made of the Welfare Clinics and mothers' clubs to get this message across to mothers that this habit had to change.[46] In 1933, health visitors met to 'compare notes and gather fresh impetus for their labours'. The report of the meeting highlights how Dundee's twenty-six health visitors 'would accompany a mother to market and show her how to lay out her money to the best advantage. Then they go to the mother's home and cook the food.' In Dundee, Glasgow, Fife and Edinburgh classes were given on 'nourishing dishes' and sample menus of shilling dinners, aimed at feeding a husband, wife and three children, were collected for distribution with recommendations that families should have three meals per day. Many families could manage this expenditure, but others had more than three children and the proposed three meals per day costing three shillings meant an expenditure of twenty-one shillings before rent and fuel costs were considered from average wages of around 50/-. Indeed, one inter-war miner's wife from Lanarkshire recalled, 'it wasn't a huge wage he got . . . If he got 27/- that was a big pay.'[47] Unemployment benefits were below this sum and it is therefore hardly surprising that these 'nourishing dishes' were not popular.

This vilification of working-class mothers and increased state supervision must have affected the morale of women, but to suggest that it undermined their power as mothers and household managers is too simplistic. The situation was complex, with tradition challenging and complementing changes in approaches to motherhood offered by the state and professionals. Indeed, access to the resources facilitated by the state's concerns for the child allowed women to enhance their household management and

---

[45] *Scotsman*, 6 Apr. 1936.
[46] *Govan Press*, 9 Jul. 1931.
[47] *Scotsman*, 17 May and 6 Oct. 1933 and Sinclair, '"Silenced, suppressed and passive"', 33.

mothering skills and thereby their power within the family. Ms Anderson was one of five children and her mother had been widowed just after the First World War. She remembered how women accepted and contested state supervision:

> We were always very thin and there was a midwife looking after the woman next door and my mother at the same time. Well she said to the next door neighbour, 'My these wee Andersons are awful thin.' The neighbour said, 'You go in and see them taking their dinner and you'll get a shock', because we were always good eaters. There was always plenty to eat and it would never cost a lot either. My mother had to be economic, but we were never starved I'll tell you that.

Ms Anderson went on to describe how her mother, and other women, kept their families 'well fed', undermining professional discourses that criticised working-class mothers:

> My mother was a very thrifty woman. If fish was cheaper in a shop a distance away she would go to that shop. While she worked cleaning offices in the meat market there was a benefit shop across from it. It sold tripe and all the different bits and my mother used to get the cheek of a cow and boil that – my mother wasn't the only one. She made all these things, economic but nourishing. So if there was any economy to be used my mother would use it. We were always well fed and we were rarely ill.[48]

In the narratives women detail how they exercised their skills as household managers, whilst emphasising the hardship they endured in this process. Mrs Gallacher, a mother of nine children, stated, 'You forget these things – you've got to, but many a hard time I've had.' She recalled how she went without food to feed her children when money was scarce and how she 'trudged' the neighbourhood to acquire cheap and 'nutritious food'. This included shopping in Robert's Market, where customers took a bowl to carry home the cheaper 'chipped eggs'. 'You could take a bucket or a big jug and go down there and Mr Roberts would fill it with stock. You'd buy a cabbage; sometimes he'd leave the pigs skin or an odd pig's foot in it. You could buy a pig's foot for 3d – that'd do two dinners.'[49]

Working-class mothers' interest in the health of their families does not mean that they were being influenced by state supervision and discourses on motherhood. Family, community and working-class socialisation were significant discursive and determining forces. Mrs Gallacher stated

> I tried to do things like my mother would have done and I had a hard time trying. Of course I had to do a bit of working myself, making their clothes and that. Well my mother used to make all our clothes

---

[48] SOHCA/019/02/Glasgow, b. 1908.
[49] SOHCA/019/015/Glasgow, b. 1909.

and she kept us all going. If we wanted anything if she had it we got it and if she didn't have it we didn't get it. That's the way I did it and I always thought, well that's what my mother done and there was never anything wrong.[50]

She also related how 'everybody called my mother Granny because she looked after kids. She loved it. She adopted one wee girl, and then her mother got married and wanted her back. She was going to America, so my mother gave her back.'[51] Elizabeth Wheeler's grandmother, who had seven dependent children, one a baby still breast-feeding, took in her deceased niece's four young daughters until their father remarried. Elizabeth and her mother also resided with her grandmother until her parents were able to afford a home of their own.[52] Mrs Kilpartick maintained

> I know I would have been hungry many a time and my children too but I went out to work. I did house-cleaning. I used to put the baby in a doll's pram and do it in the afternoon because he slept great in the afternoon. My wee daughter, I'd tell her where I was and she'd come down and take him out to the garden and hurl him up to the house and change him. She was a great help to me.[53]

Family and neighbours were fundamental to what was largely communal mothering. Mrs Parsonage recollected how 'if your children needed looked after, a neighbour would say, it's all right leave them with me, they'll be all right'.[54] The community would also take responsibility for feeding, clothing and sheltering children that they thought were being neglected by their parents.[55]

Professional advice and provisions also had to be compatible with the cultural definitions of working-class mothering and women's economic situations. In 1930, the *Govan Press* reported on how the Elderpark Welfare Centre in Govan was 'Rescuing Future Citizens'. The number of women who attended the antenatal clinic was 1,699, 286 more than the previous year. The postnatal clinic saw 4,958 children and 473 mothers and 225 children received dental care, more than twice as many as the previous year. The clinic also disseminated scientific information on mothering by providing lectures for mothers and classes on 'home nursing' for young women over sixteen years of age, prospective mothers. However, the clinic also provided weekly sewing classes that were very popular. The classes were an extension of women's support networks because in the sewing classes maternity bundles and clothes for toddlers could be made and sold for the

---

[50] SOHCA/019/015/Glasgow, b. 1909.

[51] SOHCA/019/015/Glasgow, b. 1909.

[52] Wheeler, *Cowie*, 4–5.

[53] SOHCA/019/012/Glasgow, b. 1907.

[54] SOHCA/019/026/Glasgow, b. 1917.

[55] Glasgow Caledonian University, Children 1st (RSSPCC) Archive, GB 1847 RSSPCC, Annual reports of the branches, 1896–1939.

cost of the material. In the period between 1925 and 1926, 386 garments were produced and distributed in the local community. The Elderpark Welfare Centre also established a choir in 1931, organised Fresh Air Fortnight holidays and Christmas parties and presents for the children who attended. It was the first clinic in Scotland to establish a Fathers' Council whose aim was to 'attract fathers to be co-partners in parenthood', thereby challenging the view that childcare was the sole responsibility of women. In Aberdeen's Woodside Child Welfare Clinic women also made clothing, beds and bedding for babies, expectant and nursing mothers, which they sold cheaply or distributed free to 'necessitous cases' along with clothes, prams and toys which they had collected from the public. This centre was so popular that when women were no longer eligible to attend they would borrow a neighbour's baby 'so as not to miss an afternoon in the Clubbie'.[56]

Glasgow City Council's Child Welfare Clinic in Springburn was formally opened in 1926. Mrs McNicol recalled attending the clinic:

> We went to Springburn Baby Centre and we had quite a good time there. We met a schoolteacher there. Oh her husband was a rough one. He was always getting into trouble, and the poor wean, it wasn't very nice! Well we used to take a change of clothes and we couldn't afford prams, it was a shawl we used to wrap babies in, so I took a shawl, gave it to her for her baby. I used to tell her, 'Never mind you'll come all right' and she did.[57]

These clinics did not undermine women's support networks or autonomy. The increasing number of infant welfare clinics coexisted with support networks and provided another public venue for women to reduce their isolation and to extend their access to resources, leisure and public spaces. For example, although the clinics principally concentrated on providing education for mothers in 1921 during the miners' dispute child welfare centres in the Middle Ward of Lanarkshire received 10,240 applications for assistance from mothers. This was repeated during the seven- month-long miners' lockout of 1926. School boards were also targeted to provide clothing and a hot meal each day for children and when they did not, children were often withheld from school, as was the case in Blantyre in 1926.[58]

The economic climate also limited the capacity for control and supervision of women by medical professionals which had ambiguous consequences because it also limited women's access to resources. The structure of the National Insurance Act ensured that between the wars most married women and children were denied access to healthcare, with the exception of the maternity and child welfare clinics, and hospital out-patients.

---

[56] *Govan Press*, 4 and 11 Feb. 1927, 6 and 7 Mar. 1931, and H. Mackenzie, *The Third Statistical Account of Scotland, The City of Aberdeen* (Edinburgh, 1953), 445.

[57] Glasgow City Council Minutes, 17 Jun. 1926 and SOHCA/019/015/Glasgow, b. 1909.

[58] Sinclair, "'Silenced, suppressed and passive'", 216–20.

There were some doctors who treated women and children who were unable to pay for healthcare. Many did so out of sympathy and through the self-interest of maintaining their male breadwinner patients.[59] George Robertson, a general practitioner, maintained that the depression was 'as serious for doctors as it was for patients' because they lost vast numbers of insured patients. In 1925 he had about 1,500 names on his insured list for free care, but their dependants were chargeable. He maintained that owing 'to the prevalence of poverty' at least half these dependants were given free healthcare and when individuals ceased to be insured, 'if they were well known to us we felt morally under obligation to attend to their wants when asked to do so'.[60] Mr Gordon concurred, stating, 'In those days it was three shillings for a visit and people didn't have that money so the doctors never pushed to get it – they just accepted the situation.'[61] Costs could range from between 2/- and 3/6 in the 1920s to between 2/6 and 5/- for surgery attendance. For home visits the price in the 1920s was between 2/6 and 5/- and by the 1930s it was 3/6 to 7/-. This mitigated contact with doctors, especially in the industrial and mining areas hard hit by depression that did not keep pace with the growth in access to health services.[62] Because of this, custom and culture rather than professionals often dictated how healthcare was administered.

Margaret Allan expressed the view of many working-class people when she stated that 'in these days doctors were a foreign word'. Mrs Jones explained how 'you had to pay for everything, but people hadn't the money to pay for the doctor'.[63] Margaret Allan also highlighted how, because of the expense of medical care, women 'depended on their own remedies'.

> Home remedies were passed on. Even for childbirth you never called a doctor, it was the woman next door who was the midwife. Home remedies from the old folk nearly put the doctor out of business because that was what we thrived on because the doctor cost 3/-.[64]

Mrs Galbraith agreed:

> Medicines were so expensive that you did an awful lot yourself. I know my mother used to make cough bottles which turned out an awful lot cheaper because we couldn't afford an awful lot of medicines and the same with doctors. Parents did their best to cure you before they started bringing in doctors.[65]

---

[59] A. Digby and N. Bosanquet, 'Doctors and patients in an era of national health insurance and private practice, 1913–1938', *Economic History Review*, 41, 1: 74–94 (1988).

[60] Robertson, *Gorbals Doctor*, 111–12.

[61] SOHCA/019/043/Clydebank, b. 1920.

[62] Digby and Bosanquet, 'Doctors and patients', 84–9.

[63] The Barrhead People's Story Group, *It's Funny Whit Ye Remember* and SOHCA/019/026/Glasgow, b. 1900.

[64] The Barrhead People's Story Group, *It's Funny Whit Ye Remember*.

[65] SOHCA/019/08/Glasgow, b. 1916.

Mrs McQueen's memories highlight how the skill of practising traditional medicine and the self-abnegation of care enhanced women's feminine identities. She states that 'my mother was awful kind. If any of the neighbours was in trouble, or if any of the neighbours were sick or anything it was always my mother they came for and she always helped them: put poultices on them or anything they needed.'[66] Custom and women's pride in their 'home remedies' converged with the economic conditions between the wars to facilitate continuities in women's practice of traditional medicines in their neighbourhoods. At the 1930 Scottish Labour Women's Conference, Miss Jobson provided evidence of this. Although aware of the economic impediments women faced in access to healthcare, she also stressed that

> It seems that when a woman gets married and has a family she thinks she knows everything about her health. Grandmothers are the worst of the lot. If we could do away with most of them we would have a great deal less trouble with our younger women and there would be a good deal more made of the health service. Women do not make the best use of the services available.

She went on to state, 'we need to get rid of the idea amongst women that only the very ignorant and the very poorest need advice in times of illness'.[67] Women only tended to call doctors in emergencies owing to costs. They sacrificed their own needs for those of their families and relied on their networks to assist during periods when they or their children required medical assistance. Moreover, while child welfare received immediate attention between the wars, the same cannot be said for maternity care, even though the incidence of maternal mortality was rising. Glasgow City Council approached the Scottish Board of Health in January 1923 with a proposal to establish a Child Welfare and Maternity Centre in Shettleston and Maryhill, Glasgow. The Board of Health agreed to consider child welfare clinics, but stipulated that there would be no provision for maternity care.[68] In 1924, the ILPer John Wheatley, then Minister for Health, reiterated this position, stating that 'the proper place for women to be confined is the home'.[69] The *Glasgow Herald* reported on the 'Health of Mothers' in 1929: in Glasgow '60 per cent, and in some districts as many as 80–90 per cent of confinements, were in the hands of midwives' who administered to women in their own homes.[70] However, by this point 'Glasgow's Maternity Problem' was apparent in the rising number of women dying in childbirth. The Medical Officer's Report for Glasgow discussed the 'deficiency of maternity accommodation in the city' and claimed that demand

---

[66] SOHCA/019/018/Glasgow, b. 1909.
[67] *Glasgow Herald*, 10 Jan. 1930.
[68] Glasgow City Council Minutes, 8 Jan. and 26 Feb. 1923.
[69] Glasgow City Council Minutes, 7 Aug. 1924.
[70] Glasgow City Council Minutes, 27 May 1929.

for maternity care was spreading amongst all classes.[71] Yet it was not until March 1933 that the Glasgow Division of the British Medical Association forwarded a memorandum on 'Glasgow's Maternity Problem', outlining a scheme for consideration to the Council.[72] It would appear that 'rescuing future citizens' took priority over maternal mortality that was often attributed to women having illegal abortions. The economic climate and ideological forces between the wars limited supervision by the state and the potential loss of women's autonomy as mothers.

Limited access to medical professionals ensured that other local resources, especially charitable ones, were exploited by women, not merely for healthcare but also for a range of material and psychological resources which eased the burdens of household management and allowed women to cope and make men dependent on them. For example the Glasgow Medical Missionary Society identified itself as 'strictly non-denominational'. It employed twenty-two missionaries to provide medical care, 'spiritual uplift and social improvement' to its beneficiaries in the Calton and Gorbals regions of Glasgow.[73] In 1926, the Society administered medical care to over 30,000 Glaswegians who did not qualify for assistance from a panel or parish doctor under the National Insurance Act, and stressed the importance of these provisions for women and children. These services were vital to mothering and their children and demand for them increased as the economic climate deteriorated. In 1929, the Society provided services to 33,447 individuals as well as supplying 7,000 dressings and 3,200 home visits. By 1933, 48,522 individuals received medical care.[74] Glasgow's Outdoor Medical Services for the sick poor was also used extensively: in 1931 this Service provided 113,217 consultations across the city.[75]

Local resources were significant for working-class women, allowing them to extend their assets. However, while medical attention was exploited because it released resources for other expenditure or because women were unable to afford medical care for themselves or their children, the Glasgow Mission's Christian work in saving souls was less popular. In 1933, of the 48,522 individuals who received medical assistance, only 67 were 'induced to attend church', although the majority may have already been churchgoers. Yet 272 children were encouraged to take up the offer to join the organisation's Pals Club. [76] This was a way in which women could be relieved of the burdens of childcare for a few hours each week.

Charity was often religion-based in local communities and, like religion and religious institutions, it was used to enhance womanly identities and

[71] Glasgow City Council Minutes, 9 Apr. 1929.
[72] Glasgow City Council Minutes, 3 and 15 Mar. 1933.
[73] *Glasgow Herald*, 2 Feb. and 10 Dec. 1926.
[74] *Glasgow Herald*, 27 Nov. 1929, 11 Dec. 1931, 2 Dec. 1932, 24 Mar. 1933 and 3 Nov. 1938.
[75] *Glasgow Herald*, 24 Mar. 1933.
[76] *Glasgow Herald*, 24 Mar. 1933.

their resources.[77] Through association with religious organisations women were able to enrich their respectable identities and extend their access to public spaces and their sphere of influence. Religious discourses also enhanced women's psychological resources; they allowed subordinate groups to envisage an eventual levelling of worldly fortunes and emphasised the significance of solidarity, equality, mutual aid, honesty and simplicity – ideals that permeated women's networks. Sharing and lending, although based on the concept of reciprocity, were presented as self-sacrifice, a form of Christian duty that was a 'godsend' to the recipient. This feminised and often informal form of 'philanthropy' allowed women to shore up their feminine identities as carers and givers. Clearly women's relationship with religion permeated their worldview, but whilst it could be beneficial it also held the potential to impede their progress. The clergy in Scotland may have espoused the idea that women should find love, contentment and sexual fulfilment within marriage, but unlike the Church of England, the Church of Scotland refused to countenance the use of contraception or divorce.[78] Indeed, the Church of Scotland in many respects mirrored the doctrines of its Catholic counterparts on these issues.

In Scotland sectarian anxieties were at the root of fears over the 'disintegration of the family'. Both the Catholic and Protestant clergy attributed this to interdenominational marriages, the use of contraception, separation and divorce. At a meeting held in 1935 by the Catholic Trust Society in Edinburgh, attended by 9,000 women, it was asserted by Archbishop McDonald that women 'were more open to pagan propaganda' which threatened the very foundation of the family. The pagan propaganda to which he referred was support of the use of birth control and abortion.[79] In 1937, Lady Winifred Elwes, at a 'meeting of Protestant mothers', expressed the view held by the Protestant clergy that the use of birth control would ensure that 'the nation' would 'fall into the hands of Catholics'.[80]

Parishioners were conscious of these discourses: Mrs Galbraith claimed that ministers 'didn't believe in birth control', although in defiance she also stated that 'they didn't do anything to help the women who were having the children'. Mrs Jones did not attend religious services after she married into the Catholic faith, but she recalled, 'I know real ones, good Catholics, they were warned about birth control.' Women were also made aware that ministers opposed divorce and some believed that if they had got divorced they would have been 'barred from the church'.[81] The

---

[77] For the relationship between women's identity and religion, see C. Brown, *The Death of Christian Britain* (London, 2001), 163, 180–91 and passim.

[78] For England see J. Lewis, 'Public institution and private relationship: marriage and marriage guidance 1920–1968', *Twentieth Century British History*, 1, 3: 233–65 (1990).

[79] *Times*, 25 May 1937 and *Scotsman*, 9 Feb. 1935.

[80] *Scotsman*, 9 Feb. 1935.

[81] SOHCA/019/08/Glasgow, b. 1916, SOHCA/019/018/Glasgow, b. 1909 and SOHCA/019/08/Glasgow, b. 1916 respectively.

discourse on interdenominational marriages also permeated collective mentalities. In 1933, Archbishop Mackintosh warned that there was a need to 'save the children' of Scotland, stating that 'again and again children are taken from their parents due to apathy'. He attributed this to Catholics marrying people from other religious denominations that resulted in 'disseminations in the household'.[82] Mrs McQueen, a Protestant, married a Catholic. She remembered how 'they made out it was mixed marriages that caused divorces'.[83] Regardless of the reality, the clergy glorified marriage and motherhood as a woman's rightful place and shored this up by their very vocal opposition to separation, divorce and birth control.

Women were well acquainted with the clergy's attitudes to separation, divorce and the use of contraceptives, but not all women accepted the clergy's preaching. They could embrace aspects of their discourses, but only in so far as it was compatible with their everyday lives. Mrs Kilpatrick recalled

> My father and mother were separated. Every week he belted her and she left him and got a legal separation and he never sent her money. He was bad to her and the priest would come up to my mother and tell her that she had to go back to her husband! 'You're married to him in the eyes of God.' I said, 'What happens to the eyes of God on a Saturday night when he gets a drink. He belts her.' He said, 'She's married to him, she'll have to go back to him.'[84]

Mrs Campbell, a Catholic, recalled why, and the means by which, she prevented an unwanted pregnancy: 'When I had six weans to a drunk man, and he never worked a day, I realised I'd need to stop it. A friend of mine got me a douche for there was no birth control in those days. I never had to take another.'[85]

Such support gave women a means of controlling their fertility that needed no assistance from men and many women used this resource. In Scotland, the dominant discourse that elevated the role of motherhood did not necessarily mean that women accepted that their fertility should be unrestricted. In fact, the number of women who attempted to control their fertility can be ascertained from the rising level of maternal mortality. In the early 1930s, illegal abortions accounted for about 10.5 per cent of all maternal mortality figures, but by 1934, this had risen dramatically to 20 per cent. Women's support networks 'dispersed information on the methods' of 'bringing on a period' and also the names of abortionists.[86] Mrs Lang recollected that 'there was one that lived beside us. She used to do illegal abortions and if there was anybody expecting they'd say, "Oh

[82] SVDP, Annual Report, 1933.
[83] SOHCA/019/027/Glasgow, b. 1905.
[84] SOHCA/019/011/Glasgow, b. 1917.
[85] SOHCA/019/04/Glasgow, b. 1910.
[86] Brookes, 'The illegal operation', 171–2.

that'll be another wan for Kitty Richie". She used to do them. It's a good job that there were people like her or there'd be a lot of children walking the streets.' Croy in Lanarkshire with its mere 'two hundred or so' of a population also had an abortionist.[87] Mrs MacIntosh's recollection also suggests that attitudes towards pre-marital sex and abortion were complex and situational in working-class neighbourhoods:

> There was a wee girl, she was expecting, and her mother thought that was terrible. Oh she was high and mighty! She sent for somebody to get rid of the baby and the girl lost that much blood she was taken to hospital. She was on her last legs and she got married before she died. It was sad. The mother didn't want the baby. That woman never came out the house after that.[88]

Community mores, which were shaped by the material realities of women's lives, were important in determining how working-class women viewed pre-marital sex, the use of contraception and abortion. Many working-class women accepted pre-marital pregnancy if it was accompanied by a subsequent wedding. In addition, although the identity of motherhood was very significant, and abortions could be frowned upon, women tended to distinguish between illegal abortions and 'bringing on a period', with the latter not attracting the same condemnation as illegal abortions. This was undoubtedly influenced by the ways in which the courts and the media treated women if they were prosecuted for having, or attempting to obtain, an abortion. The *Glasgow Herald* reported on 'the unsavoury nature of six cases of procuring abortions' and on the case of Elizabeth Dunn, who was sentenced to eight months in prison for attempting to procure an abortion. The duration of the sentence may also indicate that this was to ensure the birth of the child.[89]

The criminalisation of abortion affected women's subjectivities. Illegal abortions were condemned and all other attempts to abort a pregnancy were redefined as 'bringing on a period'. Yet women were aware that 'bringing on a period' was a form of abortion. Because of this, they carried the shame that the dominant gender discourses, the lack of access to contraception and abortions and community mores imposed on them. Mrs Kilpatrick remembered, 'I only wanted one but six years after that, and then another six years after that I was expecting again and I said, "There's not going be a third." I never took anything, nor did I go to a doctor or anything. I done a lot of things I shouldn't have done. I was only about three months when it all came away and I got rid of it after that, but you're the first person I've ever told.'[90] Women's attitudes and the economic realities of their lives

[87] SOHCA/019/013/Glasgow, b. 1907 and SOHCA/019/044/Lanarkshire, b. 1900.
[88] SOHCA/019/015/Glasgow, b. 1909.
[89] *Glasgow Herald*, 19 Feb. 1931.
[90] SOHCA/019/012/Glasgow, b. 1907.

moderated the ideal of motherhood as enshrined in the dominant world-view. Poverty and continual childbirth, and the desire for freedom from these obstacles, undermined the idealisation of motherhood intended to enhance and enlarge Britain's population. Abortion, or 'bringing on a period', needed no aid or approval from men. This was one way that women could control their lives. It was a resource, if relative. These women were feminists in the respect that 'a feminist is a woman who does not allow anyone to think in her place', whether that was the state or a spouse.[91]

The clergy and religious organisations may have influenced women's behaviour to some extent, but in return working-class women gained enhanced status, resources and security. Religion also bestowed a sense of comfort and hope during a period marked by economic insecurity and the increasing threat of a further war. Respondents were asked what they felt they had gained from religion and unequivocally they cited the psychological resources of strength, purpose, courage and comfort. Mrs Ingills felt her faith gave her 'comfort, definitely, anxiety too, but comfort was the main thing'. Mrs Nicol stated, 'I used to pray and I felt if I asked for something I got it. I felt that God was good.' Mrs O'Neil believed, 'God gave me strength', and, significantly, Mrs Jones noted that 'they had to have something to hang on to, they really did. They needed something to say well when I die I'll be getting something. They had to have something to hold on to, because they hadn't very much in our [sic] lives.'[92] What is fundamental in this response is the intermittent use of 'they' and 'our' in the description suggesting the collective nature of this particular resource and the need for composure in a world that is no longer perceived to understand the significance of religion.

The clergy also provided women with venues in which to socialise, informally as meeting places, and formally in religious-based organisations, allowing women to extend their public spaces and public profiles. Mr Jamieson recalled, 'once the service was over they collected outside the church and gossiped. Your mother met other ladies there and they all had families and they didn't have much time to gossip, but in the end it was a social gossip.'[93] Women also gained positions of power denied them elsewhere through their association with religious organisations. Mrs Ingills recalled, 'I was very much brought up in church. It was very important to me. I helped out whenever I could. I was a primary teacher, a Sunday school teacher, a leader of the Girls' Auxiliary. I went through all the stages.' Mrs Galbraith stated that 'The one thing that really educated me a lot was the Townswomen's Guild. It took you out to different places.'[94] It

---

[91] See Michèle Le Doeuff as quoted in Kemp and Squires, *Feminisms*, 142.

[92] SOCHA/019/010/Glasgow, b. 1907, SOHCA/019/016/Glasgow, b. 1905, SOHCA/019/014/ Glasgow, b. 1909 and SOHCA/019/011/Glasgow, b. 1917 respectively.

[93] SOHCA/019/018/Glasgow, b. 1899.

[94] SOHCA/019/010/Glasgow, b. 1907 and SOHCA/019/08/Glasgow, b. 1916.

would also have been difficult for men to contest women's involvement in these 'respectable' pursuits or to refuse to care for children while women were so occupied. In this respect women challenged the sexual division of leisure and the restrictions to their public profiles embedded in the ideal of separate spheres.

Religious institutions often provided access to charity and acted as a childminder through their children's clubs. Mrs Ferguson remembered how 'there were places where the poor could go and get things. They had one thing in town and you could put in for a holiday for the children: the Fresh Air Fortnight, and they got away for a fortnight's holiday.'[95] Again, there is a shift in the narrative from the collective 'the poor' to the personalised 'you could', which suggests that for composure there is a dissociation with poverty, but also that many women, possibly including this woman, used this kind of resource. Because of this it was difficult for socialists to challenge the influence of religion in women's lives because they feared

> alienating support, especially among women who carried the burden of life when money was more than unusually short. For these women charity could in truth be life and a heaven-sent way of getting children off their hands, lessening work and worry.[96]

According to Mrs McQueen, however, charity was dispensed strictly on religious denomination: 'some people used to get help off the St Vincent de Paul, but you had to be deep in'.[97] Yet this is not the picture presented by St Vincent de Paul. They stressed that their 'energies and sympathies' were not solely 'extended to persons of our own creed'.[98] Irrespective of the validity of the assertion, as Table 7.2 (which is only a snapshot sample of the parishes receiving relief) indicates, the Society of St Vincent de Paul was fundamental in local communities.

In 1919, the society provided relief to 45,266 families in Scotland in cash and in kind on a weekly basis as well as professional legal and medical services. However, as the economic climate deteriorated the number of individuals assisted increased. By 1932, 74,645 families received support in cash or in kind, although the level of demand ensured that relief had to be spread more widely. This was problematic because of the loss of subscribers from industries, such as Fairfield's shipyard and United Collieries Ltd, along with the reduction of funds collected at church doors because of the economic climate.[99] The increasing demands on this resource highlights how important to women the organisation was. It helped women mediate hardship and cope with household management.

---

95 SOHCA/019/07/Glasgow, b. 1911.
96 Glasser, *Growing Up in the Gorbals*, 54–5.
97 SOHCA/019/018/Glasgow, b. 1909.
98 SVDP, Annual Report, 1919–1939, especially 1925.
99 SVDP, Annual Report, 1919, 1921 and 1932.

Table 7.2 St Vincent De Paul's Relief of Families in Need, 1922–36.

Selected parishes	Relief in cash and kind* (£s)				Families relieved per weekly visit			
	1922	1925	1931	1936	1922	1925	1931	1936
Sacred Heart, Bridgeton, Glasgow	521.10	241.09	248.92	181.50	2,096	1,180	1,254	1,165
St Joseph, Blantyre	245.25	265.05	158.34	134.68	583	1688	708	312
Our Lady of the Holy Redeemer, Clydebank	308.08	143.03	149.34	153.35	761	207	1106	466
St Patrick, Coatbridge	247.41	164.04	182.71	129.09	1,304	1,209	961	554
St Mary, Greenock	1171.01	344.16	160.90	114.55	4,115	1,975	1,060	681
St Mirrin, Paisley	386.42	247.16	201.33	216.56	1,610	1,367	1,783	1,856
St John, Port Glasgow	1008.60	438.31	277.39	134.03	3,090	1,495	2,331	818

* Until 1929 and inclusive, payments in tokens, clothing and coal are listed separately. Thereafter they are grouped as payment in kind. Rent is a separate category throughout, but has been included in this data as payment in kind.

Source: St Vincent de Paul Annual Reports, 1921–36.

Like other religious organisations, the Society had a women's branch, allowing women opportunities for leadership; connections with such organisations provided an extension of their public spaces and their status through expressions of their godliness in the self-sacrifice of philanthropic activities. The needlewomen of St Vincent de Paul did this by purchasing cloth and making garments for the poor. In 1925, 2,900 such garments were distributed across Scotland. The bible women who administered medical care and spiritual guidance to the sick through the auspices of the Glasgow Medical Missionary Society expressed similar womanly identities.[100] Nor was the influence of religion on women's identities restricted to formal participation in charitable organisations. Religious identities enhanced women's status and profiles. It gave them a sense of purpose beyond the domestic sphere, enhanced their resources and moderated the sexual division of leisure.

Women's subjectivites were influenced by increased state supervision and by the shoring up of domesticity between the wars, but while the private sphere was important in shaping women's political identities, to ignore the effect of the public sphere would obscure and undervalue the choices women made. In the private and public spheres women not only responded to class and gender inequalities but they attempted to enhance their physical and psychological resources and thereby their power. They did so by adopting the language of the dominant gender discourse on womanhood, by using networks and 'women's talk' to shore up their status and identities, and by exploiting local institutions to enhance their resources. In this way they also augmented their public profiles and gained greater potential to make men reliant on them. In many respects this was a 'rough kind of feminism' which may have been situational and only one aspect of working-class women's multiple identities, but it was nevertheless an expression of the feminine as a political tactic that provided women with knowledge and resources, and helped them survive and identify themselves as good housewives, mothers and household managers. Thus, it allowed women to negotiate some degree of power and self-legitimisation within their homes and neighbourhoods.

---

[100] SVDP, Annual Report, 1925 and *Glasgow Herald*, 11 Dec. 1931.

CHAPTER EIGHT

Gender and the Politics of Everyday Life

Scotland's inter-war working-class constituency has been identified with a powerful class awareness that was expressed in extreme militancy immediately before, during and in the years after the First World War. Such was the extent of the militancy that it has generated a debate over the country's radical and 'revolutionary' potential. However, in Scottish labour historiography that story has been and remains a masculine narrative.[1] This chapter subverts that narrative by highlighting how working-class women's experiences of everyday life politicised them. Women's roles as moral guardians of home, family and community provided a basis for coalitions, especially where economic conditions threatened their identities as good household managers, but they also expressed a class awareness that was interlinked to their gender identities. Women's roles were central during protests over the effects of unemployment. Unemployment affected women directly and as wives and mothers because women were at the forefront of the adverse economic climate which diminished their resources. Like many socialist women in Scotland, working-class women responded by demanding a social wage to alleviate these conditions. To do so they became involved in protests, deputations, demonstrations and direct action on welfare issues in local communities. Yet the gendered nature of class formation that largely excluded women from institutional protest meant that neighbourhoods facilitated 'inherently non-institutional forms' of female protest.[2] These protests were a continuation of the radical populist protests which had characterised women's political activity and which were expressions of both their class and gender identities.[3]

The cost, condition and availability of decent housing had been a principal area of women's radical and subversive forms of political activity before World War I, and especially during the rent strikes of 1915. At this time the cost of fuel and food merged with housing issues to cause discontent amongst significant numbers of working-class women. Mr Ewart recalled women's politicisation over these issues in Partick during World War I:

> They were hard working people that were fed up and they wanted potatoes and couldn't get them. But they saw this lorry coming along.

---

[1] See Duncan and McIvor, *Militant Workers* and Kenefick, *Red Scotland*.

[2] See Macdonald, 'Weak roots', 6–30.

[3] For a discussion on the use of these protests in the nineteenth century see Gordon, *Women and the Labour Movement*.

This old lady, she was a member of the Orange Lodge, the opposite kind that should have been doing this – she said to the women round about, 'Come on, now's your chance. Here's the potatoes that you can't buy, but someone else can. They've got the money because you haven't, because you're not in the same class as them.' So she puts an old sack apron on and underneath that she had a bread knife. She went up to the nearest potato sack and stuck the knife in and said, 'Come on, fill your pinnies.' And they all picked up their skirts and filled them with potatoes. There wasn't a bag of potatoes went into that shop. And when a bloke went to get the rents nine times out of ten he had to get a police escort to get near the close and when he did get the police they were all bundled out into the street. They were just women anxious to see their families were being fed, that's all. It wasn't that they were trying to change anything. They were trying to prove with their existence that we had the right to be fed.[4]

The determination of the women and their aggression was a clear expression of the effects of everyday life in politicising women and also of the women's ability to usurp gender norms – these women were far from 'lady-like'. It is also evident that domestic issues provided the grounds for collective action amongst women and that this was facilitated by women's support networks. One of the women involved, a widow with five children, was prosecuted. In court she made her position clear: 'I am quite willing to go to prison knowing that my family will be looked after in my absence.'[5] The fact that there were 'Orange women, old women, young women – anyone who had the guts to do it' involved in these protests indicates that the collective identity of being working-class housewives and mothers transcended the divisions of religion and gender-based conceptions of self based on respectability.

Challenging male authority and engaging in protests was not unique to Partick women. During the rent strikes, *Forward* reported on an attempted eviction in Shettleston. In defiance of the ILP's advice, and of gender norms that demonised violent women, women appeared with weapons, paraded to the factor's home, burned an effigy and smashed his windows. The prominent ILPer John Wheatley berated the women. He informed them that the bailiffs had arrived at their intended destination and that they should be there 'protecting homes', not at the factor's house destroying them. He was informed 'in loud tones' that he had nothing to worry about: 'We have left enough behind to prevent that.'[6]

Women's protests acted as a linchpin between formal and informal politics. However, women's direct action was undermined by the appropriation of housing concerns as a political lever by groups like the ILP,

[4] SOHCA/019/031/Glasgow, b. 1908.
[5] *Daily Record*, 26 May 1917.
[6] *Forward*, 12 and 19 Jun. 1915.

the Labour Housing Association and the myriad of tenants' associations that had sprung up to represent council tenants after World War I. These organisations had a tradition of activating women in the struggle to reduce the price of rent and improve housing standards, but with the exception of the Labour Housing Association, the leadership of these groups was generally male-dominated. This resulted in the adoption of more institutional forms of protest against rent prices and housing conditions, particularly the use of deputations to the relevant councils and factors, which were mainly led by men. In 1924, the *Daily Record* reported that the Clydebank Housing Association had adopted the role of a 'trade union' between factor and tenant. The organisation proposed to offer advice, collect rents and 'act as a wholesale between factors and tenants to prevent the bullying of women by house factors'. In 1931, committees were formed in Bothwell, Chapelhall and Calderbank, all in Lanarkshire, to represent tenants and demand that 'the council and other landlords' reduce rents by 25 per cent because of 'the poor state of employment'.[7] The institutionalisation of 'domestic concerns' often displaced women's direct action, although some women did take advantage of this process by using it as a springboard into the formal political sphere. For example, in 1936 Mrs Gembles stood for election for the Haymarket Council seat in Edinburgh as a Tenants' Association candidate.[8]

Although adopting an institutional approach often eclipsed direct and spontaneous action, it did facilitate coordinated action and embraced a greater number of individuals. Concessions were also obtained: in 1932 Glasgow Corporation decided to reduce the rents of over 2,000 houses by 2/- per week. However, in 1933, the Council of Tenants' Associations, representing some 30,000 tenants, requested a meeting with Glasgow City Council so that they could forward demands for further rent reductions.[9] The Council refused to hear the deputation. It was not alone in refusing to respond to this form of protest. Mr Thomas Stewart, secretary of the Property Owners and Factors Association, Glasgow, Ltd., replied through the *Glasgow Herald* to a request from 'various bodies of workers and political parties' in Govan who sought a reduction in rents of 47.5 per cent. On behalf of the Association he let it be known that the deputation would 'not serve any useful purpose'.[10]

Housing struggles and conflict with property owners became more muted in the late 1920s and 1930s because of the less favourable economic and political context. Nevertheless, women continued to protest. Alexander McLean, the chief sanitary inspector for Renfrewshire pointed

---

[7] *Daily Record*, 24 Nov. 1924 and 21 May 1931.

[8] *Scotsman*, 4 Nov. 1936.

[9] Glasgow City Council Minutes, 30 Mar. 1933, 5 and 11 Apr. 1933 and *Glasgow Herald*, 18 Mar. 1932.

[10] *Glasgow Herald*, 13 May 1932.

out that there was considerable discontent amongst the ill-housed in the region. So bad was the discontent amongst the women that 'sanitary staff were constantly under the necessity of adopting a policy of appeasement'.[11] Other forms of protest were deployed, including comic songs sung on the day that rents were paid:

> Here comes the factor, the factor, the factor.
> Here comes the factor, the factor for his rent.
> Catch him by the waistcoat, his greatcoat, his billy-goat
> Tell him he's a nanny-goat and fling him doun the stairs.[12]

Direct action was not completely sidelined. Rent strikes continued, such as those in Renfrewshire where nearly 600 Paisley women, many with babies in their arms, took to the streets in 1938 to protest against rent increases. Accompanied by a drum-and-flute band, the women marched round the county building chanting that more rent meant less food for their families and that their 'case was one of domestic life or death'. The council responded by promising the women that there would be 'great concessions'.[13] Rent strikes and the traditions borrowed from populist protests were equally evident in strikes in Glasgow, Aberdeen, Lanarkshire, Renfrewshire and the 'spiritual home of anarchy', Clydebank, throughout the inter-war years.[14] Mrs Adams recalled in Greenock, 'there was a rent strike up our way in the new houses. They all went on strike one year and they went up and down the road shouting and singing at night.'[15] The protests that women were involved in linked a number of concerns, many of which stemmed from the level of unemployment in Scotland. Mrs Duncan recalled the rent strikes in Govan:

> Nearly every close, I'll not say every one, but the biggest majority wouldn't pay their rent, but of course there was nobody working. They were fighting the rents and they weren't getting any work so people just hadn't the rent to give them. I was just lucky. I was in a different position.[16]

The notion that it was 'luck' that differentiated those who could pay their rents from those who could not ensured that there was little or no social condemnation attached to what might otherwise have been defined as aberrant or 'rough' behaviour. Women's defence of their families made the domestic ideal a political issue and provided women with a public platform.

However, women's militancy was not confined to strictly domestic or non-industrial issues. As Chapter four highlighted, working women were

---

[11] *Glasgow Herald*, 19 Sep. 1938.
[12] SOHCA/019/031/Glasgow, b. 1908.
[13] *Daily Record*, 3 and 10 May 1938.
[14] *Daily Record*, 24 Nov. 1924 and *Forward*, 24 Nov. 1924.
[15] SOHCA/019/022/Greenock, b. 1919.
[16] SOHCA/019/05/Glasgow, b. 1912.

involved in significant numbers in the General Strike of 1926. In towns, cities and rural areas across Scotland everyday experiences of the General Strike and the miners' lockout of 1926 politicised working-class women. The government's use of the Emergency Powers Act, special police and middle-class blackleg labour, along with the experiences of being a working-class wife left to cope with limited resources during periods of industrial action, shaped women's class awareness and resulted in their providing considerable support for the disputes. Women from mining communities across Britain supported families, maintained community cohesion and safeguarded the strike from blackleg labour. They were also involved in protests, picketing and fundraising during the lockout, and this sharpened the class, community and gender identities of many of them.[17] In doing this, women in mining areas linked the bureaucratic world of 'organised' trade unionism to the more traditional custom-based community protests that had marked Edwardian Britain.[18]

The miners' lockout lasted for seven months, placing an incredible burden on their wives and families. Although there were wives who 'nagged men to go back to work', and some men returned to work of their own volition, the prolonged nature of the dispute ensured that most wives knew, more than the men, the price of the sacrifice that had already been made, and were therefore willing to sustain the cost of abandoning this 'investment'.[19] The Chief Woman Officer of the Labour Party, Marion Phillips, maintained that

> Women were deeply involved. The storm centre was the mining industry; there, women were deeply involved as mothers, wives, sisters; on them a heavy burden fell; their courage and endurance were constantly behind their men.[20]

Scottish women were actively involved in the miners' lockout; they engaged in picketing, employing 'rough music' and humiliating strikebreakers. Many of these women subverted gender norms by using obscene humour against 'scab' labour. Indeed, Scottish women demonstrated a strong sense of political cohesion and set 'collective standards of behaviour' that made strikebreaking difficult.[21] In this they were often extremely aggressive. At Lochgelly in Fife a crowd of 'hostile women' assaulted and intimidated miners who tried to go back to work. Seven of the women were arrested and imprisoned for their actions. Many of the other women who were involved were prosecuted

---

[17] See Bruley, 'Women', 243; Barron, 'Women of the Durham coalfields', 53–84; Gier-Viskovatoff and Porter, 'Women of the British coalfields', 190–230; V. Gordon Hall, 'Contrasting female identities', 107–33.

[18] See Kirk, *Custom and Conflict*.

[19] Barron, 'Women of the Durham coalfields', 53–84.

[20] M. Phillips, *The Story of the Women's Committee for the Relief of Miners' Wives and Children* (n.p., 1927), ix.

[21] Campbell, *The Scottish Miners, Vol. One*, 242.

and fined. In Ayrshire, twenty-nine women were arrested for the intimidation of two miners who had gone back to work. The women were part of what
the *Scotsman* identified as a 'hostile and alarming crowd' who carried trays
and tin cans which they beat 'furiously' whilst surrounding and following the
men along the road to the colliery. There were also disturbances involving
women in the mining districts of West Calder and Cambuslang, Lanarkshire,
where two women were imprisoned for their militancy.[22] A further thirteen
women were reported to the Procurator Fiscal, accused of shouting and
throwing mud at blackleg labour. Eight women were arrested in Shotts
and one in Blackwood, Lanarkshire, for similar behaviour.[23] Women from
Lockerbie were also arrested and imprisoned for following blacklegs home,
'bawling and shouting' to the accompaniment of a 'melodeon and a tin can
band'. Cries of 'scab' were levelled at the men and one woman was accused
of spitting on a blackleg – she was imprisoned for twenty-one days.[24] This
kind of evidence indicates that women were wholeheartedly involved in the
industrial action rather than merely supporting it.

As well as picketing, Scottish women took part in demonstrations, processions and parades in support of the miners. During the lockout, on
the day preceding the May Day celebrations, an open-top carriage drove
around the mining district of East Lothian. It was full of women singing
'The Red Flag' and waving a 'very red flag' while inviting others to join in.
In July 1926 in the Lanarkshire mining district demonstrators met to reject
the terms offered by employers for a return to work at a reduced wage of
one shilling nine and a half pence per day and an extended working week.
This included a 'considerable number of women' from Shotts, Fauldhouse,
Harthill, West Benhar and Salsburgh, who joined miners to form a crowd of
between 8,000 and 10,000 protesters.[25] Women's 'support' in Lanarkshire
was extensive and effective during the miners' strike. They not only set up
soup kitchens in washhouses but also 'engendered and maintained a spirit
of comradeship'.[26] The *Scotsman*'s report that there was 'grumbling and
grousing' among the wives of Fife's miners which was 'mostly confined to a
denunciation of the Government, the coalowners and the other capitalists
believed to be opposing the aims of the pitworkers' indicates the extent to
which the experiences of the General Strike politicised many women.[27]

Women's protests were 'exemplars' of their potential in the 'elaboration
of a class based ideology', but one influenced by experiences of gender.[28]

22 *Scotsman*, 31 May and 5 Oct. 1926.
23 Sinclair, '"Silenced, suppressed and passive"', 164–5.
24 *Scotsman*, 18 Jun. and 28 Oct. 1926.
25 *Scotsman*, 3 May and 9 Jul. 1926.
26 McLean, 'The 1926 strike in Lanarkshire', 11 and Gier-Viskovatoff and Porter, 'Women of
    the British coalfields', 202–14.
27 *Scotsman*, 4 May 1926.
28 See Macdonald, 'Weak roots', 6–30 and Knox and McKinlay, 'The Re-Making of Scottish
    Labour', 174–93.

Thus, when the miners' union 'in the interests of peace' withdrew their colliery pickets at the Castleloan and Cumloden collieries in Bo'ness, the women from the 'rows', in defiance of the union, took up the 'offensive' and caused the 'police considerable anxiety'. Police reinforcements had to be called when the women became involved in violent episodes as 'tempers' rose and they turned out 'en masse' to stop six firemen from returning to work.[29] This was highly controversial because without the return of firemen the consequences of the build-up of methane gas in the mines could have been catastrophic for the owners and the locality. The risk of an explosion might have forced owners to consider a compromise with workers. However, the union decided to concede to the employers for fear that they might close the mine down, whilst women opted for a more militant position.

Gender awareness and gender solidarities are reflected in the women's defiance of the union and the police authority. It is also palpable in the use of female forms of protest: the use of household implements as weapons and the ritualised humiliation of men. Women from Ayrshire appeared in court for intimidating two blackleg miners, one of whom was so traumatised he refused to return to work. In the court, to the laughter of those attending the trial, a female defendant claimed that she had only been in the crowd because it was 'a cheery secht to see a man in his pit claes'.[30] Indeed, a Scottish Office report insisted that the behaviour of women towards blackleg labour significantly reduced the number of men who were prepared to cross the picket lines. These women were clearly politicised by the industrial action. In Lanarkshire not only was there a significant increase in the membership of the ILP, with five women's sections being established during the dispute, but many women also joined the more militant United Miners of Scotland Women's Sections. Moreover, these women were actively encouraged to get involved in membership drives and to stand for election in Parish, Education and County Councils, and to take positions on Labour Exchanges and to involve themselves in class politics and protests, which they subsequently did.[31]

Little has been written about the participation of women who were not from mining communities during the General Strike, but it is clear that they too were actively involved in the dispute in Scotland. Like women in mining districts, much of the women's militancy may have been heightened by the use of the Emergency Powers Act to refuse bail to those arrested and to impose harsher punishments on demonstrators and pickets. Militancy might also have been fuelled by the profiteering of shopkeepers who used the transport difficulties during the General Strike to raise the price of basic foodstuffs, including potatoes and meal.[32] Additionally, it may also have

[29] *Scotsman*, 3 Sep. 1926.
[30] *Scotsman*, 29 Sep. 1926.
[31] Sinclair, '"Silenced, suppressed and passive"', 164, 173–5.
[32] *Scotsman*, 6 May and 18 Jun. 1926.

been sharpened because the army was sent to Scotland as well as by police intimidation and baton charges in cities including Aberdeen, Edinburgh and Glasgow. But as with women in mining districts, numerous working-class women were already demonstrating class consciousness before the onset of the strike. At the labour movement's May Day celebration on 2 May 1926 in Glasgow, held to rally support for the miners, it was estimated that more than 25,000 men and women turned out. The *Scotsman* identified this demonstration as having 'assumed record proportions'. Speakers spanned the spectrum of left-wing politics and included ILP MPs, socialist Councillors and communists. Glasgow was not the only venue: Stirling and Musselburgh were amongst the other locations at which men and women protested.[33]

During the General Strike there was also a number of consumer 'disturbances' over food involving women across Scotland. The East End of Glasgow was labelled 'the storm centre of the strike', where 'looting and lawlessness' were indulged in by both sexes, who not only stopped transport services but also plundered bread vans and boot warehouses and broke into shops. Amongst the East End's 'lawless' citizens in 1926 were – in contrast to the numerous men who were charged with stealing alcohol – an elderly woman who was fined £2 for stealing a tin of peaches, a small luxury, from a store which had been looted. There was also an eighteen-year-old girl who was sent to prison for thirty days for stealing a pair of boots from a shop window broken during the riot.[34]

The involvement of women outside mining communities indicates the widespread nature of female militancy. Women from Glasgow, like their counterparts in the mining district of Airdrie, were involved in violent episodes as they tried to bring transport to a standstill to resist the use of black-leg labour. Disturbances also took place in Rutherglen and Cambuslang, where women and men were arrested for throwing missiles at tramcars, whilst in Kirkcaldy and Muirend thousands of men and women blockaded factories to stop blacklegs from working.[35] Dundee women also challenged strikebreakers and they too were arrested. In Aberdeen thousands of people arrived to ensure that the Council could not re-establish motorbus services. The first bus to leave was rushed and a volunteer 'roughly handled'. The second bus, driven by a 'city clerk and well known rugby player', was also stopped and the driver 'forcibly removed'. Later, a bag of coal was stolen from a truck and the coal was used to provide missiles to attack motorbuses. However, although women were directly involved in these actions they were often treated as spectators. The Aberdeen station of the BBC strongly urged 'all women of the city to stay away from the centres of disturbance'.[36]

[33] *Daily Record*, 3 May 1926 and *Scotsman*, 3 May 1926.
[34] *Glasgow Herald*, 7 and 8 May 1926 and *Scotsman*, 10 May 1926.
[35] Glasgow Trades and Labour Council Files, 1926, Emergency Press Special Edition, 12 May 1926 and *Scotsman*, 18 Jun. 1926.
[36] *Scotsman*, 7 Jun. 1926, Arnot, 'Women workers', 277 and *Scotsman*, 8 Jun. 1926.

In Edinburgh a police baton charge resulted in numerous women being injured in what socialists identified as 'police brutality'. Although socialists may have identified women as victims in these clashes the conflict was precipitated by a group of women wearing red rosettes and red ribbons who attacked blackleg transport workers, and by the crowd of men and women who gathered to throw paper, flour and other missiles at transport blackleg labour in the city. This resulted in arrests but, undeterred, the following day, in what the *Scotsman* described as 'lively scenes' in the central district of the city, '1000s of women swelled the thong of protesters'. The women's 'cries' seemingly 'added to the general uproar' when protesters were again attacked by the police and the voluntary special constables enlisted under the Emergency Powers Act.[37] Women responded to the police baton charges: Mary Gagen, who was unemployed, was fined £3 when she was found guilty of 'having thrown earthenware vessels into the street in the direction of the police' from an open window in Edinburgh. Catherine Welsh, also from Edinburgh, was fined £1 when she was found guilty of 'inciting a crowd to attack police officers from an open window of her home'.[38]

It has been argued that in popular discourses no form of female violence, verbal or physical, was considered legitimate. Violent women have been demonised as 'insane, sub-human, and abnormal' and portrayed as lacking in femininity.[39] The press often focused on this aspect of women's behaviour, highlighting the ways in which women transgressed gender boundaries and breached the codes of motherhood by their apparently irresponsible actions. When Glasgow women were arrested and imprisoned for rioting and intimidation what particularly attracted the attention of the press were those who were mothers of large families and pregnant woman.[40] It was these women who were deemed to have transgressed most seriously the established gender codes of behaviour.

Political and rank-and-file women were also involved in relief efforts for miners' dependants and this also had a politicising effect on many women, in terms of both class and gender. Local authorities often attempted to starve the miners into capitulation by refusing their wives and children relief.[41] In Scotland there was no provision for relief for able-bodied men who were involved in industrial action or for their dependants. However, at the beginning of the miners' strike, a circular from the Scottish Board of Health directed Parish Councils to provide some form of relief for the dependants of miners, the preference being the provision of communal meals. It also dictated that the scale of relief should not exceed five shillings

[37] *Scotsman*, 6, 7 and 22 May and 18 Jun. 1926.
[38] *Scotsman*, 7 and 8 May 1926.
[39] See Rowbotham, 'Only when drunk', 155–69.
[40] *Scotsman*, 12 May 1926.
[41] Bruley, 'Women', 241–2.

for a wife and two shillings for each child and that deductions were to be made for any provision of relief in kind.[42] Initially Parish Councils did provide monetary relief to the dependants of miners but as the lockout progressed, and the costs incurred rose, feelings hardened towards the provision of relief: sixty Ayrshire ratepayers sent a petition to the Parish Council protesting against further relief being granted to the wives and children of 'fit men' who, they maintained, had been offered work, but had refused it. The petitioners pointed out that it was 'illegitimate' to provide relief and argued that it was 'an intolerable and unjustifiable tyranny' to hold them liable as ratepayers in such a manner. By August rates of relief were reduced in Ayrshire and payments ceased completely at Cambusnethan in Wishaw and at Clackmannan.[43] Thus, the role that fell to women of organising relief for the wives and children of miners became increasingly significant.

Socialist women played a critical role in ensuring that miners and their families did not starve.[44] Yet women who were not directly affiliated to any organisation also challenged local authorities to provide relief to miners' families. Miners' wives were enlisted to travel across Britain and overseas to raise funds for the relief of miners' families. Women led protests in Dalkeith, Ayr and Clackmannan over the cessation or reduction of relief payments and 'stormy scenes' took place in Wishaw in an attempt to have the decision to cease providing relief reversed. Local women marched from Ayr Parish Council to the nearby Kyle Union Poorhouse and threatened to remain there until admitted in protest at the cessation of relief. These women were only dispersed by a large police presence.[45] Further to this, forty miners' wives appeared in Ayr Sheriff Court to support thirteen women who were presenting a test case to appeal against the decision of Ayr Parish Council to refuse them relief. The women, who were unrepresented by any legal council, were unsuccessful because the magistrate supported the Parish Council's decision. He informed the first applicant that all her able-bodied husband had to do was go to the Parish and state that he was 'temporarily out of work' rather than on strike and at that point the Parish could decide whether or not they would pay any relief. All other applications were then dismissed on the same grounds. These women were quite clear where the blame for 'the burden that lay on their shoulders' should be attributed. They blamed the government for not stepping in, the owners for their 'aloof attitude' and the trade union leaders for their 'strike policy'.[46]

The women of Lanarkshire were more successful in their attempts to

[42] *Scotsman*, 10 May 1926 and 23 Feb. 1927.
[43] *Scotsman*, 6 and 27 Aug. 1926.
[44] Bruley, 'Women', 241–2.
[45] *Scotsman*, 26 and 27 Aug. 1926 and *Glasgow Herald*, Jul. 24 and 13 Aug. 1926. See also Barron, 'Women of the Durham coalfields', 75–7; Gier-Viskovatoff and Porter, 'Women of the British coalfields', 209–14.
[46] *Scotsman*, 6 Aug. 1926.

safeguard relief. In 1926, more than 200 Protestant and Catholic women from Dykehead in Shotts, a deeply sectarian area of Lanarkshire, united to contest the Council's rates of relief. The women demanded improved public assistance and also the recognition of claims of families who were strikebound. These demands were conceded and while the women did not gain significant rises in benefits, what advances they did get meant a great deal to them because it was a response to their collective action.[47] What is also clear is that the commonalities of gender and class were sufficient to overcome the sectarian divisions manifest in everyday life, at least temporarily. In Scotland these women also kept attention focused on the suffering of women and children during the miners' lockout, and this no doubt contributed to the government's highly controversial decision in 1927 to change the Scottish Poor Law so that provision for the relief of wives and dependants of workers who were engaged in an industrial dispute was enshrined in statute, or what the *Scotsman* scornfully referred to as 'rateaided strikes'.[48]

Although unemployment was identified as a problem that largely affected men between the wars its effects were far from gender-specific. As Chapter two demonstrated, the Restoration of Pre-War Practices Act, the Anomalies Act and the policies of Labour Exchanges and trade unions all guaranteed that the true level of women's unemployment was effectively disguised. However, in 1931 the *Glasgow Herald* reported that

> In the past few weeks several thousand women have had their unemployment benefits ceased because they do not qualify under the Anomalies Act. In Glasgow over 75 per cent of women in receipt of dole failed and in some districts it is as high as 99 per cent. Due to the means test these women cannot get Public Assistance.[49]

The contemporary activist Harry McShane noted how 'a lot of women could not get relief and many widows and single girls had to deal with the Parish Council who treated them very badly'. One woman from Gourock, who was made unemployed from the ropeworks factory where she had worked for more than four years, was denied benefits on the basis that she was a married woman. This was irrespective of the fact that she had lived separately from her husband for twenty-one years.[50] Thus, women had to fight to receive benefits and this led to their participation in hunger marches and also to direct conflict with Parish Councils. According to Harry McShane, 'women threatened councillors with violence and pushed hesitant men into action'.[51]

---

[47] Sinclair, '"Silenced, suppressed and passive"', 181–2.
[48] *Scotsman*, 21 and 25 Feb. and 10 Mar. 1927.
[49] *Glasgow Herald*, 17 Nov. 1931.
[50] McShane and Smith, *No Mean Fighter*, 131–3 and Sinclair, '"Silenced, suppressed and passive"', 129.
[51] McShane and Smith, *No Mean Fighter*, 131–3.

In Dundee the effects of unemployment and benefit cuts acted as cata-lysts which motivated women to become involved in demonstrations, riots and looting in 1921, 1923 and again in 1931. The women legitimised their protests by claiming that they were 'desperate for the bairns to get food'.[52] Amongst those arrested for their participation in these events were working women who were clearly in solidarity with their unemployed sisters and brothers, including Mary McNeil, Isabella Stewart and Mary Soular, all mill workers. Mary Soular was charged with using 'seditious language', because she had asked a crowd of demonstrators, 'why die in the midst of plenty?'. According to the press she knew full well that the Glasgow communist John Maclean had also been imprisoned for using these same words at a Glasgow demonstration. Moreover, Mary's speech provides evidence of the gen-dered nature of political protest because she also implored the crowd to take the food they needed for their children and that all that was between them and the food was 'plate glass'.[53]

Often when women mobilised, or were mobilised in this way, they jus-tified it on the basis of protecting their family, or their family's income. These women sought a social wage, a redistribution of resources from the state or state bodies that would provide justice and equality of treatment. They felt they had as much right to maintain their families as more affluent families had, but they also recognised that exploiting the discourse that glorified them as 'guardians of the family' was more productive than utilis-ing class-based rhetoric.

Direct experiences with the agents of social welfare could also politicise women. Mrs McNicoll recalled

> It was a November day and it was freezing and the money was getting paid out. So, I'm in this hall and there's about fifty behind me. When I got up to the table for my £2 8/- the man flung it at me. It fell on the floor. I refused to lift it. He says, 'Lift it!' 'No, I don't want to come for this money, I want to work. I'm not begging for money.' So the crowd took it up. Well you can imagine fifty people waiting for their money behind me. So the guy sitting at the table beside him says, 'If I was you I'd pick that money up and hand it to that lady because', he says, 'this crowd's going to tear you apart.'[54]

This woman subsequently joined the National Unemployed Workers' Movement [NUWM].

The contemporary socialist Harry McShane insisted that it was through the NUWM that the socialist movement came closest to women in the inter-war years.[55] Unemployment was a major problem for working-class wives

---

[52] G. Smith, 'Motherhood, health and welfare in a women's town c1911–1931', *Oral History*, 23, 1: 67–9 (1995).

[53] *Glasgow Herald*, 18 Jun. 1930.

[54] SOHCA/019/014/Glasgow, b. 1911

[55] McShane and Smith, *No Mean Fighter*, 131.

who shouldered the burden of household management. Moreover, when resources were scarce it was primarily women who made sacrifices and these factors ensured that women attempted to safeguard and secure their families' resources. Glasgow Corporation consistently heard deputations involving women who were protesting against the effects of the means test.[56] In Glasgow the NUWM and the Communist Party organised demonstrations in 1931 on two separate occasions and these involved estimated crowds of 50,000 people, many of whom were women. The *Glasgow Herald* remarked on the involvement of 'large numbers of girls and women holding babies'. 'Bannerettes' with 'Pay no Rent' and 'Fight or Starve' combined the issues that reflected women's political concerns.[57] By 1932, women were again demonstrating on the streets over the means test. In June of that year, 2,000 housewives, led by 'socialist' women councillors, marched on George Square to ask Glasgow Town Council to abolish the means test. The women insisted that the 'misery and hardship' in the city was directly attributable to the means test and also pointed out that the means test was causing 'domestic strife'. In July 1932, women approached Glasgow Corporation again to ask them to petition the government to abolish the means test, arguing that it was a 'Destitution Test'. The ILPer Jean Roberts took up the case of working-class women on Glasgow Council.[58] In the 1930s, Motherwell's working-class women were also prominent in the many demonstrations against the means test. It is also the case that, as with women's militancy during the General Strike and the miners' lockout, female protesters were often the perpetrators of violence. For example, in Coatbridge protesting women assaulted police officers, injuring a number of them. However, it was not until 1936 that 'socialist' men on the Council voted to call a public meeting of citizens to protest against the scales of relief.[59] At this time, economic circumstances were improving and the Labour Party was making more significant inroads into local government across Scotland, making it more politically expedient to adopt the practices that rank-and-file women and socialist women had engaged in throughout the 1930s.

Socialist women, many from working-class backgrounds, empathised with women's distress and campaigned incessantly against the means test, coordinating demonstrations, standing at appeals on behalf of women and protesting in political circles.[60] However, like unemployed men, working-class women had limited resources available to them to organise and coordinate protests. As a result, many of the disputes which they were involved in tended to be informal, non-institutional and aimed at the local

[56] Glasgow City Council Minutes, 1930–6, *Scotsman*, 24 Sep. 1931 and *Glasgow Herald*, 9 Oct. 1931.

[57] *Glasgow Herald*, 10 Jun. 1931.

[58] *Govan Press*, 1 Jul. 1932 and *Glasgow Herald*, 5 Aug. 1932.

[59] Sinclair, '"Silenced, suppressed and passive"', 148–71 and *Times*, 13 Aug. 1936.

[60] See Sinclair, '"Silenced, suppressed and passive"', 148–71, *Times*, 13 Aug. 1936 and *Scotsman*, 5 Aug. 1932.

agencies of the state.[61] Mrs Duncan recalled such a confrontation. When her husband was incapacitated and unable to work she approached the Parish for assistance and was given a small sum of money, 4/6, to maintain herself, her husband and her two children for four days. She owed two-thirds of this for milk and fuel and approached her mother in distress. Her mother responded thus:

> 'That'll be **** right', she says. 'I'll put on a clean overall.' They always had a clean overall and shawl to go out dressed. She went up to Govan Town Hall and said, 'Who was it?' I said, 'That man.' 'Right!' she says. 'Are you married?' He answered, 'Yes. What's it got to do with you?' 'Have you got children? Well, see if your wife could keep you and your weans on that.' So we took that long that the head man came out. He said, 'What is it?' 'How would you like it? Her man's lying ill in bed.' You'd to pay for medicine then. So he says, 'Just hold on.' He got us 18/-. He says, 'Is that better mum?' Only for my mother![62]

Such experiences enhanced women's class awareness. Mrs McNicoll maintained that

> The means test was terrible! Oh it was! They could come into your house and tell you what to sell so thank God all my stuff was second-hand so it wasn't worth selling. But they'd come in and tell you what to do. Really! Talk about Russia, Russia wasn't as bad as what they were in those days.[63]

Women used their networks to resist poundings, which were the removal by Sheriff Officers and bailiffs of furniture and household goods in lieu of debts including rent arrears. Evictions were also opposed; for example, in October 1922, a demonstration took place to urge Glasgow City Council to petition Parliament to prohibit evictions. It was 300 strong with women accompanied at the rear by unemployed men. Despite the fact that the Unemployed Committee was given an assurance by the Council that unemployed tenants would not be evicted hundreds of families were ejected from their homes.[64] Both socialist women and local women's networks were instrumental in organising resistance to evictions. In Govan a pulley system with a basket attached was used to provide families with necessities when they had blockaded doors to resist eviction officers. Other families were assisted to return to the premises from which they had been evicted by neighbours.[65] These campaigns were not discrete isolated protests. Rather,

---

[61] See G. Rawlinson, 'Mobilising the unemployed: the National Unemployed Workers' Movement in the West of Scotland', in Duncan and McIvor, *Militant Workers*, 176–97.

[62] SOHCA/019/05/Glasgow, b. 1912.

[63] SOHCA/019/014/Glasgow, b. 1911.

[64] *Glasgow Herald*, 11 and 21 Oct. 1922.

[65] SOHCA/019/05/Glasgow, b. 1912.

they were characterised by overlapping leadership and involvement, and interconnected issues.

The interconnections between unemployment, poverty, rent campaigns and eviction protests are clear from the demonstrations which took place in Cambuslang, Lanarkshire, in 1924. A family that was involved in withholding rent as a protest against housing prices and conditions had been evicted, resulting in demonstrations outside the factor's home. Many of the demonstrators were arrested and this led to further protests outside the police station. A hostile crowd also replaced the evicted woman, her children and her household goods back in the home from which they had been ejected. Sentries were placed outside the door to ensure that the family would not be re-evicted.[66] Indeed, in Lanarkshire squatting was also a response to the cost of housing, evictions and the condition of housing, with some families taking up illegal residence in unallocated council housing. Another strategy used by women to secure improved housing involved sending letters to the Department of Health. The opportunity was taken to exploit other concerns about the hazards of overcrowding, such as the dangers of incest and the welfare of children. Other women were more direct in their approach, such as Mrs Brent and Mrs Mathieson, who attended Hamilton Town Hall to protest about housing conditions in the town. These women were accused of being 'unladylike' because they had engaged in a torrent of bad language and threats in their attempt to secure council accommodation. Indeed, like many councils across Scotland, Hamilton Council also faced demonstrations over housing conditions, including one involving more than 200 men and women.[67]

Women became politicised in a multitude of ways by their everyday experiences. Throughout Britain women shared aspects of the socio-economic and political climate and were affected by the dominant discourses on gender and motherhood. Mr Parsonage grew up in Wales. He recalled the effects that unemployment had upon his mother's political identity:

> She sold off her home bit by bit to keep us in food. Well my mother had to go to the Parish for boots for me and they were tackety boots, full of studs. I could hardly lift my feet and she says to the man, 'Is this the best you can do? Look at the size of him? He couldn't wear them.' He walked away. He says, 'Take it or leave it!' She says, 'I'll leave it.' She hit him under the eye with one of the boots. Of course she was arrested, me with her. They took her down to the City Hall. They chucked her in, me and all, in the cell. She'd been charged with assault. So anyway she got fined 1/-.

Mr Parsonage insisted that his mother was worn down by poverty and oppression, that 'she had had enough' and that this explains why she

[66] *Forward*, 24 Nov. 1924.
[67] Sinclair, "'Silenced, suppressed and passive'", 50, 203–7.

became a Mosleyite between the wars, enduring police brutality for her political allegiances and involvement in protests.[68]

Women's protests reflected their oppression that was shaped by their class and their gender and this is evident in women's attitudes and behaviour during the period of the means test in the 1930s. It was working-class women as household managers who often contested the impact of the actions of the state to protect their families. The means test was widely seen as something abhorrent in working-class communities in Scotland, criticised as an intrusion of privacy and as a mechanism that broke up families. It was seen as demeaning and inhumane. In some regions of Britain, unemployment was a divisive force among the working class, fragmenting class through labels such as 'taxpayer' and 'scrounger'.[69] This was less evident where there was a high incidence of unemployment as there was in Scotland. Indeed, unemployment facilitated community cohesion to undermine the operation of the means test but the social stigma of unemployment was also mediated because many of those out of work had been skilled workers, 'respectable' men and co-workers. Ms Stewart was a member of the more affluent working class. She recalled

> Well there was an awful lot of poverty and a lot of nice people lost their job, and they had been sensible and saved when they had it. They just had to limit spending because they didn't get much money. But then the 1930s were very poor and there was a lot of suicide and a lot of children were really, really hungry.[70]

Although working-class women and the unemployed had few effective channels to overturn such legislation, they exploited fully those that were available to them. Mrs Jones recalled

> They used to come up in the middle of the night, the inspectors, and knock the door and come in to see if the one that was drawing the means test was living there. Oh! There was always arguments on the stairs because they'd come up in the middle of the night and bang you up whether there was weans in the house or not – and they were screeching and the women were screeching. Oh it was a hard time then.[71]

To resist the means test women protested, signed petitions and sent deputations to their councillors. They also participated in informal action to negate the impact of the means test so that it would not undermine family

[68] SOHCA/019/026/Wales, b. 1915.

[69] A. Deacon, 'Concession and Coercion – The Politics of Unemployment Insurance in the Twenties', in A. Briggs and J. Saville (eds), *Essays In Labour History* (London, 1977), 9–35. See also A. Deacon, *In Search of the Scrounger: the Administration of Unemployment Insurance in Britain, 1920–1931* (London, 1976).

[70] SOHCA/019/020/Glasgow, b. 1895.

[71] SOHCA/019/011/Glasgow, b. 1917.

resources. Because of the fact that benefits were allocated based on a family's combined income, Mrs Duncan, whose husband was in employment, fraudulently claimed that her brother and his friend resided with her in her one-bedroom home.[72] Mr Armstrong was working and claimed not to reside with his parents. He recalled the support of his family's female neighbour:

> There was this inspector that came round and . . . the cry got up, 'Divany's on the go.' Well I'd to go next door. Mrs Ross would say, 'Neighbours bloody help one another.' There was nobody reporting one another, but it was terrible. The means test was the worst thing! It was a harsh thing. It was inhuman.[73]

There was an awareness that the means test disempowered women as household managers, but resistance to it was also a working-class defence of family and community – a survival strategy. Women's subversion of the means test also highlights how class and gender identities overlapped, especially when it was in complete defiance of 'male authority'. Mrs Campbell exhibited such defiance when she went against the wishes of her husband to support an unemployed family member to receive benefits: 'I got married, and my brother was on the means test. My brother used to sign on and he used my address and my man didn't like it.'[74] No doubt her mother was more appreciative because it was her income that would have declined had she lost her son's contribution to the family economy.

Women's actions to moderate the means test were a defence of their identity and a means of safeguarding the spaces which offered them power. It was a protection of women's resources, physical and psychological, albeit with secondary benefits for the entire family unit. For this reason, this form of dishonesty among people who apparently placed a high value on honesty was not generally frowned upon. Ms Anderson maintained

> It never affected us, but there was a lot of twists went on and in a lot of cases you couldn't blame the families. Sometimes the public was way ahead of the people who were causing this, because they knew that it was going to mean less money coming in.[75]

Defiance of the state and male authority was facilitated by women's networks and a collective consciousness among women of the working classes of their need to support each other to safeguard against the obstacles they faced when attempting to identify with the ideals of good household management. In this sense the community was just as significant in the shaping of women's political identities, in terms of both class and gender,

[72] SOHCA/019/05/Glasgow, b. 1912.
[73] SOHCA/019/026/Glasgow, b. 1905.
[74] SOHCA/019/034/Glasgow, b. 1901.
[75] SOHCA/019/04/Glasgow, b. 1910.

as women and men's experiences of the workplace and the political arenas of Scotland.

Many women were influenced by particular images of class that derived from their experiences within their neighbourhoods and this could facilitate coalitions, even if only temporarily. The solidarity that women shared also originated experiences of gender, from close housing proximity and from mutual need. This ensured the continued operation of women's 'survival networks'. Women's roles were no less significant in shaping political identities than experiences of work and although much of the action undertaken by women was impromptu, like the rent strikes and food riots, such behaviour depended on formal organisation and an enabling tradition that was embedded in women's networks. This underpinned a collective consciousness which was in some respects a reflection of a 'rough kind of feminist' behaviour. Women usurped gender norms and entered the public world of politics, infusing it with their priorities and concerns. Working-class women responded politically to the effects of the adverse economic climate. They were actively involved in the General Strike and miners' lockout, and they organised and participated in housing protests and in campaigns against cuts in benefits. Women's political identities were shaped by gender but their political agency also suggests that the labour movement failed to exploit a political consciousness which would have been to the benefit of class awareness. Women's class awareness was born of class and gender experience and heightened by struggle. It was also a collective consciousness and one that mitigated alternative identities, including the religious and respectable identities that often fragmented class in Scotland.

Conclusion

The inter-war years were a period of extreme gender antagonism and economic insecurity in Scotland and this influenced working-class women's political identities. However, gender antagonism facilitated, even if only on a temporary basis, a 'rough kind of feminism'. Although divided by age, religion, status and income, working-class women converged on a range of issues which affected them as a group. They came together to counter the weight of the adverse economic climate, government policies and men's attempts to subordinate them in the workplace, the political arena, the home and in their communities. The formation of women's political identity in Scotland between the wars was a complex process, but it was one in which they were active participants.

In the workplace gender antagonism and discrimination were constant realities that women faced. Working-class women experienced vertical and horizontal segregation and they were perceived and labelled as a threat to men's jobs, and to male status, autonomy and wages. They also faced a discourse disseminated by employers, men and the industrial wing of the labour movement, which attempted to identify women, and have women identify with, docility, political apathy and subservience. The presentation of women as an acquiescent workforce, apathetic to the trade union movement, industrial action and the class struggle, and female militancy as merely a 'temper', was used to justify their exclusion from positions of power in work and most trade unions. Yet these characterisations of working women had little basis in reality. Indeed, it seems that it was male workers who were increasingly subject to degrees of rehabilitation due to structural unemployment, a surplus of labour and the possible introduction of monopoly capitalism. These conditions contributed to men's vulnerability and were difficult to counter. By contrast, the idea that women were usurping men, and thus masculinity, male privilege and masculine respectability, was not difficult for men to imagine. Although there were some progressive trade unions, culture, exclusionary policies and the promotion of a characterisation of women which denied them economic progress and representation, ensured that female workers endured gender discrimination as well as the exploitative conditions of their work.

Many working-class women resisted this dual exploitation. They responded to the nature of their work alongside, and often in a similar manner to, their male counterparts, especially during the most significant strikes of the inter-war years, the 1919 Strike, the 40 Hours Strike and the

1926 General Strike. Yet the gendered language of class adopted by the trade union movement and the disdain of extra-trade union and popu-list forms of pressure protest meant that expressions of women's politi-cal agency were regarded as less consequential by the male-dominated leadership of the labour movement. Women continued to be neglected as a political constituency; their struggles were trivialised and used to vindicate male perceptions of the female workers' industrial militancy as inconsequential.

Despite this, the exclusion or secondary status attributed to women in the workplace and within the structures of the trade union movement impacted upon the political identity of working-class women and was evident in the operation of their gender-specific rituals within the workplace and the maintenance of female-centred work cultures. These work cultures allowed women to develop a sense of pride, independence, collectivity and cama-raderie. They were also a rejection of attempts to identify women as docile, politically apathetic and subservient. They allowed women to contest male definitions of skill and status, permitting them to create their own occu-pational rankings. Women's work cultures thereby facilitated the capacity for self-definition, and levels of autonomy and power, and provided psy-chological resources. They were not just spaces accommodating resistance, but spheres of female influence and agency and, significantly, they were an assertion of the feminine, a political tactic, even if it was not consciously defined as such. This suggests that men and the leadership of the industrial wing of the labour movement contributed to women's subordinate posi-tion in the workplace and the trade union movement and by doing so they contributed to their own exploitation. The industrial wing of the labour movement did not do this by allowing cheap female labour to supplement men in the work-place. Women's substitution for men was not a common occurrence; rather men internalised an archaic worldview based upon the idea that women were a form of competition. These ideals had existed in nineteenth-century Scotland, but they intensified with the growing inter-war political focus on unemployment, perceived as a male problem, and one exacerbated by women's entry into the labour market in greater numbers. Therefore, working-class men's vulnerability, engendered by the potentially rehabilitating effects of mass unemployment, the possibility of the introduction of monopoly capitalism and the changing nature of work, created a defensiveness which negated sustained broader militancy by focusing upon gender as the source of their subordination. In general, women were systematically ignored in the class struggle.

The ILP were, for most of the inter-war period, the dominant political force of the labour movement, especially in the west of Scotland. They were also, by their definition, the 'Real Women's Party'. Yet in the political arena, the attitudes and actions of the male-dominated labour movement frequently ensured the continued undervaluation of working-class women as a political constituency. However, while they may have been undervalued in the political sphere, women did make political progress. The aims of the women of the labour movement in the post-war years were not equality of the sexes, nor were they for equal status for each sex. It was a combination of both. They sought to promote complementary gender roles along with equality of the sexes. To achieve this, women of the ILP, the Labour Party, the Co-operative Women's Guild and the Communist Party used the characterisation of womanhood promoted by the male-dominated labour movement to their advantage. They sought a social wage to disperse power and enhance working-class women's resources and they demanded welfare measures to improve the quality of life of working-class people. Using discursive constructions of womanhood also allowed political women to extend their presence by exploiting the socio-political realm assigned to women. In this way, they gained power without direct confrontation and competition with male members who had greater resources and a tradition of activism to draw from. In overt, covert and subversive ways socialist women challenged the sexual division of labour, advancing women's rights to freedom of choice, the right to economic independence and the right to control their fertility. Socialist women promoted a feminist agenda, invoking a range of strategies. They crossed party and organisational lines to advance women's interests, and they were often more feminist in their aims and activities than many of the self-proclaimed feminists of Scotland. Socialist women extended women's political sphere and their public profiles, challenged the sexual division of labour as well as the constraints of gender and labour movement discourses on womanhood. Although they faced many impediments these women were the dissenting domestics of the dominant male vision of the 'politics of the kitchen'.

Outside of the formal worlds of work and politics working-class women's lives were narrowly restricted, particularly after marriage and more so when children came along. Women were largely confined to the home and to the immediate locality, functioning to maintain the preservation and comforts of the family unit. This was a role which, although demanding a high degree of skill, also involved great hardship and physical sacrifice. But it was also a role, given the prevailing attempts to define and orchestrate women's behaviour, which could be held in high esteem, offering women enhanced status, autonomy and power. Yet many men were neither prepared nor equipped to concede the new status afforded to women and the result was often gender conflict. However, because of the sexual antagonism, in working-class women's relations with men a 'rough kind of feminism' could manifest itself throughout the neighbourhoods of Scotland.

Scotland was in a process of social, economic, political and ideological rupture. Noted for their relative political and industrial militancy during the period 1910–22, Scottish men experienced immense setbacks in the inter-war years. The power and privilege of the 'breadwinner' was challenged during World War I by women's entry into the formal labour market in greater numbers. The inter-war period brought little relief. The recession corresponded with the reassertion of masculinity based upon the provider ideal. Compounding matters were the effects of mass unemployment, deskilling and rationalisation. These structural forces were exacerbated by the perception engendered by various institutions, organisations, the media and the state, that women were a threat to masculinity. In an attempt to re-situate women in the private sphere as glorified wives and mothers, a polarised vision of womanhood was invented; that of the liberated usurper of men economically, politically, socially and sexually. The cumulative effects of the discursive and extra-discursive context resulted in extreme male vulnerability. The masculine insecurities which ensued were expressed through the extreme levels of gender antagonism, manifest in an exceptionally high rate of domestic violence and a retreat by men into aspects of popular culture.

'Masculine republics', the traditional areas of male popular culture, were symbolically re-invented to facilitate the expression and absorption of a sense of manliness when other forms of expression and assimilation were fragile and vulnerable. However, this entailed expenditure at a time when poverty and social deprivation were extreme in Scotland. Yet even among the more economically secure families this situation could cause conflict. Economic security offered improved life chances and status, providing access to the ideals of the companionate marriage, respectability and privacy and the new and improved living environments of the interwar years. Women, the poor and the more affluent alike, could face the problems, real and potential, associated with men's abuse of the 'family wage', and this created a basis for empathy. Male expenditure threatened women's identities as good wives, mothers and household managers. It impeded their potential subjectification of a vision of womanhood which would offer them an enhanced status and spaces of influence in the home and the neighbourhood. Thus, it encroached on women's capacity for self-legitimisation and eroded their physical and psychological resources, and therefore their autonomy and power. This was contested by women; sexual antagonism ensured that women recognised that working-class men oppressed them as much as class and this facilitated gender cohesion, expressed in networks of kin and community and in their involvement with women's groups that contested men's power.

Marginalised in the worlds of work, politics and play, and subjected to attempts by men to undermine them, a tradition of empathetic interests, shared spaces and female communication prevailed amongst women allowing them to converge on issues which affected them as a group and which might diminish their power. Like women in the worlds of work and politics, in the home and neighbourhoods of Scotland working-class women challenged gender discourses and the boundaries of separate spheres in a variety of ways. Women used their networks, along with gossip, religion and religious institutions to dictate neighbourhood norms, to extend their public profiles and resources and more importantly to make men dependent on them. This 'politics of everyday life' provided women with a medium for power, status and identity, and allowed them to contest attempts to undervalue them, while simultaneously mediating class and gender oppression where it affected them as women. They did so by uniting on specific issues, through sharing and by way of mutual support, often in defiance of men. Thus, much of their agency was an expression of 'a rough kind of feminism'. This was born of the need to survive and from the empathy engendered by sexual oppression because class and gender identities in working-class communities were not mutually exclusive.

The politics of everyday life which working-class women developed was based upon notions of respectability, spirituality and community. Although this politics largely united women, these same ideals formed the basis of stratification determined by behaviour, the family economy, local identity, religious affiliation and residence. Although the politics of everyday life could provide the basis for coalitions, it fragmented working-class women's capacity for feminist behaviour and their class-based political agency. It also gave rise to particular images of class, which moderated class awareness by linking ideas about respectability to religious affiliation and voting behaviour.

The impact on women's collective mentalities depended on individual circumstances and experience, but women's roles, influenced by their class position, were no less significant in shaping political identities. This was evident in the ways in which women's defence of their families and communities resulted in militant actions. A great deal of this protest was spontaneous but this did not mean it lacked an organisational basis. Women's involvement in rent strikes, food riots, resistance to evictions, their participation in the General strike and miners' lockout, in housing protests and in campaigns against cuts in unemployment benefits were facilitated by the traditions embedded in women's networks. Women's militancy was also feminist because it threatened gender norms and allowed women to penetrate the public world of politics and infused it with their priorities and concerns. Gender and class influenced women's political identities and their political agency and that it did, indicates that the labour movement in Scotland failed to exploit a political consciousness which would have been to the benefit of class awareness. It was also a consciousness that was collective and one that moderated alternative identities including the religious and respectable identities that often fragmented class in Scotland.

The same can be said of formal feminist organisations between the wars that neglected to consider the ways in which working-class women shared feminist goals while expressing a disavowal of a feminist identity. Moreover, this also indicates the need for a re-evaluation of feminism itself. In particular, there is a necessity for a greater analysis of the sources of working-class women's disavowal of a feminist identity as well as their capacity to share feminist objectives and to act in feminist ways. This book has gone some way in that direction, highlighting that although working-class women do indeed have fragmented identities, and that they generally reject a feminist identity, they can nonetheless unite on specific issues and behave in feminist ways. Working-class women have done so when the influence underpinning coalition was the dual experience of sexual and class antagonism.

Bibliography

PRIMARY SOURCES

Glasgow Regional Archive

TD95536, British Women's Temperance Association, Alexandria Branch, Secretary's Book, 1922–65.

TD95530, British Women's Temperance Association, Greenock Branch, Manuscript Minutes 1912–49.

TD1207/1–3 [170/1067E], Corporation of Glasgow Public Assistance Department Statistics: Abstracts of Cases [Heads of Households] 31 May 1932.

GB81HB19, Records of Glasgow Corporation: Glasgow City Council Printed Minutes.

D-ED2–6, Glasgow Education Diaries 1920–1, 1924–5 and 1929–30.

D-TC6/246, Glasgow Liberal Association, Gorbals Division, 1925.

CO2/2238–58, Greenock Parish Council Minutes, Vols XXVII–XXXIV.

TD956/23/7, ILP, Barrhead Women's Section Manuscript Minutes, 1923–31.

HB10/4/3, Redlands Hospital for Women, Admission Records 1907–35.

[TD1317] DC83, Scottish Conservative Club Records, List of Subscribers to the Political Fund 1933.

[TD1206] CWS1/39/1.12–CWS1/39/13.1, Scottish Co-operative Women's Guild Annual Report and Statement for years ending 1919–36.

[TD1206] CWS1/39/6–8, Scottish Co-operative Women's Guild Central Council Minutes 1915–20, 1920–5 and 1925–30.

HB77/1/1/1, Scottish Federation of Women's Welfare Clinics Minutes.

PA4/212, Workers Educational Association, *Growing Up in Shettleston between the Wars* (1985).

Mitchell Library Glasgow

CATHOLIC Directory for Scotland, John Burns & Sons, Glasgow (1921, 1925 and 1930).

SR187/89101/36/36, Glasgow and West of Scotland Association for Women's Suffrage, Executive Manuscript Minutes, 1902–33.

SR157/891036/3, Glasgow Women's Suffrage Society Manuscript Minutes, 1918–24.

97133/6, Glasgow Trades Council and Labour Council, 1919–30, Executive Minutes.

97133/12, Glasgow Trades and Labour Council, Misc. Files and Papers 1926 (Strike).

331.88155NAT, National Union of Paper, Bookbinding and Print Workers, Scottish District Council, Minute Books 1921–36.

331-881/R/SS/GLA, Printing and Kindred Trades Federation, Glasgow Branch Manuscript Minutes Book, October 1915–43.

33188155GLA, Printing and Kindred Trades Federation Annual Reports 1920–3 and 1928.

3724.70RAI, Railway Clerks Association, Glasgow Southern Branch Manuscript Minutes. Books 1–4, 1920–65.

Glasgow University Archive Services

GB 248 TSB 064, Records of Greenock Provident Bank, Annual Reports 1914–39

GUA, DC19/4/2/2 Records of the Scottish Temperance Movement, 'The Story Writes Itself', Crime, 1925–9, Press Cuttings.

Government publications

HMSO, Ministry of Labour Gazette, Vols XXX–XXXXIV.

Census for Scotland 1911, 1921 and 1931.

House of Commons Parliamentary Papers, *Report on the Judicial Statistics for Scotland*, 1910–36.

Old Paisley Society, 11–17 George Place, Paisley PA1 2HZ

Typed transcripts

1. Jessie Henderson, born 1923 Paisley, Renfrewshire.
2. Jessie McGregor, born 1926 Paisley, Renfrewshire.
3. Mary Neil, born 1898 Paisley, Renfrewshire.
4. Allie Wright, born 1919 Paisley, Renfrewshire.

Society for St Vincent de Paul (Scotland) Archive

Annual Reports, 1919–39.

Scottish Film Archive

Documentary 3053, Sheffield Film Co-operative, *Red Skirts on Clydeside*.

Glasgow Caledonian University

William Gallacher Memorial Library:

STUC Annual Reports 1920–5.

STUC Annual Reports 1926–30.

STUC Annual Reports 1931–5.

STUC Organisation of Women Committee Minutes.

TAPES 6 and 7: Interview with Joe and Marion Henery.

Children 1st (RSSPCC) Archive
GB 1847 RSSPCC Annual reports of the branches, 1896–1939

Sutherland Collection, University of Strathclyde
STANDING Joint Committee of Industrial Women's Organisations, *Labour Women's Report on Socialism and Our Standard of Living* (London, 1938).
The Women with the Basket: The History of the Women's Co-operative Guild, 1883–1927 (Manchester, 1927).
INTERNATIONAL Co-operative Women's Guild, *Housewives Build A New World* (Reading, 1936).
LABOUR Party, *Protect The Nations Mothers* (London, 1936).

Special collections
SUTHERS, K. B., *Mind Your Own Business: The Case for Municipal Housekeeping* (London, 1938).

PRINTED PRIMARY SOURCES/NEWSPAPERS AND CONTEMPORARY JOURNALS

Bulletin
Citizen
Daily Record
Forward
Glasgow Evening News
Glasgow Evening Times
Glasgow Herald
Govan Press
Greenock Telegraph
Labour Women
Scotsman
Scottish Temperance Annual
Scottish Worker
Times

PUBLISHED PRIMARY SOURCES/BOOKS CONTEMPORARY

BLAIR, M., *The Paisley Thread Industry and the Men Who Created and Developed It* (Paisley, 1907).
CALLEN, K. M., *History of the Scottish Co-operative Women's Guild: Diamond Jubilee 1892–1952* (Glasgow, 1952).
CLAYTON, J., *The Rise and Decline of Socialism in Great Britain 1884–1924* (London, 1926).
CUNNISON, J. and Gilfillan, J. B. (eds), *Third Statistical Account of Scotland, The City of Glasgow* (Glasgow, 1958).

HAMILTON, M. A., *A Brief Introduction to Trade Unionism for Women* (London, 1941).

MACKENZIE, H., *The Third Statistical Account of Scotland, The City of Aberdeen* (Edinburgh, 1953).

MOISLEY, H. A. and Thain, A. G., *Third Statistical Account of Scotland. The County of Renfrew* (Glasgow, 1962).

PHILLIPS, M., *The Story of the Women's Committee for the Relief of Miners' Wives and Children* (London, 1927).

RATHBONE, E., *The Disinherited Family, A Plea for Direct Provision for the Costs of Child Maintenance through Family Allowances* (London, 1927).

PUBLISHED SECONDARY SOURCES

Books

ADAMS, R., *A Woman's Place 1910–1975* (London, 1975).

BARRETT, M. and Phillips, A. (eds), *Destabilising Theory: Contemporary Feminist Debates* (Cambridge, 1992).

BARRHEAD People's Story Group, The, *It's Funny Whit Ye Remember: Shared Memories of Life Experiences from 1920 to the 1950s* (Essex, 2002).

BEDDOE, D., *Back to Home and Duty: Women between the Wars, 1918–1939* (London, 1989).

BERGER Gluck, S. and Patai, D. (eds), *Women's Words: The Feminist Practice of Oral History* (London, 1991).

BINGHAM, A., *Gender, Modernity, and the Popular Press in Inter-war Britain* (Oxford, 2004).

BOURKE, J., *Dismembering the Male Men's Bodies, Britain and the Great War* (London, 1999).

   Working-Class Cultures in Britain (London, 1994).

BRAYBON, G. and Summerfield, P., *Out of the Cage: Women's Experiences in Two World Wars* (London, 1997).

BROWN, C. G., *The Death of Christian Britain* (London, 2001).

CAINE, B. (ed.), *English Feminism 1780–1980* (Oxford, 1997).

CAMPBELL, A., *The Scottish Miners 1874–1939, Volume One: Work, Industry and Community* (Aldershot, 2000).

   The Scottish Miners, 1874–1939, Volume Two: Trade Unions and Politics (Aldershot, 2000).

CAMPBELL, B., *The Iron Ladies, Why do Women Vote Tory?* (London, 1987).

CANNADINE, D., *Class in Britain* (London, 2000).

CHARLES, N. and Hughes-Freeland, F. (eds), *Practising Feminism: Identity, Difference, Power* (London, 1996).

CHINN, C., *Better Betting With a Decent Feller: Bookmaking, Betting and the British Working Class, 1750–1990* (London, 1991).

   They Worked All Their Lives: Women of the Urban Poor in England, 1880–1939 (Manchester, 1988).

CLAPSON, M., *A Bit of a Flutter: Popular Gambling and English Society c. 1823–1961* (Manchester, 1992).

CLARK, A., *The Struggle For The Breeches: Gender and the Making of the British Working Class* (London, 1997).

CLARK, D. (ed.), *Marriage, Domestic Life and Social Change: Writings for Jacqueline Burgoyne (1944–1988)* (London, 1991).

COLLETTE, C., *For Labour and for Women: The Women's Labour League 1906–1918* (Manchester, 1990).

COOTE, A. and Patullo, P., *Power and Prejudice: Women and Politics* (London, 1990).

CRAIG, F. W. S., *British Parliamentary Election Results 1918–1949*, 3rd ed. (Chichester, 1983).

DAVIDOFF, L. and Westover, B. (eds), *Our Work, Our Lives, Our Words* (London 1986).

DAVIES, A., *Leisure, Gender and Poverty: Working-class Culture in Salford and Manchester 1900–1939* (Buckingham, 1992).

DEACON, A., *In Search of the Scrounger: the Administration of Unemployment Insurance in Britain, 1920–1931* (London, 1976).

DE Groot, G., *Blighty: British Society in the Era of the Great War* (London, 1996).

DIGBY, A. and Stewart, J. (eds), *Gender, Health and Welfare* (London, 1996).

DOWNES, D. M. et al. (eds), *Gambling, Work and Leisure* (London, 1976).

DUNCAN, R. and McIvor, A. (eds), *Militant Workers: Labour and Class Conflict on the Clyde 1900–1950. Essays in Honour of Harry McShane* (Edinburgh, 1992).

DUNNING, E. et al. (eds), *The Sociology of Sport: A Selection of Readings* (London, 1971).

FARMER, L., *Criminal Law, Tradition and Legal Order: Crime and the Genius of Scots Law, 1747 to the Present* (Cambridge, 1997).

FRASER, W. H. and Maver, I. (eds), *Glasgow Volume II* (Manchester, 1996).

GALLAGHER, T., *Glasgow, The Uneasy Peace: Religious Tension in Modern Scotland* (Manchester, 1987).

GIBB, A., *Glasgow: The Making of the City* (London, 1983).

GILES, J., *Women, Identity and Private Life in Britain, 1900–1950* (London, 1995).

GITTINS, D., *Fair Sex: Family Size and Structure in Britain, 1900–39* (London, 1982).

GLASSER, R., *Growing up in the Gorbals* (London, 1987).

GORDON, E., *Women and the Labour Movement in Scotland 1850–1914* (Oxford, 1991).

GORDON, E. and Nair, G., *Public Lives: Women, Family and Society in Victorian Britain* (London, 2003).

GRAVES, P. M., *Labour Women: Women in British Working-class Politics 1918–1939* (Cambridge, 1994).

GYFORD, J., *The Politics of Local Socialism* (London, 1983).

HAMMERTON, J., *Cruelty and Companionship: Conflict in Nineteenth-Century Married Life* (London, 1992).

HANNAM, J. and Hunt, K., *Socialist Women: Britain, 1880s to 1920s* (London, 2001).

HARRISON, B., *Prudent Revolutionaries: Portraits of British Feminists between the Wars* (Oxford, 1987).

HEY, V., *Patriarchy and Pub Culture* (London, 1986).

HOLLIS, P., *Ladies Elect: Women in English Local Government, 1895–1914* (Oxford, 1987).

HOLTON, S. Stanley, *Feminism and Democracy: Women's Suffrage and Reform Politics in Britain, 1900–1918* (Cambridge, 1986).

HOWKINS, A. and Lowerson, J., *Trends in Leisure 1919–1939* (London, 1979).

HUDSON, P. and Lee, W. S., *Women's Work and the Family Economy in Historical Perspective* (Manchester, 1990).

HUNT, K., *Equivocal Feminists: The Social Democratic Federation and the Woman Question 1884–1911* (Cambridge, 1996).

JONES, S. G., *Workers At Play: A Social and Economic History of Leisure 1918–1939* (London, 1986).

KEATING M., *The City That Refused To Die, Glasgow: the Politics of Urban Regeneration* (Aberdeen, 1988).

KEMP, S. and Squires, J. (eds), *Feminisms* (Oxford, 1997).

KENEFICK, W., *Red Scotland! The Rise and Fall of the Radical Left, c. 1872 to 1932* (Edinburgh, 2007).

KING, E., *Scotland Sober and Free: the Temperance Movement* (Glasgow, 1979).

KINGSLEY Kent, S., *Making Peace, the Reconstruction of Gender in Inter-War Britain* (Princeton, 1993).

KIRK, N., *Custom and Conflict in the 'Land of the Gael': Ballachulish, 1900–1910* (Monmouth, 2007).

KNOX, W. W., *Industrial Nation: Work, Culture and Society in Scotland 1800–Present* (Edinburgh, 1999).

LAW, C., *Suffrage and Power: The Women's Movement, 1918–1928* (London, 1997).

LAYBOURN, K., *Britain on the Breadline: A Social and Political History of Britain Between the Wars* (London, 1990).

The General Strike: Day by Day (London, 1999).

LEE, C., *British Regional Employment Statistics* (Cambridge, 1979).

LEVY, H., *Drink: An Economic and Social Study* (London, 1951).

LEWIS, J., *The Politics of Motherhood: Child and Maternal Welfare in England 1900–1939* (London, 1980).

Women in England 1870–1950 (Hemel Hempstead, 1984).

LIDDINGTON, J., *The Life and Times of a Respectable Rebel: Selina Cooper 1864–1946* (London, 1984).

The Long Road To Greenham: Feminism and Anti-Militarism in Britain Since 1820 (London, 1989).

LIDDINGTON, J. and Norris, J., *One Hand Tied Behind Us* (London, 1977).

LISTER, R., *Citizenship: Feminist Perspectives* (Houndmills, 1997).

LLEWELLYN Davies, M. (ed.), *Maternity Letters from Working Women* (London, [1915] 1978).

MACDONALD, C. M. M., *The Radical Thread: Political Change in Scotland, Paisley Politics, 1885–1924* (Edinburgh, 2000).

MACDOUGALL, I., *Voices from the Hunger Marches: Personal Recollections by Scottish Hunger Marchers of the 1920s and 1930s* (Edinburgh, 1990).

MACNICOL, J., *The Movement for Family Allowances 1918–45: A Study in Social Policy* (London, 1980).

McINTYRE, S., *Little Moscows* (London, 1980).

McKINLAY, A. and Morris, R. J. (eds), *The ILP on Clydeside 1893–1932: From Foundation to Disintegration* (Manchester, 1991).

McLEAN, I., *The Legend of Red Clydeside* (Edinburgh, 1983).

McSHANE, H. and Smith, J., *No Mean Fighter* (London, 1978).

MELLING, J., *Rent Strikes: People's Struggle for Housing in West Scotland 1890–1916* (Edinburgh, 1983).

MITCHELL, G., *The Hard Way Up: The Autobiography of Hannah Mitchell, Suffragette and Rebel* (London, 1977).

MORRIS, M., *The General Strike* (London, 1976).

MURRAY, B., *The Old Firm: Sectarianism, Sport and Society in Scotland* (Edinburgh, 1990).

NASH, D. G., *The Crucial Era: The Great Depression and World War II, 1929–1945* (New York, 1992).

PACIONE, M., *Glasgow: the Socio-spatial Development of the City* (Chichester, 1995).

PEDERSON, S., *Family Dependence and the Origins of the Welfare State: Britain and France* (Cambridge, 1993).

PENNINGTON, S. and Westover, B., *A Hidden Workforce: Homeworkers in England, 1850–1985* (London, 1989).

PHILLIPS, G. A., *The General Strike: The Politics of Industrial Conflict* (London, 1976).

POLLARD, S., *The Development of the British Economy 1914–1967* (London, 1968).

PUGH, M., *The Making Of Modern British Politics 1867–1939* (Oxford, 1993).
  Women and the Women's Movement in Britain 1914–1950, 2nd ed. (London, 2000).

RILEY, D., *'Am I That Name?' Feminism and the Category of 'Women' in History* (London, 1988).

ROBERTS, E., *A Woman's Place: An Oral History of Working-class Women 1890–1940* (Oxford, 1984).

ROBERTSON, G. G., *Gorbals Doctor* (London, 1975).

ROSS, E., *Love and Toil: Motherhood in Outcast London 1870–1918* (Oxford, 1993).

ROUNTREE, G., *A Govan Childhood The Nineteen Thirties* (Edinburgh, 1993).

SAVAGE, M. and Miles, A., *The Remaking of the British Working Class 1840–1940* (London, 1994).

SCOTT, G., *Feminism and the Politics of Working Women: The Women's Co-operative Guild 1880 to the Second World War* (London, 1998).

SCOTT, J. (ed.), *Feminism and History* (Oxford, 1996).

SCOTT, J. C., *Domination and the Arts of Resistance: Hidden Transcripts* (London, 1990).

SIMONTON, D., *A History of European Women's Work: 1700 to Present* (London, 1998).

SMART, C. (ed.), *Regulating Womanhood: Historical Essays on Marriage, Motherhood, Marriage and Sexuality* (London, 1992).

SMOUT, T. C., *A History of the Scottish People 1830–1950* (London, 1990).

SMYTH, J. J., *Labour in Glasgow 1896–1936: Socialism, Suffrage and Sectarianism* (Edinburgh, 2000).

SPRING Rice, M. *Working-Class Wives: Their Health and Condition*, reprinted (London, 1981).

SUMMERFIELD, P., *Reconstructing Women's Wartime Lives: Discourse and Subjectivity in Oral Histories of the Second World War* (Manchester, 1998).

TEBBUTT, M., *Making Ends Meet: Pawnbroking and Working-Class Credit* (Leicester, 1983).

THANE, P., *The Foundations of the Welfare State: Social Policy in Modern Britain* (London, 1989).

TIGER, L., *Men in Groups* (London, 1969).

TITMUSS, R. M., *Essays on the Welfare State*, 3rd ed. (London 1976).

TODD, S., *Young Women, Work and Family in England, 1918–1950* (Oxford, 2005).

TUCKETT, A., *The Scottish Carter* (London, 1967).

The Scottish Trades Union Congress, the First 80 Years 1897–1977 (Edinburgh, 1986).

VOET, R., *Feminism and Citizenship* (London, 1998).

VOVELLE, M., *Ideologies and Mentalities* (Oxford, 1990).

WALBY, S., *Patriarchy at Work, Patriarchal and Capitalist Relations in Employment* (Cambridge, 1986).

WARD, P., *Unionism in the United Kingdom, 1918–1974* (Basingstoke, 2005).

WHEELER, E., *Growing Up in Cowie and Bannockburn* (Stirling, 2006).

WHITESIDE, N., *Bad Times: Unemployment in British Social and Political History* (London, 1991).

WIENER, M., *Men of Blood: Violence, Manliness, and Criminal Justice in Victorian England* (Cambridge, 2004).

YOUNG, J. D., *Women and Popular Struggles: A History of Scottish and English Working-class Women 1500–1984* (Edinburgh, 1985).

Articles in books

ANDERSON, K. and Jack, C. D., 'Learning to listen: interview techniques and analysis', in S. Berger Gluck and D. Patai (eds), *Women's Words: the Feminist Practice of Oral History* (London, 1991), 11–26.

ANDERSON, M., 'Population and family life', in A. Dickson and J. H. Treble (eds), *People and Society in Scotland Vol. III 1914–1990* (Edinburgh, 1992), 14–43.

AYERS, P., 'The making of men: maculinities in interwar Liverpool', in M. Walsh (ed.), *Working Out Gender Perspectives from Labour History* (Aldershot, 1999), 66–83.

AYERS, P. and Lambertz, J., 'Marriage relations, money and domestic violence in working-class Liverpool 1919–39', in J. Lewis, *Labour and Love: Women's Experience of Home and Family, 1850–1940* (Oxford, 1986), 195–210.

BENNETT, R., 'Gendering cultures in business and labour history: marriage bars in clerical employment', in M. Walsh (ed.), *Working Out Gender Perspectives from Labour History* (Aldershot, 1999), 191–209.

BERGER Gluck, S. and Patai, D., 'Introduction', in S. Berger Gluck and D. Patai (eds), *Women's Words: The Feminist Practice of Oral History* (London, 1991), 1–6.

BORLAND, K., '"That's not what I said": interpretive conflict in oral narrative research', in S. Berger Gluck and D. Patai (eds), *Women's Words: The Feminist Practice of Oral History* (London, 1991), 63–76.

BROOKES, B., 'The illegal operation: abortion, 1919–39', in London Feminist History Group (eds), *The Sexual Dynamics of History: Men's Power Women's Resistance* (London, 1983), 165–176.

BROWN, C. G., 'Popular culture and the continuing struggle for rational recreation', in T. M. Devine and R. J. Finlay (eds), *Scotland in the Twentieth Century* (Edinburgh, 1996), 210–29.

BROWN, C. G. and Stephenson, J., '"The view from the workplace": Stirling women and work 1890–1950', in E. Breitenbach and E. Gordon (eds), *Out of Bounds: Women in Scottish Society 1800–1945* (Edinburgh, 1992), 7–17.

BRULEY, S., 'Women', in J. McIlroy, A. Campbell and J. Gildart (eds), *Industrial Politics and the 1926 Mining Lockout, The Struggle for Dignity* (Cardiff, 2004), 229–48.

BURNESS, C., 'The long slow march: Scottish women MPs, 1918–1945', in E. Breitenbach and E. Gordon (eds), *Out of Bounds: Women in Scottish Society 1800–1945* (Edinburgh, 1992), 151–73.

BURNETT, J., 'Exposing the "inner life": the Co-operative Guild's attitude to cruelty', in S. D'Cruze (ed.), *Everyday Violence in Britain, 1850–1950, Gender and Class* (Harlow, 2000), 136–53.

BUTT, J., 'Working-class housing in Glasgow 1900–1939', in I. MacDougall, *Essays in Scottish Labour History: a Tribute to W. H. Warwick,* John Donald Publications (Edinburgh, 1978), 143–69.

CLARK, A., 'Humanity or justice', in C. Smart (ed.), *Regulating Womanhood: Historical Essays on Marriage, Motherhood and Sexuality* (London, 1992), 187–206.

CONLEY, Carolyn A., 'Atonement and domestic homicide in late Victorian Scotland', in R. McMahon (ed.), *Crime, Law and Popular Culture in Europe, 1500–1900* (Cullompton, 2008).

COTT, N., 'Feminist theory and feminist movements', in J. Mitchell and A. Oakley (eds), *What is Feminism?* (Oxford, 1986), 49–62.

COWMAN, K., '"Giving them something to do": how the early ILP appealed to women', in M. Walsh (ed.), *Working Out Gender Perspectives from Labour History* (Aldershot, 1999), 119–34.

DAVIES, A., 'Leisure in the "classic slum"', in A. Davies and J. Fielding (eds), *Workers' Worlds: Culture and Communities in Manchester and Salford 1880–1939* (Manchester, 1992), 101–27.

DAVIS, T., '"What kind of women is she?" women and communist party politics, 1941–1955', in R. Brunt and C. Rowan (eds), *Feminism, Culture and Politics* (London, 1982), 85–108.

DEACON, A., 'Concession and Coercion – The Politics of Unemployment Insurance in the Twenties', in A. Briggs and J. Saville (eds), *Essays In Labour History* (London, 1977), 9–35.

DELMAR, R. 'What is feminism?', in J. Mitchell and A. Oakley (eds), *What is Feminism?* (Oxford, 1986), 8–33.

FINCH, J. and Summerfield, P., 'Social reconstruction and the emergence of companionate marriage 1945–59', in D. Clark (ed.), *Marriage, Domestic Life and Social Change: Writings for Jacqueline Burgoyne (1944–1988)* (London, 1991), 7–32.

FINDLAY, R., 'The Labour Party in Scotland, 1888–1945: pragmatism and principle', in G. Hassan (ed.), *The Scottish Labour Party* (Edinburgh, 2004), 21–33.

FRASER, W. H., 'Trades councils in the Labour movement in nineteenth century Scotland', in I. MacDougall (ed.), *Essays in Scottish Labour History: a Tribute to W. H. Warwick* (Edinburgh, 1978), 1–28.

GORDON, E., 'Women and working-class politics in Scotland 1900–1914', in H. Corr and L. Jamieson, *State, Private Life and Political Change* (London, 1990), 224–42.

GRAVES, P., 'An experiment in women-centred socialism: Labour women in Britain', in H. Gruber and P. Graves, *Women And Socialism, Socialism And Women: Europe Between The Two World Wars* (Oxford, 1998), 180–214.

HANNAM, J., '"In the comradeship of the sexes lies hope of progress and social regeneration": women in the West Riding ILP, 1890–1914', in J. Rendall (ed.), *Equal or Different* (Oxford, 1987), 214–38.

   'Women and politics', in J. Purvis (ed.), *Women's History: Britain, 1850–1945* (London, 1995), 217–43.

HANNAM, J. and Hunt, K., 'Gendering the stories of socialism: an essay in historical criticism', in M. Walsh (ed.), *Working Out Gender Perspectives from Labour History* (Aldershot, 1999), 102–18.

HUGHES, A. and Hunt, K., 'A culture transformed? Women's lives in Wythenshawe in the 1930s', in A. Davies and S. Fielding (eds), *Workers' Worlds: Culture and Communities in Manchester and Salford 1880–1939* (Manchester, 1992), 74–101.

HUMPHRIES, J., 'Women and paid work', in J. Purvis (ed.), *Women's History: Britain, 1850–1945* (London, 1995), 85–106.

HUTCHISON, I. G., 'Scottish issues in British politics 1900–1939', in C. Wrigley (ed.), *A Companion to Early Twentieth Century Britain* (Oxford, 2002), 72–86.

INNES, S. and Randall, J., 'Women, gender and politics', in L. Abrams, E. Gordon, D. Simonton and E. J. Yeo (eds), *Gender and Scottish History since 1700* (Edinburgh, 2006), 43–83.

JAGGER, A., 'Love and knowledge: emotion in feminist epistemology', in S. Kemp and J. Squires (eds), *Feminisms* (Oxford, 1997), 188–93.

JEFFREYS, S., 'Sex reform and anti-feminism in the 1920s', in London Feminist History Group (eds), *The Sexual Dynamics of History: Men's Power, Women's Resistance* (London, 1983), 177–202.

JOHNSON, P., 'Credit and thrift and the British working class 1870–1939', in J. Winter (ed.), *The Working Class in Modern British History: Essays in Honour of Henry Pelling* (London, 1983), 150–70.

KINGSLEY Kent, S., 'Gender reconstruction after the First World War', in H. L. Smith (ed.), *British Feminism in the Twentieth Century* (Aldershot, 1990), 66–83.

KNOX, W. W., 'Introduction', in W. W. Knox (ed.), *Scottish Labour Leaders 1918–1939* (Edinburgh, 1984), 15–53.

'Class, work and trade unionism in Scotland', in A. Dickson and J. H. Treble (eds), *People and Society in Scotland, Vol. III 1914–1990* (Edinburgh, 1992), 108–37.

LAMBERTZ, J., 'Feminism and the politics of wife-beating', in H. L. Smith (ed.), *British Feminism in the Twentieth Century* (Aldershot, 1990), 25–46.

LAWSON, J., Savage, M. and Warde, A., 'Gender and local political struggles over welfare policies', in L. Murgatroyd et al. (eds), *Localities, Class and Gender* (London, 1996), 195–217.

LEWIS, J., 'In search of a real equality: women between the wars', in F. Gloversmith (ed.), *Class, Culture and Social Change: A New View of the 1930s* (Brighton, 1980), 208–39.

MAVER, I., 'The Catholic community', in T. M. Devine and R. J. Finlay, *Scotland in the Twentieth Century* (Edinburgh, 1996), 269–83.

MAY, M., 'Violence in the family: an historical perspective', in P. J. Martin (ed.), *Violence and the Family* (Chichester, 1978), 135–68.

MacDOUGALL, I., 'Some aspects of the General Strike in Scotland', in I. MacDougall (ed.), *Essays in Scottish Labour History: A Tribute to W. H. Warwick* (Edinburgh, 1978), 170–206.

McIvor, A., 'Gender apartheid? Women in Scottish society', in T. M. Devine and R. J. Finlay (eds), *Scotland in the Twentieth Century* (Edinburgh, 1996), 188–209.

'Were Clydeside employers more autocratic? Labour management and the "labour unrest"', in A. McIvor and W. Kenefick (eds), *The Roots of Red Clydeside 1900–1914: Labour Unrest and Industrial Relations in the West of Scotland* (Edinburgh, 1996), 40–65.

'Women and work in the 20th century', in A. Dickson and J. H. Treble (eds), *People and Society in Scotland, Vol. III 1914–1990* (Edinburgh, 1992), 138–173.

McKinlay, A., 'Doubtful wisdom and uncertain promise', in A. McKinlay and R. J. Morris (eds), *The ILP on Clydeside, 1893–1932: From Foundations to Disintegration* (Manchester, 1991), 123–53.

Moorhouse, J. J., 'Shooting stars: footballers and working-class culture in twentieth century Scotland', in R. Holt (ed.), *Sport and the Working Class in Modern Britain* (Manchester, 1990), 178–89.

Pugh, M., 'Domesticity and the decline of feminism, 1930–1950', in H. L. Smith (ed.), *British Feminism in the Twentieth Century* (Aldershot, 1990), 144–66.

Purvis, J., 'From "women worthies" to poststructuralism? Debate and controversy in women's history in Britain', in J. Purvis (ed.), *Women's History: Britain, 1850–1945* (London, 1995), 1–22.

Rawlinson, G., 'Mobilising the unemployed: the National Unemployed Workers' Movement in the West of Scotland', in R. Duncan and A. McIvor (eds), *Militant Workers: Labour and Class Conflict on the Clyde 1900–1950. Essays in Honour of Harry McShane* (Edinburgh, 1992), 176–97.

Rowan, C. '"Mothers, vote Labour!" The state, the Labour movement and working-class mothers, 1900–1918', in R. Brunt and C. Rowan (eds), *Feminism, Culture and Politics* (London, 1982), 59–84.

Rowbotham, J., '"Only when drunk": the stereotyping of violence in England, c.1850–1900', in S. D'Cruze (ed.), *Everyday Violence in Britain, 1850–1950, Gender and Class* (Harlow, 2000), 155–69.

Savage, M., 'Urban politics and the rise of the Labour Party', in H. Corr and L. Jamieson (eds), *State, Private Life and Political Change* (London, 1990), 205–23.

Scott, J., 'Experience', in J. Butler and J. W. Scott (eds), *Feminists Theorise the Political* (New York, 1992), 27–40.

Sowerwine, C., 'Socialism, feminism and the socialist women's movement from the French Revolution to World War II', in R. Bridenthal, S. M. Stuard and M. E. Wiesner (eds), *Becoming Visible Women in European History* (New York, 1998), 357–88.

Tebbutt, M., '"Women's talk?" Gossip and women's words in working-class communities 1880–1939', in A. Davies and J. Fielding (eds), *Workers' Worlds: Culture and Communities in Manchester and Salford 1880–1939* (Manchester, 1992), 42–68.

THANE, P., 'The women of the British Labour Party and feminism, 1906–1945', in H. L. Smith (ed.), *British Feminism in the Twentieth Century* (Aldershot, 1990), 124–43.

'Visions of gender in the making of the British welfare state: the case of women in the British Labour Party and social policy 1906–1945', in G. Bock and P. Thane (eds), *Maternity and Gender Policies: Women and the Rise of the European Welfare States 1880s–1950s* (London, 1991), 93–118.

'Women since 1945', in P. Johnson (ed.), *Twentieth Century Britain: Economic, Social and Cultural Change* (London, 1994), 94–110.

WALBY, S., 'Post-post-modernism? Theorising social complexity', in M. Barrett and A. Phillips (eds), *Destabilising Theory: Contemporary Feminist Debates* (Cambridge, 1992), 31–52.

WALKER, G., 'Varieties of Scottish Protestant identity', in T. M. Devine and R. J. Finlay, *Scotland in the Twentieth Century* (Edinburgh, 1996), 250–68.

Journal articles

ALEXANDER, S., 'Men's fears and women's work: responses to unemployment in London between the wars', *Gender and History*, 12, 2: 401–25 (2000).

BARRON, H., 'Women of the Durham coalfields and their reaction to the 1926 miners' lockout', *Historical Studies in Industrial Relations*, 22: 53–84 (2006).

BEAUMONT, C., 'Citizens not feminists: the boundary negotiated between citizenship and feminism by mainstream women's organisations in England, 1928–1939', *Women's History Review*, 9, 2: 413–26 (2000).

BERGER Gluck, S., 'Reflections on oral history in the new millennium: roundtable comments', *Oral History Review*, 26, 2: 1–27 (1999).

BINGHAM, A., '"An era of domesticity?" histories of women and gender in interwar Britain', *Cultural and Social History*, 1, 2: 225–34 (2004).

BLACKBURN, S., 'Interpreting sweating and women's paid work at home', *Labour History Review*, 56, 3: 10–16 (1991).

BOURKE, J., 'Housewifery in working-class England 1860–1914', *Past and Present*, 143: 167–97 (1994).

BREITENBACH, E., Brown, A. and Myres, A., 'Understanding women in Scotland', *Feminist Review*, 58: 44–65 (Spring 1998).

BROWN, C. G., 'Sport and the Scottish Office in the twentieth century: the control of a social problem', *The European Sports History Review*, 1: 164–82 (1999).

'Sport and the Scottish Office in the twentieth century: the promotion of a social and gender policy', *The European Sports History Review*, 1: 183–202 (1999).

BUXTON, N. K., 'Economic growth in Scotland between the wars: the role of production structure and rationalisation', *Economic History Review*, 33, 4: 538–55 (1980).

Cook, B. W., 'Female support networks and political activism', *Chrysalis*, 3: 43–61 (1977).

Cott, N. F., 'Comment on Karen Offen's "Defining feminism: a comparative historical approach"', *Signs*, 15, 1: 203–6 (1989).

Cowman, K., '"Incipient Toryism"? The Women's Social and Political Union and the Independent Labour Party, 1903–14', *History Workshop Journal*, 53: 129–48 (Spring 2002).

Creighton, C., 'The rise of the male breadwinner family: a reappraisal', *Comparative Studies in Society and History*, 38, 2: 310–39 (1996).

Damer, S., 'Farewell to the Wine Alley', *Scottish Labour History Review*, 11: 9–11 (Winter 1997/Spring 1998).

De Groot, G. and Schrover, M., 'Between men and machines: women workers in the new industries 1870–1940', *Social History*, 20: 279–96 (1995).

Gall, G. and Jackson, M., 'Strike activity in Scotland', *Scottish Labour History Journal*, 33: 97–122 (1998).

Gier-Viskovatoff, J. and Porter, A., 'Women of the British coalfields on strike in 1926 and 1984: documenting lives using oral history and photography', *Frontiers: A Journal of Women's Studies*, 19: 190–230 (1998).

Giles, J., 'A home of one's own: women and domesticity in England, 1918–1950', *Women's Studies*, 16, 3: 239–53 (1993).
    'Narratives of gender, class and modernity in women's memories of mid-twentieth century Britain', *Signs*, 28, 1: 221–41 (2002).

Gordon, E., 'Women, work and collective action: Dundee jute workers 1870–1914', *Journal of Social History*, 21, 1: 27–46 (1987).

Grayson, J., '"But it's more than a game it's an institution": feminist perspectives on sport', *Feminist Review*, 13: 5–16 (Spring 1983).

Hall, G. V., 'Contrasting female identities: women in coal mining communities in Northumberland, England, 1900–1939', *Journal of Women's History*, 13, 2: 107–33 (2001).

Hammerton, J., 'The targets of rough music: respectability and domestic violence in Victorian England', *Gender and History*, 3, 1: 23–44 (1991).

Hore, B. D., 'Alcohol and crime', *Alcohol and Alcoholism*, 6: 435–9 (1988).

Hughes, A., 'The economic and social effects of recession and depression on Greenock between the wars', *International Journal of Maritime History*, 13, 1: 281–306 (2006).

Iacovetta, F., 'Post-modern ethnography, historical materialism and decentring the (male) authorial voice: a feminist conversation', *Histoire Sociale/Social History*, 53, 64 (Nov. 1999), 289–93.

Innes, S., 'Constructing women's citizenship in the interwar period: the Edinburgh Women Citizens' Association', *Women's History Review*, 13, 4: 621–7 (2004).

Kelber, L. K., 'Separate spheres, female worlds, woman's place: the rhetoric of women's history', *The Journal of American History*, 75, 1: 9–39 (1988).

KINGSLEY Kent, S., 'The politics of sexual difference: World War I and the demise of British feminism', *Journal of British Studies*, 27, 3: 232–53 (1988).

KLEIN, L. E., 'Gender and the public/private distinction in the eighteenth century: some questions about evidence and analytic procedure', *Eighteenth-Century Studies*, 29, 1: 97–109 (1996).

KNOX, W. W. and McKinlay, A., 'The Re-making of Scottish Labour in the 1930s', *Twentieth Century British History*, 6, 2: 174–93 (1995).

LEWIS, J., 'Gender, the family and women's agency in the building of welfare states: the British case', *Social History*, 19, 1: 37–55 (1994).

'Public institution and private relationship – marriage and marriage guidance 1920–1968', *Twentieth Century British History*, 1, 3: 233–65 (1990).

MACDONALD, C. M. M., 'Weak roots and branches: class, gender and the geography of industrial protest', *Scottish Labour History*, 33: 6–30 (1998).

McKAY, J., 'Red Clydeside after 75 years: a reply to Iain McLean', *Scottish Labour History Society*, 31: 85–94 (1996).

McKINLAY, A. and Hampton, A., 'Making ships, making men: working for John Brown's between the wars', *Oral History*, 19, 1: 21–8 (1991).

McLEAN, J., 'The 1926 strike in Lanarkshire', *Our History*, CPGB Publication (Spring 1976).

McNEILL, F., 'Remembering probation in Scotland', *Probation Journal*, 52, 1: 23–38 (2005).

MELLING, J., 'The Glasgow Rent Strike and Clydeside Labour – some problems of interpretation', *Scottish Labour History Society Journal*, 13: 39–44 (1979).

MITCHELL, M., 'The effects of unemployment on the social condition of women and children in the 1930s', *History Workshop*, 19: 105–26 (1985).

NASH, D., Reconnecting religion with social and cultural history: secularization's failure as a master narrative', *Cultural and Social History*, 1, 3: 302–25 (2004).

NOLAN, M., '"The women were bloody marvellous": 1951, gender and New Zealand industrial relations', *Historical Studies in Industrial Relations*, 16: 117–39 (2003).

NORQUAY, N., 'Identity and forgetting', *Oral History Review*, 26, 1: 1–12 (1999).

OFFEN, K., 'Defining feminism: a comparative historical approach', *Signs*, 14, 1: 119–57 (1988).

PASSERINI, L., 'Memory', *History Workshop Journal*, 15: 196–7 (1983).

PEDERSEN, S., 'The failure of feminism in the making of the British Welfare State', *Radical History Review*, 43: 86–110 (1987).

PHILLIPS, A., 'Women on the shop floor: the Colchester rag trade 1918–1950', *Oral History*, 22, 1: 56–66 (1994).

PUGH, M., 'Popular Conservatism in Britain: continuity and change 1870–1987', *Journal of British Studies*, 27, 3: 254–82 (1988).

ROBERTS, E., 'Women, the family economy and homework: North West England 1900–1970', *Labour History Review*, 56, 3: 16–17 (1991).

ROSE, S. O., 'Gender antagonism and class conflict: exclusionary strategies of male trade unionists in nineteenth century Britain', *Social History*, 13, 2: 191–208 (1988).

'Gender and labour history: the nineteenth century', *International Review of Social History*, 38: 145–62 (1993).

ROSS, E., 'Fierce questions and taunts: married life in working-class London 1870–1914', *Feminist Studies*, 8, 3: 575–97 (1982).

'Survival networks: women's neighbourhood sharing in London before World War I', *History Workshop*, 15: 4–27 (1983).

ROWAN, C., 'Women in the Labour Party, 1906–1920', *Feminist Review*, 12: 74–91 (1982).

SAVAGE, M., 'Trade unionism, sex segregation and the State: women's employment in "new" industries in inter-war Britain', *Social History*, 13, 2: 209–30 (1991).

SCOTT, P. 'Did owner-occupation lead to smaller families for inter-war working-class families?', *Economic History Review*, 61, 1: 99–124 (2007).

SMITH, G., 'Motherhood, health and welfare in a women's town c1911–1931', *Oral History Society*, 23, 1: 63–77 (1995).

SMITH, H. L., 'Sex vs. class: British feminists and the Labour movement 1919–1929', *Historian*, 47, 1: 19–37 (Nov. 1984).

SMITH, J., 'Labour tradition in Glasgow and Liverpool', *History Workshop*, 17: 32–56 (1984).

STEVENSON, J., 'Writing Scotland's history in the twentieth century: thoughts from across the border', *The Scottish Historical Review*, 76, 201: 103–14 (Apr. 1997).

SUMMERFIELD, P., '"They didn't want women back in that job": the Second World War and the construction of gendered work histories', *Labour History Review*, 63, 3: 83–103 (Spring 1998).

THOMPSON, D., 'Gender, work and the family', *Labour History Review*, 56, 3: 4–9 (1991).

WALKER, G., 'The Orange Order in Scotland between the wars', *International Review of Social History*, 38, 2: 177–206 (1992).

WILSON, G., 'Women's work in offices and the preservation of men's "breadwinning" jobs in early twentieth-century Glasgow', *Women's History Review*, 10, 3: 461–82 (2001).

UNPUBLISHED

Theses

ARNOT, J., 'Women workers and trade union participation in Scotland, 1919–1939', Ph.D. thesis (University of Glasgow, 1999).

BLACK, J., 'An assessment of the impact of the Temperance (Scotland)

Act 1913', B.A. Independent Study Project (University of Strathclyde, 1999).

CAIRNS, D., 'Women and the Clydeside labour movement', M.Phil. thesis (University of Strathclyde, 1996).

CLARK, P. C., 'The Greenock labour movement and the General Strike', B.A. dissertation (University of Strathclyde, 1986).

CUSHMAN, J., 'Negotiating the shop floor: employee and union loyalties in British and American retail, 1939–1970', Ph.D. thesis (University of Glasgow, 2003).

HUGHES, A., 'Popular pastimes and wife assault in inter-war Glasgow', B.A. dissertation (University of Strathclyde, 1996).

McKEE, J., 'Glasgow working-class housing between the wars 1919–1939', M.Phil. thesis (University of Strathclyde, 1976).

SINCLAIR, L., '"Silenced, suppressed and passive": a refocused history of Lanarkshire women, 1920–1939', Ph.D. thesis (University of Strathclyde, 2005).

Conference papers

BROWNE, S. and Tomlinson, J., 'Dundee: A women's town?' Paper presented at the Twentieth Century Conference, 26 Mar. 2009, University of Dundee.

INTERNET RESOURCES

MAVER, I., 'Women', *The Clydebank Story*, http://www.theclydebankstory.com, accessed 1 Apr. 2008.

Oxford Dictionary of National Biography, Oxford University Press, 2004, http://www.oxforddnb.com, accessed 12 Apr. 2008.

TUC History on-line: http://www.unionhistory.info, accessed 6 Aug. 2008.

ORAL TESTIMONIES

University of Glasgow

CD-ROM No. 0155: Stephenson, J. D., Stirling women's oral history archive, Smith Art Gallery and Museum, Stirling, 2007.

Scottish Oral History Society, Department of History, University of Strathclyde

INTERVIEWS with author and profiles. All names have been changed to preserve anonymity

SOHCA/019/01: Questionnaire.

1. SOHCA/019/02/Dennistoun/Glasgow/1908/A: Ms Anderson
Father's occupation: warehouseman.
Left school: 14.
Employment: textile/factory worker.

Religion: Protestant.
Voted: ILP.
Marital status: unmarried.
Children: none.

2. SOHCA/019/03/Calton/Glasgow/1907/B: Mrs Bruce
Father's occupation: shipyard worker.
Left school: 11.
Employment: packer/machinist/factory.
Religion: Protestant.
Voted: ILP.
Marital status: married.
Children: two.

3. SOHCA/019/04/Bridgeton/Glasgow/1910/C: Mrs Campbell
Father's occupation: tradesman.
Left school: 14.
Employment: factory/rag-store owner.
Religion: Protestant (Catholic after marriage).
Voted: ILP.
Marital status: married.
Children: five.

4. SOHCA/019/05/Govan/Glasgow/1912/D: Mrs Duncan
Father's occupation: coal merchant.
Left school: 14.
Employment: shop assistant/domestic servant/cleaner.
Religion: Catholic.
Voted: ILP.
Marital status: married.
Children: three.

5. SOHCA/019/06/Oatlands/Glasgow/1907/E: Mrs Edwards
Father's occupation: stone worker.
Left school: 14.
Employment: textile/machinist.
Religion: Protestant.
Voted: ILP.
Marital status: married.
Children: one.

6. SOHCA/019/07/Anderson/Glasgow/1911/F: Mrs Ferguson
Father's occupation: labourer.
Left school: 14.
Employment: book-binder.

Religion: Protestant.
Voted: Labour.
Marital status: married.
Children: one.

7. SOHCA/019/08/Townhead/Glasgow/1916/G: Mrs Galbraith
Father's occupation: manager of public house.
Left school: 14.
Employment: office.
Religion: Protestant.
Voted: Conservative.
Marital status: married.
Children: two.

8. SOHCA/019/09/Tradeston/Glasgow/1900/H: Mrs Harrison
Father's occupation: foreman.
Left school: 14.
Employment: textile/munitions/textile/machinist.
Religion: Protestant.
Voted: Conservative.
Marital status: married.
Children: two.

9. SOHCA/019/010/Dennistoun/Glasgow /1907/I: Mrs Ingills
Father's occupation: packer/church officer.
Left school: 14.
Employment: paper trade.
Religion: Protestant.
Voted: Conservative.
Marital status: married.
Children: two.

10. SOHCA/019/011/Cowcaddens/Glasgow/1917/ J: Mrs Jones
Father's occupation: moulder.
Left school: 15.
Employment: shop assistant/factory.
Religion: Catholic.
Voted: Conservative.
Marital status: married.
Children: none.

11. SOHCA/019/012/Anniesland/Glasgow/1907/K: Mrs Kilpatrick
Father's occupation: railwayman.
Left school: 15.
Employment: shop assistant/factory.

Religion: Protestant.
Voted: Conservative.
Marital status: married.
Children: two.

12. SOHCA/019/013/Dennistoun/Glasgow/1907/L: Mrs Lang
Father's occupation: plane-maker.
Left school: 14.
Employment: factory/entertainer.
Religion: Protestant.
Voted: ILP.
Marital status: married.
Children: five.

13. SOHCA/019/014/Springburn/Glasgow/1911/M: Mrs MacIntosh
Father's occupation: railway foreman.
Left school: 14.
Employment: print/domestic servant.
Religion: Catholic.
Voted: Labour.
Marital status: married.
Children: none.

14. SOHCA/019/015/Bridgeton/Glasgow/1909/N: Mrs Nicol
Father's occupation: blacksmith.
Left school: 14.
Employment: weaver/char/shop assistant.
Religion: Protestant (Catholic after marriage).
Voted: ILP.
Marital status: married.
Children: ten

15. SOHCA/019/016/Townhead/Glasgow/1905/O: Mrs O' Neil
Father's occupation: furnace worker.
Left school: 14.
Employment: textile.
Religion: Protestant.
Marital status: married.
Children: one.

16. SOHCA/019/017/Calton/Glasgow/1909/P: Mrs Patterson
Father's occupation: carter.
Left school: 14.
Employment: book-binder.
Religion: Catholic.

Marital status: married.
Children: four.

17. SOHCA/019/018/Camlachie/Glasgow/1909/Q: Mrs McQueen
Father's occupation: metalworker.
Left school: 14.
Employment: textile.
Religion: Protestant (Catholic after marriage).
Marital status: married.
Children: four.

18. SOHCA/019/019/Calton/Glasgow/1907/R: Mrs Reid
Father's occupation: boiler worker.
Left school: 14.
Employment: factory/brewery/shop assistant.
Religion: Catholic.
Voted: ILP.
Marital status: married.
Children: three.

19. SOHCA/019/020/Pollokshields/Glasgow/1895/S: Ms Stewart
Father's occupation: office clerk.
Left school: 16.
Employment: office.
Religion: Protestant.
Voted: Conservative.
Marital status: unmarried.
Children: none.

20. SOHCA/019/021/Camlachie/Glasgow/1909/T: Mrs Thompson
Father's occupation: labourer.
Left school: 14.
Employment: factory.
Religion: Catholic.
Voted: Labour.
Marital status: married.
Children: four.

21. SOHCA/019/022/Greenock/Renfrewshire/1919/U: Mrs Adams
Father's occupation: distribution.
Left school: 14.
Employment: textiles/shop assistant.
Religion: Protestant.
Voted: Conservative.
Marital status: married.
Children: two.

22. SOHCA/019/023/Greenock/Renfrewshire/1904/V: Mrs Burns
Father's occupation: metalwork.
Left school: 14.
Employment: shop assistant.
Religion: Protestant.
Voted: Conservative.
Marital status: married.
Children: four.

23. SOHCA/019/024/Port Glasgow/Renfrewshire/1901/W: Mrs Church
Father's occupation: store owner.
Left school: 14.
Employment: textiles.
Religion: Catholic.
Voted: Labour.
Marital status: married.
Children: six.

24. SOHCA/019/025/Ireland (1914)/Paisley (1921)/Renfrewshire/1914/
     X: Mrs Johnson
Father's occupation: labourer.
Left school: 14.
Employment: office.
Religion: Protestant.
Voted: Conservative.
Marital status: married.
Children: six.

25A. SOHCA/019/026/Govan/Glasgow/1917/Z: Mrs Parsonage
Father's occupation: coal merchant.
Left school: 14.
Employment: shop assistant/factory.
Religion: Protestant.
Voted: Conservative.
Marital status: married.
Children: two.

25A. SOHCA/019/026/Cardiff/Wales/1915/Z: Mr Parsonage
Father's occupation: labourer.
Left school: 14.
Employment: shipyard.
Religion: Protestant.
Voted: Conservative.
Marital status: married.
Children: two.

26. SOHCA/019/027/Gorbals/Glasgow/1905/AA: Mr Armstrong
Father's occupation: hewer.
Left school: 14.
Employment: labourer/tramwayman/machine-operator.
Religion: Protestant.
Voted: ILP.
Marital status: married.
Children: five.

27. SOHCA/019/028/Govan/Glasgow/1905/AB: Mr Beattie
Father's occupation: night watchman.
Left school: 14.
Employment: distillery/personal service/mill-worker.
Religion: Protestant.
Voted: Labour.
Marital status: married.
Children: none.

28. SOHCA/019/029/Townhead/Glasgow/1909/AC: Mr McCallum
Father's occupation: railway foreman.
Left school: 14.
Employment: woodworker.
Religion: Catholic.
Voted: Labour.
Marital status: married.
Children: five.

29. SOHCA/019/030/Bridgeton/Glasgow/1900/AD: Mr Davidson
Father's occupation: milkman.
Left school: 14.
Employment: foundry/labourer/baker.
Religion: Protestant.
Voted: ILP.
Marital status: married.
Children: none.

30. SOHCA/019/03/Partick/Glasgow/1908/AE: Mr Ewart
Father's occupation: hewer.
Left school: 14.
Employment: butcher/labourer/dock-worker.
Religion: Protestant.
Voted: ILP.
Marital status: married.
Children: five.

31. SOHCA/019/032/Charing Cross/Glasgow/1914/AF: Mr McMillan
Father's occupation: motor salesman.
Left school: 16.
Employment: electrician.
Religion: Protestant.
Voted: Conservative.
Marital status: married.
Children: three.

32. SOHCA/019/033/Oatlands/Glasgow/1914/AG: Mr Gray
Father's occupation: tradesman.
Left school: 14.
Employment: fireman.
Religion: Protestant.
Voted: Conservative.
Marital status: married.
Children: two.

33. SOHCA/019/034/Govan/Glasgow/1901/AH: Mr Troy
Father's occupation: riveter.
Left school: 14.
Employment: baker.
Religion: Catholic.
Voted: Labour.
Marital status: married.
Children: seven.

34. SOHCA/019/035/Kelvinside/Glasgow/1893/AI: Mr Watson
Father's occupation: skipper.
Left school: 14.
Employment: shop assistant.
Religion: Protestant.
Voted: Labour.
Marital status: married.
Children: four.

35. SOHCA/019/036/Townhead/Glasgow/1899/AJ: Mr Jamieson
Father's occupation: clerk.
Left school: 16 (University educated).
Employment: chartered accountant.
Religion: Protestant.
Voted: Conservative.
Marital status: married.
Children: none.

36. SOHCA/019/037/Shettleston/Glasgow/1921/AK: Mr McKenna
Father's occupation: bottle-blower.
Left school: 14.
Employment: steel-worker.
Religion: Protestant.
Voted: Labour.
Marital status: married.
Children: none.

37. SOHCA/019/038/Townhead/Glasgow/1900/A: Mr Murray
Father's occupation: stableman.
Left school: 14.
Employment: truck driver.
Religion: Protestant.
Marital status: married.
Children: five.

38. SOHCA/019/039/Possilpark/Glasgow/1918/AM: Mr Neilson
Father's occupation: labourer.
Left school: 14.
Employment: shop assistant.
Religion: Catholic.
Voted: Labour.
Marital status: married.
Children: four.

39. SOHCA/019/040/Govan/Glasgow/1913/AN: Mr Orr
Father's occupation: labourer.
Left school: 14.
Employment: shop assistant.
Religion: Catholic.
Voted: Labour.
Marital status: married.
Children: four.

40. SOHCA/019/042/Anderson/Glasgow /1915/AO: Mr Scott
Father's occupation: undertaker.
Left school: 14.
Employment: railway signalman.
Religion: Protestant.
Marital status: married.
Children: two.

41. SOHCA/019/043/Clydebank/Dunbartonshire/1920/AP: Mr Gordon
Father's occupation: foreman.

Left school: 14.
Employment: shipyard labourer.
Religion: Catholic.
Voted: Labour.
Marital status: married.
Children: none.

42. SOHCA/019/044/Croy/Lanarkshire/1900/AQ: Mr Logan
Father's occupation: labourer.
Left school: 14.
Employment: agricultural labourer.
Religion: Protestant.
Voted: ILP.
Marital status: unmarried.
Children: none.

43. SOHCA/019/046/Greenock/Renfrewshire/1906/AR: Mr Coyle
Father's occupation: printer/local councillor.
Left school: 16 (University educated).
Employment: teacher.
Religion: Protestant.
Voted: Liberal.
Marital status: married.
Children: two.

Index